D1593167

AVERROES AND HIS
PHILOSOPHY

Averroes
and his Philosophy

OLIVER LEAMAN

CLARENDON PRESS · OXFORD
1988

Oxford University Press, Walton Street, Oxford OX2 6DP
Oxford New York Toronto
Delhi Bombay Calcutta Madras Karachi
Petaling Jaya Singapore Hong Kong Tokyo
Nairobi Dar es Salaam Cape Town
Melbourne Auckland
and associated companies in
Beirut Berlin Ibadan Nicosia

Oxford is a trade mark of Oxford University Press

Published in the United States
by Oxford University Press, New York

British Library Cataloguing in Publication Data
Leaman, Oliver
Averroes and his philosophy.
1. Averroes
I. Title
181'.9   B749.Z7
ISBN 0-19-826540-9

Library of Congress Cataloging in Publication Data
Leaman, Oliver
Averroes and his philosophy/Oliver Leaman.
Bibliography: p.   Includes index.
1. Averroes, 1126–1198.   I. Title
B749.Z7L43   1988
181'.9—dc19   87-25956
ISBN 0-19-826540-9

Set by Cotswold Typesetting Ltd, Gloucester
Printed and bound in Great Britain by
Biddles Ltd, Guildford and King's Lynn

In loving memory of Zoe Ruth Marks

PREFACE

THIS book has a clear purpose. It is intended to provide an introduction to the philosophical thought of a remarkable thinker, ibn Rushd, whose name was Latinized to Averroes. I have taken the rather self-indulgent line of dealing with those aspects of his thought which interest me most, and which strike me as the most significant. This book is in no way an exhaustive account of his philosophy, nor of his work on Aristotle and in the many other fields of theology, law, medicine, and so on which he explored. Nor is it primarily concerned with the historical phenomenon of Averroism and its effect upon the development of philosophy in the Christian and Jewish worlds. It does not deal at any length with the response to Averroes' thought in the Muslim world today. All these issues are touched on, but they are not central to the book itself. I am mainly concerned with the way in which Averroes develops his arguments to defend his view of the importance of philosophy in acquiring an understanding of the world, the principles behind its structure, and the language we use to describe it.

The study of Islamic philosophy is something of a minority activity at the moment, and it is unfortunate that so much acerbity characterizes the relationships between its various practitioners. Many commentators fail to regard Islamic philosophy as really philosophy at all, and tackle it with the instruments of philological scholarship and literary criticism. This book is firmly opposed to any such approach and argues throughout that Averroes produced intriguing and complex philosophical theories which require and deserve serious philosophical analysis. I am sure that I have not managed to produce the definitive guide to Averroes' philosophy, and I have not even made the attempt. But I hope that by the time readers approach the end of the book they will feel that the philosophical thought of Averroes is a considerable intellectual achievement which raises many profound and exciting questions.

There are a number of people and institutions which I should like to thank for their assistance in writing this book. The Leverhulme Trust kindly provided me with a grant to assist with the research. Many librarians in a number of academic libraries were very helpful, and those in my own college particularly so. My work was constantly encouraged by Dr Erwin Rosenthal, whose enthusiasm for *falsafa* has only increased with his years. I have had many fruitful and enjoyable discussions with Alan

Sinyor on Averroes. Peter Edwards has provided a lot of help. I am very grateful for the help of Hilary Walford in improving the style of the book. My thanks go to them all. Any errors which remain are to be laid directly at my door.

O.N.H.L.

Liverpool
April 1987

CONTENTS

NOTE ON THE TEXT

Where there are Oxford Classical Texts of the works of Plato and Aristotle these have generally been used, and the Oxford translation employed, although sometimes modified.

The following abbreviations of Aristotle's works have been used:

Cat.   Categories
De an.   De anima
De int.   De interpretatione
Met.   Metaphysics
NE   Nicomachean Ethics
Phys.   Physics
Rhet.   Rhetoric

The following abbreviations of Averroes' works have been used:

APR   Averroes' Commentary on Plato's 'Republic', ed., trans., and int. E. Rosenthal (University of Cambridge Oriental Publications, 1; Cambridge University Press: Cambridge, 1956; repr. 1966 and 1969); references are to the page- and line-numbers of the Hebrew in this edition; translations are taken from Averroes on Plato's 'Republic', trans. and int. R. Lerner (Cornell University Press: Ithaca, 1974); references with lower-case roman page-numbers are to Lerner's introduction.

CPR   Averroes' Commentary on Plato's 'Republic', ed., trans., and int. E. Rosenthal (University of Cambridge Oriental Publications, 1; Cambridge University Press: Cambridge, 1956; repr. 1966 and 1969); references are to the page- and line-numbers of the Hebrew, and translations are also taken from this edition.

Damīma   Appendix to the Faṣl al-maqāl; page-references are to the Arabic in Philosophie und Theologie von Averroes, ed. M. J. Müller (Munich, 1859); all translations are taken from Averroes on the Harmony of Religion and Philosophy, trans. and int. G. Hourani (Luzac: London, 1961; repr. 1967 and 1976).'

Discourse	*Discourse on the Manner of the World's Existence*; page-references are to the translation in B. Kogan, 'Eternity and Origination: Averroes' *Discourse on the Manner of the World's Existence*', in M. Marmura (ed.), *Islamic Theology and Philosophy: Essays in Honor of George F. Hourani* (State University of New York Press: Albany, 1984).
FM	*Faṣl al-maqāl* (Decisive Treatise on the Harmony of Religion and Philosophy); page-references are to the Arabic in *Philosophie und Theologie von Averroes*, ed. M. J. Müller (Munich, 1859); all translations are taken from *Averroes on the Harmony of Religion and Philosophy*, trans. and int. G. Hourani (Luzac: London, 1961; repr. 1967 and 1976).
Long Comm.	Long Commentary on the *De anima*; page-references are to the Latin in *Averrois Cordubensis commentarium magnum in Aristotelis De anima libros*, ed. F. S. Crawford (Medieval Academy of America: Cambridge, Mass., 1953); translations are by the author, but part of the text is available in translation by A. Hyman in A. Hyman and J. Walsh (eds.), *Philosophy in the Middle Ages* (Harper and Row: New York, 1967), 314–24, and in G. Klubertanz, *The Discursive Power* (The Modern Schoolman: St Louis, 1952).
Manāhij	*Kitāb al-kashf 'an manāhij al-adilla* (Exposition of the Methods of Argument concerning the Doctrine of Faith); page-references are to the Arabic in *Philosophie und Theologie von Averroes*, ed. M. J. Müller (Munich, 1859); all translations are taken from *Averroes on the Harmony of Religion and Philosophy*, trans. and int. G. Hourani (Luzac: London, 1961; repr. 1967 and 1976).
Middle Comm.	*Averroes' Middle Commentaries on Aristotle's 'Categories' and 'De Interpretatione'*, ed., trans., and int. C. Butterworth (Princeton University Press: Princeton, 1983); unless otherwise indicated in footnotes, page-references are to the translation in this edition.
NE (Heb.)	Middle Commentary on Aristotle's *Nicomachean Ethics* (Hebrew), Camb. MS Add. 496, Cambridge University Library; references are to the folio numbers in this MS; all translations are taken from E. Rosenthal, *Political*

Thought in Medieval Islam (Cambridge University Press: Cambridge, 1958).

Short Comm.   *Averroes' Three Short Commentaries on Aristotle's 'Topics', 'Rhetoric' and 'Poetics'*, ed., int., and trans. C. Butterworth (State University of New York Press, Albany, 1977); page-references are to the translation in this edition.

Tafsīr   *Tafsīr mā baʿd al-ṭabīʿ ah* (Long Commentary on the Metaphysics), ed. M. Bouyges (4 vols., Bibliotheca Arabica Scholasticorum, Série Arabe; Imprimérie Catholique: Beirut, 1938–52), iii; page-references are to this edition; unless otherwise specified, translations are taken from *Ibn Rushd's Metaphysics: A Translation with Introduction of Ibn Rushd's Commentary on Aristotle's 'Metaphysics', Book Lām*, ed. C. Genequand (Islamic Philosophy and Theology Texts and Studies, 1; Brill: Leiden, 1984).

TT   *Tahāfut al-tahāfut*, ed. M. Bouyges (Bibliotheca Arabica Scholasticorum, Série Arabe, 3; Imprimérie Catholique: Beirut, 1930); page-references are to this edition; all translations are taken from *Averroes' Tahafut al-tahafut* (The Incoherence of the Incoherence), trans. and int. S. Van den Bergh (2 vols.; Luzac: Leiden, 1954; repr. 1969 and 1978), i.

Passages from the Qur'ān are generally taken from the Arberry version, with the sura in Roman and the lines in arabic numbers.

Works cited in footnotes are generally not cited in the bibliography.

Introduction: The Cultural Context

MUSLIM Spain (*Andalūs*) and North Africa (*Maghrib*) were unpromising
territory for the growth of a serious philosophical movement. This region
maintained the character of a frontier area for some time, with its
accompanying tensions and adherence to orthodoxy. Unlike the eastern
Muslim region, which had become fairly settled ethnically and politically,
Western Islam was in close and aggressive contact with anti-Islamic
forces, both within and without, and there was a tendency for Berber
groups from North Africa to invade and take over the small principalities
in Spain. The legal school which dominated the West was that of Mālik
ibn Anas, which specified a clear set of answers to legal problems which
arose within the context of Muslim society. The cultural atmosphere was
discouraging to theology, let alone philosophy. When Yūsuf ibn Tashfīn
left North Africa in the early 1090s to conquer Andalūs and establish the
Almoravid dynasty, he brought in a regime based exclusively on Malikite
law to solve all potential problems which arose. It is not difficult to see an
explanation for this in the personal characteristics of the ruler and the
social conditions of the country. Military leaders do not tend on the whole
to favour complex theoretical solutions to difficulties in interpreting
scripture; they rather accept relatively simple solutions to conceptual
problems, being men of action rather than people who enjoy contemplation. Perhaps more important, though, was the existence in the country
they ruled of a considerable network of legal authorities, the *fuqahā'*, who
were wedded to the Malikite school and whose support was politically
vital.

In spite of the suspicion which obviously existed under the Almoravid
regime of theology and any attempt at innovation and independent
thought, philosophy made a solid entrée. Both ibn Bājja and ibn Ṭufayl
worked within the Almoravid cultural context, and they were considerable
thinkers in the tradition of the *falāsifa* who were mainly concerned with
the works of Plato and Aristotle. They managed to work successfully in
local conditions due to the lack of total control of the state by any one
element. Their work did not seem to contravene the thinking of the
fuqahā' and was very closely related to the development of the more
practical sciences such as medicine and astronomy with which political
forces had no quarrel. The point that there was little antagonism between

the Maliki lawyers and the Aristotelian philosopher comes out nicely in the fact that the Islamic Aristotelian *par excellence*, Averroes, had no difficulty in producing both a Malikite law text, the *Bidāyat al-mujtahid* (The beginning for him who interprets the sources independently) and a whole stream of Aristotelian works. There is a wide gulf between the essentially practical issues with which the *fuqahā'* dealt, and the highly theoretical issues of the *falāsifa*. It was not until the introduction of theology into Western Islam that philosophy was faced with a foe which sought to occupy the same theoretical territory on which philosophy had made its home. It is worth pointing out in addition that the *falāsifa* in this period were very sensitive to the difficult position in which they were placed given the literalist interpretation of scripture which prevailed, and they took measures to restrict the influence of their writings only to sympathetic readers and listeners. There is something of a theme in the work of ibn Bājja and ibn Ṭufayl of the philosopher as a solitary and isolated individual, out of step with the rest of his society.

Philosophy came to take much more of a public stance with the overthrow of the Almoravids by the Almohades around the middle of the twelfth century. The victor, ʿAbd al-Muʾmin, was a Zahirite and believed that there was no necessity for the legal structure of Mālik in settling problems of interpretation of *sharīʿa*. A literal grasp of the text would be sufficient to answer the issue, according to the Zahirites, and the complicated *furūʿ* or 'branches' of the law which constitute the Malikite hermeneutic were abandoned. But the new ruler could not abandon the well-established network of Malikite *fuqahā'*, whose allegiance had to be acquired if the Almohades were to have any hope of survival. So the official doctrine of the state remained Malikite, and the *fuqahā'* coexisted with an expansion of *kalām* and scholarship into Andalus encouraged by ʿAbd al-Muʾmin and his son Abū Yaʿqūb Yūsuf who succeeded him. Abū Yaʿqūb is reported to have been very interested in conversations with ibn Ṭufayl, who introduced him to Averroes and set in train the great compilations of commentaries on Aristotle. It is worth quoting at length the account which Marrākushī gives of the meeting in 1168/9 which set Averroes off officially on his task:

This Abū Bakr continued to draw men of learning to the Prince from every country, bringing them to his attention and inciting him to honour and praise them. It was he who brought to the Prince's attention Abul-Walīd Muḥammad ibn Aḥmad ibn Muḥammad ibn Rushd; and from this time he became known and his ability became celebrated among men. Ibn Rushd's pupil . . . told me that he had heard the philosopher Abul-Walīd say on more than one occasion: 'When I entered into the presence of the Prince of the Believers, Abū Ya'qūb, I found him with Abū Bakr ibn Ṭufayl alone. Abū Bakr began praising me . . . the Prince asked me . . . "What is their opinion about the heavens?"—referring to the philosophers—"Are they eternal or created?" Confusion and fear took hold of me, and I began to make excuses and deny that I had ever concerned myself with philosophic learning; for I did not know what ibn Ṭufayl had told him on the subject. But the Prince of the Believers understood my fear and confusion, and turning to ibn Ṭufayl began talking about the question of which he had asked me, mentioning what Aristotle, Plato and all the philosophers had said, and bringing in besides the objections of the Muslim thinkers against them . . . Thus he continued to set me at ease until I spoke, and he learned what was my competence in that subject; and when I withdrew he ordered for me a gift of money, a magnificent robe of honour and a steed!'

That same pupil of his also told me that ibn Rushd had told him: 'Abū Bakr ibn Ṭufayl summoned me one day and and told me, "Today I heard the Prince of the Believers complain of the difficulty of expression of Aristotle and his translators, and mention the obscurity of his aims, saying 'If someone would tackle these books, summarise them and expound their aims, after understanding them thoroughly, it would be easier for people to grasp them.' So if you have in you abundant strength for the task, perform it. I expect you will be equal to it, from what I know of the excellence of your mind, the purity of your nature, and the intensity of your application to science. . . ." Abul-Walīd said: 'This was what led me to summarize the books of the philosopher Aristotle.'[1]

There are many interesting aspects of this encounter. Firstly, it is significant that ibn Ṭufayl and the ruler were alone when they summoned ibn Rushd. Despite his power and authority, Abū Ya'qūb was not eager to broadcast widely his patronage of philosophy nor his own knowledge of the area. Even ibn Rushd did not know of his interest and ability before the interview, and was nervous initially in his response to his question about creation. Lastly, as we shall see, ibn Rushd followed the Prince's instructions to the letter when compiling his variety of types of commentary. (Of course, since this is an *ex post facto* account, it might well be that ibn Rushd is being a little creative here.)

Averroes had the full name of Abul Walīd Muḥammad ibn Aḥmad ibn Muḥammad ibn Rushd and was born in 1126 AD (520 AH) in Córdoba. He belonged to a distinguished family of lawyers and public servants, naturally of the Maliki school. His grandfather was a legal thinker of some

---

[1] A. Marrākushī, *Kitāb al-mu'jib fī talkhīṣ akbār al-Maghrib* (2nd edn.; ed. R. Dozy: Leiden, 1885), 174–5. Translated by G. Hourani, in *Averroes on the Harmony of Religion and Religion* (Luzac: London, 1961), 12–13.

note and some of his writings are still extant today.[2] Ibn Rushd, his father, and grandfather all served as judges (*qāḍī*) in Córdoba. Ibn Rushd's education seems to have comprised a thorough grounding in the Maliki approach to jurisprudence and an Ash'arite introduction to theology. The Ash'arites, such as Ghazālī and Juwaynī, put forward an interpretation of *sharī'a* and Islam which emphasizes the power and influence of God over all things, an emphasis which leads them to abandon the objectivity of causality, ethics, and the world as an eternal entity. As we shall see, ibn Rushd spent most of the rest of his life arguing against this approach in all its various forms. When he was eighteen ibn Rushd went to Marrakesh to the court of 'Abd al-Mu'min, who was succeeded by his son described in the interview. As a result of this patronage ibn Rushd became a royal physician (*ṭabīb*) and later *qāḍī* of Córdoba in succession to his father. Even the death of the ruler did not interfere with ibn Rushd's philosophical activities, since his successor, Abū Yūsuf, maintained the close relationship between ruler and philosopher.

When ibn Rushd was seventy a rift occurred between him and the caliph, and the philosopher was banished with his supporters for about a year. An official proclamation was issued forbidding people to study philosophy, and, although after a fairly short time ibn Rushd was rehabilitated personally, the ban on philosophy and related studies remained in force. Ibn Rushd died a year later, at the age of seventy-two. There exists a variety of explanations for the persecution of the philosopher and philosophy itself, but the most likely is that it came about through local political infighting around the caliph, with the latter wishing to satisfy the aspirations of the *fuqahā'* within the state. It was no doubt highly useful to have a group of apparently unorthodox thinkers connected to the court who could be punished when it became convenient to make a public assertion of orthodoxy and adherence to traditional jurisprudence. Although records suggest that the opponents of philosophy wanted ibn Rushd to be put to death, he actually seems to have spent his imprisonment in house confinement, and his rehabilitation may have had a political message for the *fuqahā'*, that a wider interpretation of Islam was still available to the caliph and his adherence to Malikism should not be taken for granted. This persecution obviously hurt ibn Rushd a great deal in personal terms, in that he had earned the reputation as a bad Muslim, and on one occasion was actually driven from the mosque in Córdoba by

---

[2] Some of his judgements (*fatāwa*) are to be found in the Bibliothèque Nationale, Paris, Arabic section, no. 398

an angry crowd of worshippers. Indeed, his reputation within the Islamic community did not remain high after his death, and there is little evidence that he influenced the development of thought within Islam until quite recently. He had a far more successful afterlife among the Jewish communities in the medieval world, and a widespread effect upon the Christian world.

Before leaving the account of the context within which ibn Rushd worked, it is worth adding a couple of points which are not generally made. It is usually argued that the caliph Abū Yūsuf Yaʿqūb al-Manṣūr (r. 1184–99) punished ibn Rushd to placate the orthodox *fuqahāʾ* and *ʿulamā*, the lawyers and religious authorities, in Andalūs. Yet this same ruler at one stage ordered the burning of Malikite books on *furūʿ* and supported a literalist approach to the interpretation of law. There was something of a spirit of Andalusian separateness from the rest of the Islamic world, and not just for geographical reasons. In the West there was a tradition of literalness, starting with ibn Ḥazm (d. 1064), reinforced by ibn Tūmart, the founder of the Almohad movement (d. 1130), and continuing with ibn Rushd. The latter adhered to a literalness with respect to Aristotle, criticizing the other (generally Eastern) philosophers for misunderstanding and misrepresenting the Greek philosopher's views. Along with this literalness in philosophy went a literalness in theology and a refusal to accept as useful the conceptual apparatus constructed by the different schools of *kalām* within Islam, schools which themselves are solidly based within the East.[3]

Philosophy in the Islamic world had been introduced with the wave of translations of Greek texts into Arabic from the eighth century onwards, and for much of the time existed in a rather tense relationship with the other Islamic sciences. The foreign nature of philosophy (*falsafa*, as it was often called in direct reflection of the Greek *philosophia*) was bitterly resented and disparaged by the intellectual élite of the Islamic world. There were those who believed that the best way to discover the truth about important theoretical issues was by more specifically Islamic techniques. For examples, there was in existence a highly developed Arabic grammar, which dealt in detail with issues of meaning relating to complex theoretical terms, and a system of jurisprudence (*fiqh*) which represented itself as capable of settling all problems in interpretation of Islamic law (*sharīʿa*) in the very varying local conditions to which it might

[3] This point is clearly made by A. Sabra, 'The Andalusian Revolt against Ptolemaic Astronomy', in E. Mendelsohn (ed.), *Transformation and Tradition in the Sciences* (Cambridge University Press: Cambridge, 1984), 133–153; pp. 143–4.

be applied. The religion of Islam itself was often seen as fairly clear and unproblematic in the answers it gives to difficult problems, and the Qur'ān together with the reliably attested sayings of the Prophet and his followers (*ḥadīth*) have been taken to provide unambiguous answers to the important questions concerning how people ought to live, how the world was created, what sort of state should be constructed, which types of behaviour are valid and which wicked, and so on. In addition to all these theoretical frameworks, there existed a tradition of mysticism through which appropriate people might achieve nearness to and direct awareness of God. Finally, and probably most significantly for the work of ibn Rushd, a highly sophisticated theological system arose in close connection with the different schools of legal interpretation, which sought to establish distinct techniques for solving theoretical problems as and when they arose within the system of belief and practice specified by Islam.

Arguments went on between these different schools of thought, and on occasions they were supported by physical and political persecution. Islam represents itself as a very tolerant religion, and in many ways this is justified when one contrasts it with Christianity, for example. Yet it must be taken into account that the rapid growth of Islam led to the incorporation of many minorities and the military and cultural opposition of many powerful infidel states which militated against a total consolidation of Muslim society along a particular version of what that society ought to be. Different interpretations of Islam became acceptable as interpretations which did not debar the adherent from the community (*umma*) itself. They might be misguided, but they represented mistakes in reasoning rather than wickedness and lack of faith. Philosophy was rather out on a limb by comparison with grammar, theology, jurisprudence, and mysticism because of its unashamably foreign origins. Not only did the philosophers (*falāsifa*) claim that they and only they had the key to ultimate truth on a wide range of issues which were also tackled by other methods; the philosophers appeared to idolize thinkers like Aristotle and his commentators such as Themistius and Alexander of Aphrodisias, thinkers who were unashamably not Muslims. If a thinker like Aristotle could without the aid of Islam produce such valuable theoretical work, one might wonder what the value of Islam is with respect to those theoretical issues. The *falāsifa* did not mince their words when it came to expressing their feeling of superiority to theology and the other Islamic sciences. They did not argue that Aristotle provides an interesting series of arguments on difficult questions, questions which are also illuminatingly dealt with by a body of knowledge within Islam itself. They argued that

Aristotelian philosophy provides the only secure means of establishing truth on theoretical issues, and every other technique is fatally flawed by comparison. It is hardly surprising, then, that there should be hostility between the philosophers and the supporters of alternative approaches to the truth.

It is worth emphasizing the point that the conflict between philosophy and the Islamic sciences was not so much a conflict between different propositions as between different methodologies. Each methodology claimed exclusive validity for itself. The discussion of Islamic philosophy has tended to concentrate upon the different propositions which philosophy and Islam seem to establish, and, while this is a very important aspect of the confrontation, it is the clash between different approaches which is more significant. The opponents of *falsafa* could produce a variety of arguments to support their position. One is to rule out philosophy bluntly as *kufr*, as unbelief, because it proves propositions which are counter to Islam. The difficulty with this position is that the *falāsifa* had a complicated account of the relationship between religious and philosophical language such that the apparently un-Islamic propositions in the latter could be translated into appropriately orthodox propositions in the former. In addition, the *falāsifa* seem to argue that nothing which they can demonstrate philosophically contradicts anything revealed by religion, although their opponents and many interpreters of their thought today take this to be dissimulation (*taqīya*) of their genuinely cavalier view of Islam. Another strategy is to deny the validity of philosophical methods themselves, given the clear and all-embracing doctrine of Islam itself. If Islam specifies what is to be known and how it is to be known, what need is there of any alternative route to knowledge? A problem with this approach is that it refuses to take seriously the limitations which any religion has in answering all the questions which might be put to it. For example, religions do not establish empirical laws, nor on the whole do they specify how scientific research is to be pursued. A third line is to accept for the sake of the argument the philosophical methodology which the Peripatetics use and try to show that they reach the wrong conclusions thereby. It is also possible to argue that the philosophers' arguments are only valid up to a certain point, and if they run counter to the conclusions established by revelation they must bow down before that higher and more secure form of authority.

All these strategies were adopted at some time or another by the opponents of *falsafa*, and they will all be considered later on in the book.

8 INTRODUCTION

The response on which most attention will be placed is that by al-Ghazālī (1058–1111), who tried to beat the philosophers at their own game by showing not just that they supported propositions which embody unbelief but also that they err in their philosophical reasoning. In his fascinating work *Tahāfut al-falāsifa* (The Refutation of the Philosophers) he sought to undermine completely the claims which the Greek tradition of philosophy in the Islamic world tried to establish.[4] The thinker he had firmly in his sights is ibn Sīnā (Avicenna) who was also Persian and who lived from 980 to 1037. Avicenna is an immensely creative philosopher on any criterion, and we shall spend some time later looking at his work. Ghazali took Avicenna as the chief representative of the Peripatetic tradition in Islam, and in this he was surely justified. Avicenna embodies a major tendency in Islamic philosophy, namely, the incorporation of Neoplatonic concepts into the explication of Aristotle and Greek thought in general. In his defence of philosophy Averroes is obliged to distinguish his views quite sharply on occasion from those of Avicenna, whom he regards as an inaccurate guide to the views of Aristotle himself. It would be wrong to think of Averroes as a slavish follower of Aristotle, though, or as completely immune from the influence of Neoplatonism. We shall see that he argues that Avicenna's approach to philosophy leads logically to Ghazali's critique, so that these two thinkers are not so much extremes which Averroes seeks to mediate as two sides of the same coin. Both Avicenna and Ghazali were impressed by the phenomenon of mysticism and possessed exciting spiritual lives. Averroes, by contrast, seems to have been distinctly cool towards mystics and the reports of their experiences, and spent a spiritually unremarkable existence. He seems to have worked steadily throughout his life on his commentaries and other works without the protracted all-night sessions of Avicenna or the spiritual crises of Ghazali. In some ways he seems to have adopted the persona of Aristotle himself as someone primarily concerned with the commonsensical nature of the world, by contrast with the mystics, poets, and prophets of his religion.

Averroes' style is on the whole sober, careful, and considered. He makes his points fairly repetitively in many of his works in an attempt at expressing clearly what it is he is trying to say. It is customary to divide his work up into different categories—commentaries and the rest—and there is some point in this. He commented on all the Aristotelian corpus as he

O. Leaman, *An Introduction to Medieval Islamic Philosophy* (Cambridge University Press: Cambridge, 1985), 38–40.

knew it, and most texts received three sorts of commentary. There are short commentaries (*jawāmi'*) which act as summaries of the text and which often include a good deal of additional material to help relate the philosophical discussion to contemporary theological and legal matters. They vary in their accuracy as explications of the text. The middle commentaries (*talkhīṣ*) are naturally longer than the short commentaries or epitomes, and tend to come closest to the text itself. The large or 'great' commentaries (*tafsīr*) deal at considerable length with the text, but frequently with diversions to discuss related issues. Very few of the commentaries remain extant in Arabic, and it is largely due to the influence of Averroes in the Jewish and Christian worlds that we owe their survival in Hebrew, in Arabic in Hebrew letters, and especially in Latin. Averroes also produced commentaries on Plato's *Republic*, on Galen, on Porphyry's *Eisagoge*, and on his predecessors in the Islamic world, Avicenna and al-Fārābī. Apart from his commentaries he wrote on medicine and on law, and a variety of philosophical texts which express his views on philosophical controversies which interested him. We shall be looking in some detail at these in the book, but at this stage it is important to say something about what line the book is going to take on how Averroes' work is to be interpreted, that is, is it to be divided up into exoteric and esoteric works?

A very popular interpretative approach to Averroes, and to Islamic philosophy in general, is to separate out its products into two categories. One sort of writing presents Aristotle and Greek philosophy in general as fully in accord with Islam, and represents them as merely sharper analytical instruments for understanding and demonstrating the truth of religion. The *falāsifa* did not really believe this to be the case, though, but wrote in such a way as to deflect criticism from the enemies of philosophy within their community. The other sort of writing consists of a serious philosophical analysis of concepts which are obviously damaging to the pretensions of Islam as a guide to truth. For example, such an analysis establishes the eternity of the world, the mortality of the soul, and the relative ignorance of the deity, all of which are in opposition to the doctrines of Islam. The *falāsifa* have to disguise their adherence to these dubious beliefs (from a religious point of view) and they employ a number of different methods. One is to present them as someone else's view (for example, Aristotle, or the Greeks in general) or to write about them in as technical and difficult a manner as possible in order to dissuade all but sympathetic readers from the text. Since I have written elsewhere about my view on this approach to the interpretation of Islamic philosophy at some length,[5] I shall only summarize them here. Basically, in my opinion this hermeneutic strategy is based upon a mistaken understanding of philosophy as a matter more of literary style than of logical arguments. It puts all the emphasis upon the way in which the *falāsifa* write as opposed to the sorts of arguments they analyse, and results in serious misunderstanding of how philosophers set about arranging and assessing arguments.

Towards the end of the book I hope to establish in some detail that a demarcation of Averroes' works between those which are purely 'philosophical' and those which are 'orthodox' is a mistake. It will be argued that he presents a common view in all his works, although he expresses this view in different ways. I take it that there is no evidence in his work of the practice of dissimulation (*taqīya*). There certainly do exist inconsistencies, as exist in the work of all philosophers, and he changed his mind on some issues. I shall adopt the attitude from the outset that he presents just one view in his writings, and towards the end seek to show why this attitude is justified. A point which is made about Averroes by most commentators is that he makes a sharp distinction between 'demonstrative' and 'dialectical' texts. The former involve valid reasoning from premisses which are genuinely known to be true, and represents the highest form of reasoning. By contrast, dialectical reasoning works from premisses which do not achieve this level of truth, and most commonly are propositions which some other philosopher seeks to establish. Averroes tries to disprove these less certain propositions in his dialectical works, where he is in the business of knocking down arguments rather than directly establishing valid conclusions. It has been argued that what he means by this is that his commentaries represent the acme of philosophical labour in which he can frankly give his own views on the truth of the philosophy of Aristotle, while in his more 'popular' writings which deal with the assaults of Ghazali and others on Peripateticism he can give a version of the truth which disproves their arguments and hints at the truths present in the work of Aristotle. My approach is entirely different from this and stands in contrast to most of the ways of interpreting Averroes both in the West and in the Islamic world today.[6] I am taking it to be the case that he presents a broadly similar line of argument in all his works, whether commentaries or essays, and that analysis of his arguments

---

[5] O. Leaman, 'Does the Interpretation of Islamic Philosophy rest on a Mistake?', *International Journal of Mid Eastern Studies*, 12 (1980), 525–38. See also Leaman, *Introduction*, ch. 6, pp. 182–201.

[6] A list of some recent Arabic works on Averroes is provided in the Bibliography.

will establish that this is the correct approach to take. In short, he will be treated in this book as an ordinary philosopher with ordinary philosophical problems. The implications of this approach will be assessed at the end of the book.

PART I
Metaphysics

INTRODUCTION

THE response which Averroes provided to the critique of philosophy offered by Ghazali is interesting for a number of reasons, chief among which is the high standard of philosophical argument involved on both sides of the dispute. Averroes objects to the ways in which philosophy has been tarred with the Avicennan brush, and we shall see in this part how he tries to construct an account of philosophy which is independent of Avicenna. He does not just argue that Avicenna presents views which are alien to Aristotle, and so must be invalid, as is so often assumed. Averroes rather seeks to establish a logical connection between the very different views of Avicenna and Ghazali and then attempts to demolish them both together. Ghazali is regarded as taking Avicenna to his logical conclusion, thereby revealing the infelicities in that whole approach to philosophy. We will go through some of the discussions in the *Tahāfut al-tahāfut* (Incoherence of the Incoherence) in combination with other texts to show how this general line can be made plausible. This is a very lively series of discussions and ties in well with Averroes' more directly technical writings. Although Averroes had the last word, in many ways Ghazali had the last laugh, since the form of philosophy represented and defended by Averroes went into a sudden decline in the Islamic community after his death. By contrast, the status of Ghazali has remained formidable up to today. In the dispute there is something of a theme shared by both parties, and that is concerned with the appropriate use of language to discuss God and his relationship with the world. Ghazali keeps on pressing the philosophers to admit that their model of God and his influence over the world is very different from a full-blooded religious view. He implies that the philosophical model of the world could do without a deity quite easily since there is no central and significant role for such an entity. The response by Averroes is to accuse Ghazali of only being prepared to accept a concept of a God which is remarkably similar to that of a very powerful human being, God with a status rather similar to that of Superman. We shall eventually see what implications their views have for their understanding of how language works. Their disagreement reveals intriguing features of language when pushed to its limit and is very far from being a medieval argument of nothing but historical interest.

The Incoherence of the Incoherence

The First Proof

In his First Discussion Ghazali sets out to discuss 'those proofs that make an impression on the mind' (*TT* 4) in favour of the eternity of the world. He is opposed to these proofs, not merely on the religious grounds that he believes they contravene an acceptable concept of the deity as omnipotent creator, but because he argues that they are invalid as proofs. It is very important throughout to grasp that this is his main rationale for his argument. In the First Proof he characterizes one of the philosophers' proofs as following from the impossibility of the temporal coming from the eternal. If it is accepted that God is eternal, and if it is inconceivable for the temporal to emerge from the eternal, then God could not create a world at a particular time. It would follow that, since the world exists, it must be eternal. The argument is that, if something eternal could exist without the world also existing, then the existence of the world is merely a possibility, something waiting to be brought to actuality. When this event eventually does occur, i.e. the world is brought to existence, then some change must have occurred to bring this about. If no change did occur, then no world would result. If a change does occur, the question arises as to why it occurs now and not before, a question which leads to an infinite regress since it can be asked of every putative time at which the world came into being. This argument form is taken to support the view that the world must have been in existence eternally.

Averroes is in the fortunate position of not having to agree with everything his philosophical predecessors propounded, and he certainly does not agree with this argument form as it stands. He condemns the argument as: 'in the highest degree dialectical . . . does not reach the level of demonstrative proof. For its premises are common notions, and common notions come close to being equivocal, whereas demonstrative premises are directed towards things belonging to the same kind' (*TT* 5). In his attack on the argument he is particularly scathing on the way it employs the notion of possibility, where it raises the status of the world as a mere possibility. Averroes points out that we talk about something possible taking place in a number of different ways, and it is not always the case that something outside the agent brings about the change. He gives the example of 'the transition in the geometer from non-geometrizing to geometrizing, or in the teacher from non-teaching to teaching' (*TT* 6) which can be explained in terms of the characteristics of the agents involved without calling up an infinite regress. Averroes' point in this section is that the philosophical issues involved in the question of something eternal causing something else to happen and how change is brought about are complicated and difficult topics which require detailed and careful discussion, and the sketch of a philosophical argument which Ghazali produces is only a caricature of a proper philosophical argument.

Ghazali goes on to put the blunt question:

> Why do you deny the theory of those who say that the world has been created by an eternal will which has decreed its existence in the time in which it exists, its non-existence lasting until the time it ceases and its existence beginning from the time it begins, while its existence was not willed before and therefore did not happen, and that at the precise moment it began it was willed by an eternal will and so began? What is the objection to this theory and what is absurd in it? (*TT* 7).

Ghazali is trying to establish the acceptability of the common-sense view that God just existed by himself for a time, then decided he would bring the world into existence, did it, and so it is now in existence. What is wrong with thinking about an eternal will ordering the world to come into existence at a particular time, so that the question of why it did not come into existence earlier, nor later, is answered by saying that it came into existence precisely when it was told to by God, and not a moment earlier or later? After all, I can sit in front of a blank piece of paper in my typewriter, decide to type some material on it, and then set about accomplishing the task. There will indeed be a gap between my decision and the implementation of the decision. Averroes argues that this sort of approach ignores the disanalogy between an eternal and a temporal will. We have reasons for doing things, we have dispositions to act, and we can choose what we are going to do. God's will has been in existence forever and we cannot really think of things occurring to it in the same casual way as things occur to us. If God had decided to do something, what could make him change his mind? After all, before the world is created there is nothing else in existence to change his mind. Once God has decided to do something, why should its instantiation be delayed? There exists nothing to delay it, since nothing but God exists in the first place, and even if it did it would be incapable of defying the divine fiat. As Ghazali quite accurately characterizes the philosophers' argument, 'At one moment the object of will did not exist, everything remained as it was before, and then the object of will existed. Is this not a perfectly absurd theory?' (*TT* 10).

Ghazali goes on to wonder whether the divine will is not more similar to the temporal will than we might think. He gives the example of a man delaying a divorce until his spouse actually commits an offence, or an offence takes place, and we might also think of the example of a postdated cheque. Can we not want something to happen in the future, and yet at the same time delay its instantiation? As Averroes puts it:

In the same way as the actual divorce is delayed after the formula of the divorce till the moment when the condition of someone's entering the house, or any other, is fulfilled, so the realization of the world can be delayed after God's act of creation until the condition is fulfilled on which this realization depends, i.e. the moment when God willed it. But conventional things do not behave like rational (*TT* 12).

This is a strange way of putting his point. God might regard rational events as paradigmatically conventional. For example, the natural events of the world might appear to be conventional in the sense of being lawlike regularities which have been divinely established. Yet Averroes goes on to claim that, 'in this matter there is no relation between the concept drawn from the nature of things and that which is artificial and conventional' (*TT* 13). Ghazali follows up his argument with the suggestion that the eternal will is really very unlike the temporal will, so that arguments which the philosophers might use about the workings of our own minds to draw conclusions about God's will are unsatisfactory. Just because *we* cannot generally delay the effects of our actions and decisions if there is not an obstacle to the existence of those effects, it does not follow that God cannot. Averroes is very scathing about this approach, and rightly so. The philosophers have argued that there are serious difficulties in making sense of the proposition that God could delay a decision about the creation of the world, and they argue that this suggests that the world must be regarded as eternal. They have tried to demonstrate logically the incompatibility between an eternal will and a temporal creation, and it is just not good enough for Ghazali in this opening section to hint that the philosophers do not present a valid argument form, but only an appeal to intuition (*TT* 13).

Ghazali decides to throw in another argument to suggest that the philosophers go awry in maintaining the eternity of the world. This argument is based upon the infinity of the revolutions of the planets on the assumption that the universe is eternal. If the latter is the case, then the revolutions of the planets have been going on forever. Yet they are acknowledged to move at different rates and it is possible to establish proportional relationships between them. If all the movements are infinite, how can it be possible to establish such relationships, and specify precisely what they are? How can we even determine whether such proportions are even or uneven (*TT* 16)? Averroes' rather scornful response to this approach is solidly based upon his support for an Aristotelian understanding of the nature of infinity. Aristotle allowed the existence of accidental and potential infinites, but not essential and actual infinites. He puts it in this way:

> Our adversaries believe that, when a proportion of more or less exists between parts, this proportion holds good also for the totalities, but this is only necessary when the totalities are finite. For where there is no end there is neither 'more' nor 'less'. The admission in such a case of the proportion of more or less brings with it another absurd consequence, namely that one infinite could be greater than another. This is only absurd when one supposes two quantities which are actually infinite, for then a proportion does exist between them. When, however, one imagines things potentially infinite, there exists no proportion at all. This is the right answer to this question, not what Ghazali says in the name of the philosophers (*TT* 19).

Averroes accepts the existence of accidental but not essential infinite series. An infinite causal chain such as that of human beings replicating themselves with descendants must not be regarded as a totality which can be measured and compared with other totalities. Infinite quantities have no beginning and no end, and when we think about the beginning of everything Averoes claims that 'The starting point of his acts is at the starting point of his existence; for neither of them has a beginning' (*TT* 23).

Ghazali goes on to suggest that the philosophers do acknowledge at least one actual infinite quantity:

> According to your principles it is not absurd that there should be actual units, qualitatively differentiated, which are infinite in number; I am thinking of human souls, separated through death from their bodies. How will you refute the man who affirms that this is necessarily absurd in the same way as you claim the connexion between an eternal will and a temporal creation to be necessarily absurd? This theory about souls is that which Avicenna accepted, and it is perhaps Aristotle's (*TT* 25–6).

Averroes rejects this claim with some vehemence, pointing out with some accuracy how distant such a conception of the afterlife is from Aristotelian philosophy where 'the impossibility of an actual infinite is an acknowledged axiom . . . equally valid for material and immaterial things' (*TT* 27). We shall return to this point in more detail when we come to consider Averroes' views on the soul. For the moment it is important to grasp that

Averroes and Ghazali are offering two different accounts of the nature of infinity, a difference which later on in the *Tahāfut* becomes quite crucial.

This discussion of the issues involved in making sense of the temporal emerging from the eternal is really just preliminary skirmishing before we reach the main point at *TT* 34. Here Ghazali faces squarely the problem of explaining how God can be taken to choose to create the world at a particular time when for him all times are the same. How is he motivated to create the world at one time rather than at another time? What could encourage him to create then rather than earlier or later? What principles could he have had in mind when thinking about when to create the world? The main problem is to explain how God could choose a particular time to create when there is no way of distinguishing one time from another time. As Averroes points out, it is difficult to see how Ghazali makes out his case:

for two similar things are equivalent for the willer, and his action can only attach itself to the one rather than to the other through their being dissimilar, i.e. through one's having a quality the other has not. When, however, they are similar in every way and when for God there is no differentiating principle at all, his will will attach itself to both of them indifferently and . . . it will attach itself either to the two contrary actions simultaneously or to neither of them at all, and both cases are absurd (*TT* 36).

Ghazali argues very interestingly here that not only can the divine will differentiate between two similar alternatives, but the human will can too:

Suppose two similar dates in front of a man who has a strong desire for them, but who is unable to take them both. Surely he will take one of them through a quality in him the nature of which is to differentiate between two similar things . . . Everyone, therefore, who studies, in the human and the divine, the real working of the act of choice, must necessarily admit a quality the nature of which is to differentiate between two similar things (*TT* 37–8).

This is a very interesting suggestion. When faced with two equivalent alternative courses of action, we have to select one if we are to act, and we must have a reason for selecting that one. Yet if there is no difference between the courses of action as such apart from the fact that they are distinct, we as choosers must provide the reason for selecting one rather than another. If even we can do it, then surely there is no difficulty in conceiving of God just choosing when the world should begin regardless of the similarity of all the competing starting dates. Ghazali suggests that any difficulty in accepting this proposition is no more than a failure in human imagination rather than a conceptual difficulty. Yet Averroes' reply to this argument is entirely effective. He argues that, where we have a choice between two similar alternatives, the choice is really between accepting one of the alternatives and rejecting both. For instance, if one is hungry and is presented with equivalent dates, the choice may seem to be between the dates, but really it is between eating and not eating. Either date will satisfy one's hunger, and in choosing a date one is choosing not to remain hungry. The actual date one goes for is entirely incidental to the purpose in hand. But does this matter? Cannot Ghazali still use this example to show how God can arbitrarily choose a particular time to create the world? The problem with his argument here is that it is designed to suggest that the divine will can establish a difference where none previously exists, whereas the truth of the matter is that in the example a choice is made between alternative courses of action where a difference does already exist (*TT* 40–1).

Ghazali broadens his argument to suggest that the world could have a different physical structure than it does have without any interference in the workings of the world. He produces examples of facts with variations which might easily be very different from their present state. He discusses the differences in the directions of the movements of the spheres, and the choice of a pair of definite points in the outer sphere to serve as poles around which the heavens revolve. As far as the latter is concerned, since all parts of the sphere are of the same character, nothing could render any one pair of opposite points preferable to another as a locus of the poles. In addition, what is the necessity of accepting that the movements of one of the heavenly spheres to the west and the others to the east represent the only way in which such spheres could move? Ghazali argues that the same effects would certainly be achieved in a universe which moves in the opposite direction, with the highest sphere moving to the east rather than to the west. If this is true, then the existing organization of the universe is entirely arbitrary. This line of argument is designed to establish that there are instances in the universe of the existence of one kind of arrangement which is very similar to a kind of arrangement which does not exist, and so a choice was made of one state of affairs as against other similar alternatives. In that case, exactly the same determining factor which selected the locus of the poles and the direction of the movements of the spheres could have chosen a time for creation even though all times are similar.

Averroes' response to this attack seems rather weak, and takes the form of claiming that one could show why the world must have the particular features it does have for it to operate in the way in which it does. He goes on to quote two Koranic passages (xviii. 103–4 and vi. 75) which assert that the world should be seen as a divinely created structure, arranged in the very best and wisest manner. Averroes' argument, such as it is, is not a very strong one. He recommends that we look on the spheres as being organisms:

And just as it would be ridiculous to say that a certain movement in a certain species of earthly animal could be in any part whatever of its body, or in that part where it is in another species, because this movement has been localized in each species in the place where it conforms most to its nature, or in the only place where this animal can perform the movement, so it stands with the differentiation in the heavenly bodies for the place of their poles (*TT* 49).

When Ghazali questions the inconceivability of the arrangement of the spheres he is, according to Averroes, questioning the perfect positioning of legs on animals. The means of movement which animals possess are in the very best part of their bodies for the purpose of movement, and wondering whether they could be anywhere else is to doubt the wisdom of their organization. Now, one might think that this point requires more in the way of defence. Some sort of argument should be produced to prove demonstratively that the way in which movement is organized in animals *is* the optimal arrangement. Averroes' assumption, which is clearly expressed in the Ninth Discussion, is that everything is made with wisdom, and as such reveals in principle intelligent organization. He suggests that:

when one has observed a work with respect to its quantity and quality, and asked why the maker of this work chose this quantity or that quality to the exclusion of all other possible quantities and qualities, there is no worse mistake than to answer 'Not because of the intrinsic wisdom and thoughtfulness in the product itself, but because he willed it' (*TT* 412).

To oppose this point, Ghazali would have to argue that the creatures in the world were not created wisely and well adapted to their environment. But he could suggest that it is possible to think of improvements to the way things are arranged without criticizing the divine wisdom which went into the world. After all, for Ghazali God is under no obligation to create the very best sort of world, since the very notion of God being under an obligation is suspect. He has created the world he has created, and he could have created a different kind of world, out of pure will, and the reasons which he had for that sort of creation did not impel him in a particular direction. God created a certain kind of world because he wanted to, and it is irrelevant for us to speculate as to his motives or rationale.

This might strike us as a surprising view for a religious philosopher to adopt, and we shall see later how Averroes tries to chip away at the totality of Ash'arite philosophy of which this position is a logical consequence. But it is worth pointing out that Ghazali is pulled towards this position by his understanding of the *falāsifa* and the apparent lack of a role for a creative deity in their system. As he says: 'according to you philosophers, God has made the world consequent upon his essence by nature and by necessity, not through will and choice . . . this kind of occurrence, although it may be called an act, does not imply knowledge at all' (*TT* 437). The will of God appears to be identical with his knowledge. This implies that there is no role for God to choose between the alternatives which he may consider. He *must* choose the best of the possible states of affairs which he contemplates, thus limiting his ability and freedom to act. Averroes argues that this is not really the case, and we should beware of treating God's will as though it were like human will:

> The philosophers only attribute a will to God in the sense that the acts which proceed from him proceed through knowledge, and everything which proceeds through knowledge and wisdom proceeds through the will of the agent, not, however, necessarily and naturally, since the nature of knowledge does not imply (as he falsely affirms of the philosophers) the proceeding of the act. For if the nature of knowledge did imply this, then, when we say that God knows the opposites, it would be necessary that the opposites should proceed from him together, and this is absurd (*TT* 438).

The important aspect of the argument here is that Averroes wants to distinguish clearly our choosing which 'implies a deficiency in the willer and a being affected by the object willed' (*TT* 438) from that properly attributed to God, who has no deficiencies and is unaffected by the existence of objects. After all, 'the Creator is too exalted to possess an attribute which should be an effect' (*TT* 439). His strategy is to argue that 'the term "will" is attributed to the divine will and the human in an equivocal way, just as the term "knowledge" is attributed equivocally to eternal knowledge and to temporal' (*TT* 439). And yet, while Ghazali is accused of trying to identify the divine will with the human will, he does have a point in asking precisely what we mean when we say that God chooses a certain form for the world if he does not have any real alternative action. Averroes is surely disingenuous when he suggests that if the world proceeded from God's knowledge only then both the world and its alternatives would have proceeded from his knowledge. While God may be taken to contemplate a variety of actions, being God he can only accept one as viable:

when a thing passes into existence from non-existence . . . it cannot be doubted that existence is better for it than non-existence [see also *De generatione et corruptione*, 2. 10, 336ᵇ 28]. It is in this . . . way that the primal will is related to existing things, for it chooses for them eternally the better of two opposites, and this essentially and primally (*TT* 39).

Has Averroes successfully defended the notion of God's freedom to choose and act as he himself determines? One might think that, as God knows the best course of action, he then has no option but to follow it, and there is no place for any genuine choice. We could take up Averroes' point here, though, and suggest that it would be misguided to ascribe wilfulness to God such that he could be capable of going awry in his decisions concerning how to act. We can have good grounds for believing that the best action in a particular situation is A, and yet fail to A for all sorts of reasons, running from weakness of will to confusion and inefficiency. The very fact that one acts in accordance with one's nature is not in itself any indication of a lack of freedom, provided that it is possible to conceive of alternatives which remain physically open to one to perform. To take an Aristotelian example, if we as human beings have essential natures which specify to a degree what it is for us to live well, then this will have implications for our moral behaviour. If we are to act in morally appropriate ways, this view of our nature must come into our considerations and guide them. This does not imply, however, a radical lack of freedom on our side when it comes to moral choice. It is just that, being the sorts of creatures we are, moral choice must presuppose certain aspects of human nature. Since God also has a particular nature, choice for him must take that nature into account, and this does not represent an attack upon his power of agency or his freedom of action.

Ghazali returns to the main issue, namely, how can the temporal be produced by an eternal being? God is eternal, and his existence gives rise to the temporal series of events which make up the world. The philosophers derive the existence of a first mover from the problems in making sense of an infinite chain of causes which would otherwise have to be used as an explanation for the natural events with which we are familiar. Since the philosophers are not prepared to accept the concept of actual infinity, Ghazali wonders how they are going to avoid having to accept the existence of a cause for the world as a whole. After all, if everything in the world has a cause, we can in principle follow these causes into ever increasing generalities until we arrive at the first cause. What is then wrong with the idea that God brings into existence the world at any time he wishes to select? As Ghazali puts it, 'we must either come to an infinite regress or arrive at an eternal being out of which a first temporal being proceeds' (*TT* 61). Averroes' response to this problem is interesting: 'the temporal proceeds from the first eternal thing, not in so far as it is temporal but in so far as it is eternal, i.e. through being eternal generically, though temporal in its parts' (*TT* 61). His argument is that we should not think in terms of an eternal being directly causing a non-eternal and temporal event, 'for an eternal act has an eternal agent, and a temporal act a temporal agent' (*TT* 63). Temporal events have accidental causes which have their place in an infinite series of other temporal events. The entire series of temporal events is none the less itself eternal and brought about essentially by an eternal being acting upon the totality. This being is an essential cause in that it brings about its effects at the same time as it exists, which is not normally the case with accidental causal production. The eternal cause is only indirectly a cause of the temporal events themselves; it is directly the cause of the whole series of temporal events. This makes possible Averroes' claim that God does not act directly in time without at the same time having to accept the existence of an actual infinite series of temporal events. This does not seem very satisfactory as an explanation, though. Does not the eternal cause set in motion the series of temporal events at some time? What Averroes has in mind here is a version of Aristotle's account of essential or substantival change, which is very different from qualitative and quantitative change. Writing this book consists of assembling a certain number and type of pieces of paper with writing on them (quantitative and qualitative change), yet all this material is essentially changed into a book when it is finished. The change from a series of pieces of paper to a book takes no time at all. It did take time to fill the pieces of paper, and one could date quite precisely when the first word was written and the last full stop added. But none of these times represents the time when the new thing was brought into existence; it came into existence because of what all these temporal events *mean*. Given God's nature, he would not need any time to create new substances even in the oblique way in which we create them, and the substance of the world would have been created simultaneously with his own existence. He set in train the series of temporal events which make up our world by establishing a new substance of which they are a part, by giving that series a particular *meaning*. The world as a whole is essentially a divine product, while the events in the world are only accidentally effects of his being. We shall see in the rest of this part how Averroes tries to evade the charge that this theory is guilty of separating God from his world in an unacceptable way from a religious and philosophical point of view.

The Second Proof

Ghazali renews the attack in this section, now concentrating upon the notion of time. He wants to establish the proposition that time was created when the world was created, and that there is no enormous difficulty from a conceptual point of view in thinking of God existing before and without time:

> The meaning of our words that God is prior to the world and to time is: he existed without the world and without time, then he existed and with him there was the world and there was time . . . the world is like a particular individual, so that were we to say for example that God existed without Jesus, and then existed with Jesus, we assert nothing more than, firstly, the existence of an essence and the non-existence of an essence, and then the existence of two essences, and there is no need to assume here a third essence, time, even though our imagination finds it impossible not to presuppose it. We should not be fooled by the errors of imagination (*TT* 65–6).

Ghazali is trying to establish the acceptability of the notion that before the creation of the world God existed even if we adhere to an Aristotelian account of time. On the latter, time is not like a matrix on which all events can be identified, but rather a measure of change. Time is one movement measuring other movements by comparing and contrasting the number of times the one takes place while the others take place. Following Aristotelian premises, the existence of time presupposes the existence of movement and hence of a moving body. Since time is the measure of movement, if it can be established that time is eternal, then it would follow that a moving being, in other words the world, is eternal. For Aristotle, then, it is not just a matter of imagination that connects disparate events in terms of before, now, and after. It is a vital aspect of any language involving change and movement. In this proof Ghazali represents quite accurately the Aristotelian thesis that there could really be no start or end to time. Whatever it was that is taken to have produced the first change must itself change to act, which gives rise to an infinite regress, for something else must have changed to produce that change, and so on. Again, were time to come to an end, we could no longer measure change beyong a certain point, yet, if a measurer still existed to stand in a determinate relation to that end time, we could not rule out future changes.

Ghazali clearly has to face the difficulty of explaining how we can conceive of God existing before the world exists and yet not existing in time. Our language seems to compel acceptance of his temporal priority to the world, and, once this has been granted, the sorts of conclusions which the *falāsifa* press concerning the eternity of the world seem inevitable. Ghazali puts the stress on the way in which a picture of the relationship between disparate events and time misleads us (a point which he will repeat with even greater vigour when discussing causation and the way it is also taken to link disparate events). He needs to show, then, that the imagination misleads us when it invariably includes time in relations of priority and posteriority. He argues that:

This resembles the inability of the imagination to admit a limited body, e.g. overhead, without anything beyond its surface, so that it is imagined that behind the world there is a space either occupied or empty; and when it is said there is above the surface of the world no beyond and no farther extension, this is beyond the grasp of the imagination. Similarly, when it is said that there is no real predecessor to the existence of the world, the imagination refuses to believe it (*TT* 72).

In his response to this attack Averroes accuses Ghazali of spatializing time:

Ghazali treats the quantity which has no position and does not form a totality, i.e. time and motion, as the quantity which possesses position and totality, i.e. body. He makes the impossibility of endlessness in the latter a proof of its impossibility in the former, and he treats the action of the mind in imagining an increase in the quantity which is assumed to be actual, i.e. body, as if it concerned both quantities. This is manifest error (*TT* 76).

Averroes provides a very interesting argument, or rather series of arguments, to back up his critique. Firstly, he defends the logical connection between movement and time while at the same time rejecting the existence of such a connection between one space and another space in which the former ends. Now, one might think that the role of the instant, the 'now' in time was equivalent to the role of the point in space. This would be a mistaken identification, however. A 'now' is not a period of time (as indeed a point is not a part of space) but a limit which brings one time period to an end and marks the start of another. There is then time on both sides of it, and there could not be a first 'now' with no time before it, nor a last 'now' with no time after it, and so no beginning or ending of time. (*TT* 76–7; *Phys.* 8.1, 251ᵃ, 9–28). Yet: 'This, however, does not apply to the point, for the point is the end of the line and exists at the same time as the line, for the line is at rest. Therefore one can imagine a point which is the beginning of a line without its being the end of another line, but the instant cannot exist without the past and the future' (*TT* 77).

Averroes' argument is that the logical link between the instant and the time which surrounds it is very different from the difficulty which we might have in thinking of a point without space surrounding it. He suggests that:

the act of the imagination that a body with straight dimensions must end in another body is not false; no, this is a necessary truth, for the body with straight dimensions has the possibility of increasing, and . . . must end in the circumscribing circular body, since this is the perfect body which is liable neither to increase not to decrease (*TT* 78).

Averroes insists on the existence of 'an absolute above and an absolute below, but no absolute beginning and no absolute end' when it comes to discussing the nature of space (*TT* 82). This thesis leads Ghazali to a clever riposte, when he uses the arguments of the philosophers in support of the impossibility of a first creative event to establish the variability of the size of the world. After all, if the idea that the world was created at *t* can be criticized by the suggestion that an omnipotent God could surely create it a bit earlier than *t*, similarly the notion that the world has a certain size can be criticized by the possibility that God might have created it a bit bigger, or smaller (*TT* 87). Averroes replies to this charge that it is no threat to the notion of God's omnipotence that he is unable to do the impossible, and altering the size of the world by even a tiny amount is said to fall into the category of the impossible (*TT* 90).

What sort of impossibility is involved here? It is clearly not the 'same as regarding it as possible to identify black with white and existence with non-existence', as Ghazali puts it (*TT* 90). Averroes claims that the impossibility involved is more subtly connected with the concepts of the world and space which we use:

if it is assumed that the world might be larger or smaller than it is, it follows that outside it there would be occupied or empty space. And from the supposition that there is outside it occupied or empty space, some of the greatest impossibilities follow; from empty space the existence of mere extension existing by itself, while from occupied space a body moving either upwards or downwards or in a circle which therefore must be part of another world. Now it has been proved in the science of physics that the existence of another world at the same time as this is an impossibility and the most unlikely consequence would be that the world should have empty space. For any world must have four elements and a spherical body revolving around them (*TT* 91).

It might be thought here that Averroes goes too far in calling a different sort of physics which might account for a different view of space impossible. Such a science might be a poor explanatory model for our present world, but what is there to say that it might not serve well for a bigger or smaller world? On the Aristotelian approach, a finite space is necessary since otherwise the observable and regular properties of the heavens and the theory of natural motion would be impossible. An infinite space would additionally involve an infinite chain of causes of a given event, and we would not then be able to grasp the explanation of that event, given that we are finite creatures limited in our understanding of our world. We can know the explanations of things, we can produce explanations for the natural events of our world, and so the latter must be finite.

Ghazali is ready for this sort of answer, because he wonders whether the world must be necessary, rather than just possible, since its size is determinately established from the beginning. It could not have another and different size. Would it not follow then that the world is not in need of a creator at all? If it is necessary, what place is there for someone to bring it about? Averroes replies here very appropriately that this is a mistaken objection, since something can necessarily have the form and matter it has if it is to satisfy the description we give to it. He gives the example of a saw, which he claims must be of metal and have a particular shape before we count it as a saw, and yet there is no implication here that 'the saw has necessity of being' (*TT* 92). Ghazali's third line of attack is to put pressure on the notion of alternative sizes for the world being possible before its creation. If it is impossible for God to create the world at a particular time because he could have created it earlier, why is it not similarly impossible for God to have created the world a particular size because he could have created it a different size, perhaps 'bigger or smaller by the width of a nail' (*TT* 93)? Averroes' response to this argument is not very satisfactory. He tries to turn the tables on Ghazali by suggesting that: 'He, then, who assumes that from the eternal there proceeds only a temporal act presumes that his act is constrained in a certain way and in this way therefore does not depend on his choice' (*TT* 97). This does not really deal with the problem of the apparent comparability of space and time when it comes to the question of their finitude. Averroes seems to argue that one can deduce from reason alone the existence of a finite space, and God with his omnipotence and benevolence would create the optimal universe for his creatures which takes the structure of the universe we know. Were it to be infinite we could not establish laws of nature or grasp the laws of movement. Yet one might wonder whether the same difficulty does not arise for an infinite time, since apparently lawlike regularities can only be observed to hold over a finite period, and in the future, or in the past, which stretches away from us into infinity beyond the limits of our awareness, these laws and regularities might fall apart and change.

The Third Proof

In the Third Proof Averroes is faced with an attack upon the account of modality which the *falāsifa* employ to establish the eternity of the world. The philosophers argue that the existence of the world before it actually existed, were there to be such a state of affairs, was always possible. It must always have been possible since now it is actual. In just the same way the state of affairs describable as my smoking a pipe must always have been possible, even before either I or pipes were thought of, because it is now actual. Anything which has always been possible 'must exist eternally of necessity, for what is eternal cannot be destroyed, except in the case where the corruptible can become eternal' (*TT* 98). The argument is supposed to show that what must have been always possible can be deduced from what is now actual, which seems quite plausible, but it is then taken to establish that since a state of affairs has always been possible it must always be actual too, and so the world is eternal and not corruptible. This very strange argument would as it stands seem to show that I have always been in existence smoking my pipe, a palpably ridiculous proposition.

Van den Bergh suggests that an unstated assumption which makes the argument plausible is that the world as a whole is ungenerated.[1] An ungenerated thing can never go out of or come into existence, and so is eternal. The world is possible and we know that it exists at some time, and it is ungenerated, so that if it exists at some time it must have existed at every time. This comment is unhelpful, since were this to be the hidden assumption here Ghazali would have been likely to have spotted it. What is implicit in the argument is what has been called the principle of plenitude, according to which there is a logical connection between the eternally possible and the actual. Averroes argues that:

The man who assumes that before the existence of the world there was one unique, never-ending possibility must accept that the world is eternal. The man who asserts, with Ghazali, that before the world there existed an infinite number of

---

[1] *Averroes Tahafut al-tahafut (The Incoherence of the Incoherence)*, trans. and int. S. Van den Berg (Luzac: London, 1954; repr. 1978), ii. 43; the second volume of this work is referred to hereafter as *Notes*.

possible worlds, must admit that before this world there was another world, and before this second world a third, and so on ad infinitum, as is the case with human beings (*TT* 98–9).

Yet one wants to ask here why we are forced to assume that, if there is a possibility of God's creating a world before creating our world, he must actually have created an infinite series of them. Could God not just be thought of as considering when to create our world, and what form it should take? We might take Averroes' point that it would be peculiar to understand by a sequence of divinely created worlds a series rather like that of the infinite sequence of human beings, yet still remain in the dark over the question of why it is not possible to *think* about such alternative possible worlds. Averroes' argument is that, if these worlds are genuinely possible, then something will eventually necessitate their existence, and so they must at some point come to exist in a sort of series before our world was created, rather in the way that previous generations of human beings led to our generation. This is not a very helpful analogy, though, since, even if we do think of a series of worlds existing before this world, we do not have to think of them as causally interlinked. First there could be a world in which pigs could fly, then a world without any pigs, flying or otherwise. There is no need to contemplate an explanation of how a possible world with flying pigs becomes replaced with a world without them on the lines of a scientific hypothesis. Why must this imaginary series of worlds be connected along the causal lines which Averroes suggests? One answer lies in something he says in this section, that 'if God had the power to create another world before this, and before this second world yet another, the series must continue indefinitely' (*TT* 99). If the world is created at a finite time, then God could have created another world before it, and another world before that one, and so on. Yet Ghazali might wonder why the fact that he *could* create such a series is used to show that he *would* have brought it about, which seems rather arbitrary. Again, it is the principle of plenitude which becomes important here, for according to it anything which is eternally possible is actualized at some time or another. If the world is created at a finite time, God could always have created preceding worlds, and if he could always have created them, then he must eventually create them. He must have some motive for creating them, so the notion of development becomes important here. One world might be thought to lead to another in terms of perfection, and this is a highly inappropriate model for us to have of the world's generation. Averroes concludes that it is much simpler to think of the world as eternal and unique, and does not involve us in the conceptual difficulties of dealing with a whole series of worlds which stretch to infinity. As we have already seen, the plausibility of Averroes' approach here is entirely dependent upon the strength of the principle of plenitude and his critique of the notion of an actual infinity.

It is clear that the account of possibility which Averroes employs is very different from some commonsense notions of possibility. One thing we might say about possibility is that if something is possible then it might or might not happen, whereas if it is actual it has happened and if it is necessary it must happen. Averroes finds in Aristotle the doctrine that if something is possible then it must happen at some time or another, and if this possibility is never actualized then it was never a possibility. Aristotle has a variety of arguments in this area, some of which are based upon the idea that if we ascribe a certain power to a thing, if we say that it has a particular ability, we must delineate the range of this ability. One of the important limitations on this ability is the time over which it is said to extend. That is, my ability to type is limited both in terms of time and skill. I can type at a certain rate (so many words per minute) and for a particular period of my life. If I were to enjoy an infinitely long existence, there would be something rather odd about saying that I had a natural tendency to type which was never fulfilled. Were I to live for an infinite time and never type during that time, we should be committed to saying that a capacity can exist for an infinite time and also not exist for an infinite time, which again strikes Aristotle as contradictory. This kind of argument has been summarized by Jaako Hintikka under the useful label of the 'principle of plenitude' according to which for Aristotle something is necessary if it always was and always will be so and something is possible if it has happened or will happen at some time.[2].

In *De caelo*, I. 12, 281^b3–32, we find the argument that a world which exists at all times does not possess the capacity to cease to exist. On the face of it this is a very poor argument. The same reasoning would establish that, if during my life I never committed adultery, I did not possess the ability to commit adultery. Aristotle appreciates that a thing can at the same time possess the capacities for existing and for not existing, without appreciating that it can at the same time possess the capacity for existing at one time together with the capacity for not existing at that time. If the world always exists, he argues that there is no time left with respect to which it can have a capacity for not existing. Or, if matter is never

[2] J. Hintikka, *Time and Necessity: Studies in Aristotle's Theory of Modality* (Oxford University Press: Oxford, 1973), ch. 5.

organized into a world, then it is incapable of being so organized. If matter can remain unorganized at every time, then there is no time with respect to which it can have the capacity for being organized. Why is he so insistent that opposed powers or capacities cannot relate to the same time? He is concerned that if this is permitted it will make possible the contradiction of their being instantiated at the same time.

It is not clear that his concern here is justified. When he claims 'It is not allowable that it is true to say "this is possible, but will not be"' (*Met.* 9. 4, 1047^{b}3) he is suggesting that what is possible must conceivably occur. Imagine it occurring but assume at the same time that it will not occur. In that case imagining it to happen contradicts the assumption that it will not happen. There is some point in distinguishing between something like a cloak and things which exist forever and are continually active (*De int.* 9, 19^{a}9–18). Since the stars exist forever, for the whole of time, possibilities with respect to them cannot remain forever unactualized. If it were possible for the stars to stop, then, given the whole of time, they would indeed stop eventually. While Aristotle's argument is directed more towards everlasting things and their eternal properties than towards contingent and changeable phenomena, it is not clear why his thesis should not be transferred with equal justification to corruptible things. Although a cloak which has been destroyed by fire no longer possesses the capacity to be consumed by a goat, it does forever possess the negative property of not being consumed by a goat. It is worth noting here that Aristotle does accept that things can continue to possess negative properties after they have gone out of existence (*Cat.* 10, 13^{b}26–35; *De int.* 3, 16^{b}11–15). If there is no time left during which a capacity to be consumed by a goat could be actualized, then the cloak should be incapable of being consumed by a goat. In the whole of time it will not be consumed by a goat. Although Aristotle seeks to restrict his principle of plenitude to eternal things—'In everlasting things, there is no difference between being possible and being the case' (*Phys.* 3. 4, 293^{b}30)—it seems that the category of everlasting things can be extended to take in quite ordinary propositions about objects in the world of generation and corruption.

This interpretation of Aristotle might seem to come too close to the doctrine of the Megarians, with which Aristotle was plainly in dispute. According to them possibility is equivalent to the actual exercise of a technical skill, so that a carpenter is only a carpenter when he is practising his skill. When he is lying in the bath, he does not possess the capacity to work with wood (*Met.* 8. 3, 1046^{b}29–32; 1047^{a}19–20). The Megarian approach emphasizes an important aspect of possibility: its presence is only apprehended when it is embodied in some act and can only be known to be present when the act takes place. Aristotle's argument against this strategy is to stress the cultivation of skills through habit over a period of time, and he points out that we do not lose a skill as soon as we stop practising it (*Met.* 9. 3, 1047^{a}1–2). The Megarian view implies that someone who is sitting or standing will always be sitting or standing. Only what is actually changing may be said to be able to change (*Met* 9. 3, 1047^{a}10, 12–17). By contrast, Aristotle operates with a model of reality which is based upon change and development, where the world is a coherent entity in which individual beings interact constantly (*Phys.* 3. 2, 201^{a}22). Although the world exists eternally, the individual things in it only last for a limited period of time. It would be difficult to argue that all possibilities present in individual beings will at some time be actualized. Not all creatures actualize all the possibilities which they possess, and human beings in particular contain a whole list of virtues which they individually tend not to perfect to their utmost degree. Yet the idea that the world as a whole does not include the actualization of all these possibilities in someone or other is one which Aristotle dismisses. If throughout the course of the eternal world no one ever reached the highest levels of moral perfection, for instance, there would be no point in arguing that human beings possess the capacity to reach it at all.

Aristotle wonders whether something could always exist, without beginning or end, and yet still possibly not exist (*Met.* 12. 6, 1071^{b}24). He cannot see how this could be true. If something could cease to exist, it must at some time stop existing. If everything has the capacity to not exist, then at some point in the future nothing will exist. The argument here is that, if everything has the ability to not exist, then the whole of existence can not exist, and this is only a real possibility if it is realized at least once. The conclusion he draws is that at least one thing must exist necessarily without being able to not exist. The existence of at least one such entity guarantees the world from the threat of a complete collapse of existing things. In Averroes' work this notion of 'real' possibility, of possibility as having a stronger sense than that provided by logic, is very important. It plays a crucial part in the response to Ghazali in the *Tahāfut*. This move from the claim that it is possible that *p* to *p* seems highly suspect, though. Surely the whole point of distinguishing between possibility and actuality is in order to be able to talk about states of affairs which do not and may never take place, and yet which are not ruled out for any logical reason, as are square circles, for example.

One way of explaining how Aristotle and Averroes came to hold this unlikely analysis of possibility is to be found in their account of how a possibility is transformed into an actuality. No possibility could be actualized automatically. It requires transformation by something else which itself possesses the characteristic of the actual thing. This is easy to grasp when we think in terms of things moving against their natural tendency, as when a rolling stone is stopped from continuing down a slope by an intervening rock. It is possible for the stone to stop, and this possibility is actualized when it comes into contact with something static, or capable of stopping something which is moving. As we shall see, even in the case of human thought Aristotle and Averroes insist on the presence of an external cause to enable us to carry out this perfectly natural process. The possible intellect can only be actualized by an object which is what the Latin philosophers called 'intelligible in act', which in other words represents the principles of thought themselves (*De an* 3. 4, 429^{b}29–31). Other material things are not by themselves capable of actualizing the capacity to think. Only a creative principle can be an appropriate cause which brings us from the state of merely being able to think to thinking itself (*De an.* 3. 5, 430^{a}14–18). An appropriate example here is the way in which a teacher must already possess the knowledge which he wants to transmit to the pupils, and the cause of their eventual learning and knowing is the information which he has, together with the intention to pass it on.

Aristotle's model of the universe is of a dynamic and teleological complex. The potential for change and development lies in the capacity to receive from outside a perfection to which things are directed. This perfection is embodied in an act which must exist already if it is to be able to actualize the possibility which it does. For the individual it seems that the potentiality comes first and then is brought to actuality by the agent, but this is not the way things really are. As Aristotle puts it, 'Actual knowledge is identical with its object; in the individual, potential knowledge is in time prior to actual knowledge, but in the universe as a whole it is not even prior in time' (*De an.* 3. 5, 430^{a}20–5). There exists a process of interaction which explains the evolution of the universe as a striving in the direction of the good of individual things and ultimately towards that which represents perfection and immutability. We can accept this model and still wonder why Aristotle wishes to retain the principle of plenitude. We might accept that for a possibility to become an actuality it must be acted upon by something which is already actual without having to assert that any possibility must be actualized at some time or another.

To add plausibility to the principle of plenitude we should recall its reliance upon a particular view of infinity. Were time to be finite, then of course there could be potentialities which were unactualized, and which can remain as potentialities. But since time is infinite, any possibility must be actualized at some time or another. In an infinite period of time, anything which can happen does and must happen at some time or other. If we take the example of tossing a coin, then over an infinite period of time one would expect an equal number of heads and tails to be called. On an individual day it might well be that we get more heads than tails, but over an infinite period this should be evened out to take account of the fact that there is a 50 per cent chance of either heads or tails. Indeed, we might explain equality of heads and tails on a particular day as being due to the frequency of tosses and the laws of probability. Yet we could not explain in the same way my cat having kittens. In the past many cats have had kittens, and over an infinite period of time there will be a great many events describable as cats having kittens, yet this does not in itself provide an explanation for my cat having kittens. As an explanation we should need to identify a cause which brings her potential motherhood to become an actual motherhood, and, if that cause does not appear, then neither will the result. Are we obliged to claim that, if she never has kittens, then she never could have had kittens? There is no reason to agree with this claim. In the absence of a cause to bring something from potentiality to actuality, that particular thing will remain only a possibility.

The only plausible aspect of the principle of plenitude is the idea that, if an infinite number of events have taken place by a particular time, then certain types of events will have taken place by that time. If rain is possible, and an infinite amount of time transpires, then rain will take place on some occasions, when the appropriate causal antecedent conditions obtain. This sort of approach would fit in with the general principle adhered to by Aristotelians that nature does not do anything in vain. In other words, if nature has created a set of possible events (in the sense of potential activities and entities), then at some point these must be actualized. If they are to remain unactualized, why has nature bothered to construct such potentialities? It would be possible to argue here, not that unactualized potentiality is impossible in an individual, but that it cannot occur to an entire species, or type, or event or thing. This would connect well with Aristotle's insistence upon an agent in the route from potentiality to actuality, since an agent can be expected to exert its influence at some point of an infinite period of time to bring about a type of event, since the world is a complex of interacting bodies which change continually. The result is much weaker than the original principle of plenitude, though, since it suggests that, if something is possible, then that *type* of event must occur at some point or another in time.[3] For example, not all human beings attain moral perfection, and we all achieve degrees of such moral excellence. Given the infinity of time and given the principle that nature does nothing without a purpose, we could not as a species be potentially perfected morally if it was not the case that at least one person would achieve the ideal. What would be the point of holding it out as a possibility if no one managed to achieve it out of the species of human being even if the species was given an infinite amount of time to produce such a person? Of course, it remains logically conceivable that a species could fail to produce such an individual given any amount of time, yet it is not what Averroes calls 'really' possible. It cannot happen given the way in which the world is organized and what we can know about the constituents of the world.

The Fourth Proof

The status of modal concepts is the main object of discussion in this section, with some interesting comments upon the nature of matter. Averroes sums up Ghazali's account thus:

everything that becomes is possible before it becomes, and that possibility needs something for its subsistence, namely the substratum which receives that which is possible . . . there remains as a vehicle for possibility the recipient of the possible, i.e. matter. Matter, in so far as it is matter, does not become; for if it did it would require other matter and we should have an infinite regress. Matter only becomes in so far as it is combined with form. Everything which comes into being comes into being from something else, and this must either give rise to an infinite regress and lead directly to infinite matter which is impossible . . . for there is no actual infinite; or the forms must be interchangeable in the ingenerable and incorruptible substratum, eternally and in rotation (*TT* 101–2).

While the world as a totality is ungenerated and uncorruptible, the parts of the world are continually changing. Change can only come about if matter acquires different forms and then brings about new things. Matter must always exist since it is the necessary substrate of any change and so cannot itself be subject to change and only possible. It is itself necessary (albeit not necessary in itself—a divine prerogative) and cannot be affected

---

[3] For more detail on the weaker version, see D. Conway, '"It would have happened already": On One Argument for a First Cause', *Analysis*, 44/4 (1984), 159–66.

causally by other matter in order to come into existence, since this would lead to an infinite regress. Ghazali is not happy with this account of how change is possible since it seems to rule out the sort of first change which he takes God to have undertaken in the creation of the world.

Before we get on to Ghazali's criticisms, let us look more closely at the sort of Aristotelian account of change which Averroes is defending here. There is taken to be a persistent element in change, a subject which remains the same through the change taking place. This is indeed a reflection of our language here, since we talk about the same thing changing from one state to another. Substantival change does take place where one substances goes out of existence (a pile of leaves) and another comes into existence (a pile of ash). In this sort of case the generation of one substance presupposes the destruction of another. What persists in this sort of case is not a particular subject in the same form, as when I switch my matches from my left pocket to my right, but the matter that was elsewhere. Previously it was in the leaves and now it is in the ash. Change involves three stages, a substratum, a form, and a privation. The substratum is the subject that is changing, the form is the end towards which the change is directed, and the privation reveals that the form was not present at the beginning of the change. Had the privation been present there could not have been any change in the first place. As Averroes expresses it, the relation between the beginning and the end of a change is that of contraries or opposites so that any change in the colour of something from white has to be either to black or to some colour in between white and black.

Ghazali has to meet the objection to his account of creation that the Aristotelian account of change seems to rule out creation *ex nihilo*. The latter form of creation does not, for instance, work with already existing matter, since it is *ex nihilo*. Ghazali's strategy is rather like that which he followed in the Third Proof. He will suggest that if we can *think* of change taking place without matter, then there is nothing logically wrong with such a possibility being available to God:

The objection is that the possibility of which you speak is a judgement of the intellect, and anything whose existence the intellect supposes, provided no obstacle presents itself to the supposition, we call possible and, if there is such an obstacle, we call it impossible and, if we suppose that it cannot be supposed not to be, we call it necessary. These are rational judgements which require no real existent which they might qualify (*TT* 102).

The force of his argument lies in the last proposition. If indeed our modal notions make perfectly good sense regardless of whether they refer to

anything or not, then we can just think about things coming into existence
without having to presuppose the existence of matter. Ghazali goes on to
claim that the vacuity of the philosophical account of modal notions is
revealed when it comes to asking what the corresponding existent to
impossibility is, to which he responds 'impossibility has no real existence,
and there is no matter in which it occurs and to which it could be related'
(*TT* 103).

Averroes makes no apology for his correspondence theory of truth:
'That possibility demands an existing matter is clear, for all true
intellectual concepts need a thing outside the soul, for truth, as it has been
defined, is the agreement of what is in the soul with what is outside the
soul' (*TT* 103). He agrees that impossibility requires a substratum, and
claims that impossibilities such as the existence of empty space, and the
equivalence of one and two are impossible because they really cannot exist.
Yet if they cannot exist, it is difficult to see why they require a substratum.
Presumably one of the reasons why they cannot exist is the unavailability
of a substratum for them. In his next objection, Ghazali seeks to show 'that
the intellect in order to decide whether something is possible need not
admit an existing thing to which the possibility can be related' (*TT* 104).
He argues that, if possibility presupposes the existence of matter, it would
be impossible to conceive of certain properties as possible when they are
unrelated to matter. That is, we can think of white and black without
necessarily thinking about white and black things. If it is possible to
conceive of a colour without at the same time conceiving of a coloured
thing then no essential connection holds between attributes and their
material substrate. Averroes argues that, if we think more deeply about
what is involved in applying colour attributes to objects, or just applying
them in general, we shall see that non-existence of a colour cannot become
existence of the colour without passing through a middle stage, where this
latter is matter. If some state of affairs is possible then it can come into
existence from its contrary, and if it is to come into existence from its
contrary it must come from somewhere and a material cause must be
available to explain its transition from one state to another. Ghazali tries to
show that we can think of things as possible without being actual, an
opinion with which Averroes concurs (*TT* 106), and he derives from this
distinction the proposition that we can conceive of things independently of
their instantiation in reality. In that case it could not be validly argued that
the notion of possibility depends upon or presupposes the notion of
actuality or existence, in this case the eternal existence of matter as a
substratum.

Averroes insists that what is significant about the notion of possibility is that it identifies states of affairs which are potentially real or actual. He is adhering here to a broad interpretation of the principle of plenitude according to which 'It is not allowable that it is true to say "this is possible, but it will not be"' (*Met.* 9. 4, 1047^{b}3). Talking about possible states of affairs is only meaningful if we can think in terms of their eventual transformation into real states of affairs, and the logic of this change must follow the account of change which Averroes defends. Characteristically, Ghazali himself points to the sorts of responses which the *falāsifa* would make to his arguments (*TT* 108–9) and cleverly abstracts the notion of modality as that which misleads them on this issue. For:

To reduce possibility, necessity and impossibility to rational concepts is correct, and as for the assertion that the concepts of reason form its knowledge, and knowledge implies an object of knowledge ... yet these objects have no real existence in the external world, and the philosophers are certainly right in saying that universals exist only in the mind, not in the external world ... it can be said that possibility is a form which exists in minds, not in the external world (*TT* 109–10).

This is an intriguing suggestion. Ghazali is here using the philosophical theory of concept formation to throw doubt on the referential nature of our concepts. If he can break the link between our concepts and the way the world is, he can argue that we can imagine states of affairs very different from existing states of affairs, and so we can imagine alternatives which God did not in fact actualize, although he could have. This would lend support to the idea that he contemplated a variety of different plans for creation, and then used one at some finite point in the past. The beauty of Ghazali's technique is that the only premises of his argument are those shared by the *falāsifa*, namely, that the only things which exist in the external world are things, that is particulars, and the mind abstracts from those particulars to establish an abstract form in terms of a concept. Concepts are aspects of our rationality, while individual existents are apprehended through our sensory equipment. Possibility, just like other concepts, should be seen as an entirely rational concept, with a role and status in abstraction and isolation from the objects of our senses. In that case, it has a far wider scope in allowing a range of alternatives for creation than is the case on the philosophical account.

This argument is not a very good one, though. Averroes has little problem in extricating himself from it. He points out that concepts 'exist potentially, not actually in the external world' (*TT* 111). He means that, while we can use universal concepts to describe phenomena in the external world, and so those universals exist there potentially, it does not follow that there are universals in the external world. They must not be taken to be just another item among the great variety which exist there. Concepts do not exist in the external world in the way in which individual things exist. We can point to instances of concepts being applied in the world in the sense that we can point to white things, and heavy things, but we cannot point in the same way to redness and heaviness existing by themselves. Ghazali takes this to mean that when we use concepts of colour and weight we are in possession of ideas in our minds about these attributes, and these attributes can exist in our minds without having any corresponding material objects on which to settle. If colours are ideas in the mind without being aspects of the real world, in the sense that they are not primarily to be found in the world, then possibility can also be regarded as merely a mental phenomenon which cannot limit God's freedom of action to shape the world as and when he wishes.

Averroes seeks to counter this approach by showing that 'in a way the universal has an existence outside the soul' (*TT* 112). The fact that we can use universals implies according to him that they must succeed in abstracting features of the external world which really do exist:

for it cannot be doubted that the judgements of the mind have sense only with respect to the nature of things outside the mind. If there were outside the soul nothing possible nor impossible, the judgement of the mind that things are possible or impossible would be of as much point as no judgement at all, and there would be no difference between reason and illusion (*TT* 113).

Similarly, we can identify possible and impossible states of affairs in the external world, we can use these modal notions to describe our experience, and this suggests that they are not just formal concepts which only incidentally have an empirical use. Averroes is not arguing that our use of universals and modal notions to describe aspects of the real world is a guarantee that they are accurately so used on particular occasions. This would, no doubt, be a matter for specific investigation limited to the particular judgement considered. He is arguing, though, that the sense of these abstract notions is intimately linked with their empirical application, and they are indeed derived in part from experience which we have of ordinary objects in the external world. In the clash between Ghazali and Averroes over modal notions we are presented not just with a dispute over the proper interpretation of these terms, but rather with opposing theories of meaning. For Ghazali abstract terms have meaning in themselves, regardless of their connection with their referents in the external world. In order to use such terms we need only represent to ourselves a series of pictures or images in which the events are characterized by colour, or possibility, or weight. We can then talk about God realizing these states of affairs in isolation from any explanation of how they are linked to other states of affairs in the real world. Change can be thought to come about by sleight of divine hand, without the preconditions which are necessarily involved in analysing change which occurs in the external world. Averroes' argument is based upon the principle that it is not enough to have a series of images in one's mind to prove the meaningfulness of the states of affairs corresponding to those images. For example, we can think of God creating the world at a particular time in the sense that we form a picture of what this would be like. Averroes argues that we should not be misled by the fact that we can do this into thinking that we know what we are talking about. A proper use of terms is acquired through their connection with the framework in which they make sense, and this framework is firmly grounded in the way in which the world works. Since our universal concepts are abstracted from the individuals in the world, this is hardly surprising. Ghazali seems to think that we do not require such a framework to give our concepts meaning; so long as a sensible picture corresponds to those concepts we can be assured that they are being properly used. This clash comes out much more clearly in the discussion of the nature of causation and the notion of philosophy which are still to be analysed.

What Can God Do?

How far apart are the philosophers and the theologians on creation?

THE philosophers and the theologians seem to be very far apart on the question of the creation of the world. As we have seen, Averroes supports the notion of an eternal world not created in time, while for Ghazali and the Ash'arites the only genuine causal agent is God, who holds in being the world, consisting as it does of transitory atoms and accidents, from one instantaneous period to the next. The world was not only created *ex nihilo*, but it is kept in existence by a process of continual recreation out of nothing, with God's power and will being the only real explanation for its continuation. The philosophical position seems to diminish God's role, while the theologians seek to emphasize it. Yet Averroes argues on more than one occasion that there is really not much difference between the philosophers and the theologians on this issue. If we adopt the esotericist view there would be no problem in grasping his point, for he would obviously be dissimulating his real views and pretending they accorded with religious orthodoxy. This easy way out is not available to us here, though, and it is worth spending some time trying to see why Averroes thought these two apparently very different positions quite similar.

It is necessary to look at a fairly extensive quotation from his *Faṣl al-maqāl* (Decisive Treatise on the Harmony of Religion and Philosophy):

Concerning the question whether the world is pre-eternal or came into existence, the disagreement between the Ash'arite theologians and the ancient philosophers is in my view almost resolvable into a disagreement about naming. . . . For they agree that there are three classes of being: two extremes and one intermediate between the extremes. One extreme is a being which is brought into existence from something other than itself and by something . . . and . . . its existence is preceded by time. . . . All alike, ancients and Ash'arites, agree in naming this class of being 'originated'. The opposite extreme to this is a being which is not made from or by anything and not preceded by time; and here too all members of both schools agree in naming it 'pre-eternal'. This being is apprehended by demonstration; it is God . . .

The class of being which is between these two extremes is that which is not made from anything and not preceded by time, but which is brought into existence by something, i.e. by an agent. This is the world as a whole. . . . the theologians admit that time does not precede it, or rather this is a necessary consequence for them since time according to them is something which accompanies motion and bodies. They also agree with the ancients in the view that future time is infinite and likewise future being. They only disagree about past time and past being: the theologians hold that it is finite . . . while Aristotle and his school hold that it is infinite (*FM* 11–12).

In his *Discourse on the Manner of the World's Existence* Averroes likewise claims that there is no contradiction between this theological view and that of the philosophers. He actually says that:

The intention in this discourse is for us to make clear that what the Peripatetics believed and what the *mutakallimūn* among the people of our region believe regarding the manner of the world's existence [approximate one another] in meaning and that most of their disagreements are due to only the equivocality of what is [called] pre-eternal and temporally originated (*Discourse*, p. 207).

As he suggests in the *Faṣl al-maqāl*, when discussing time 'in truth it is neither really originated nor really pre-eternal, since the really originated is necessarily perishable and the really pre-eternal has no cause' (*FM* 12).

It seems rather strange that Averroes should try to reconcile the philosophical account of creation with the views of the theologians given the wide gap which exists between the contrasting views. He does have an interesting argument for his thesis, though. It comes from his interpretation of an Aristotelian view on how becoming takes place. An event in time comes from something, it has a material cause (*Phys.* 2. 3, 194^{b}24 = *Met.* 5. 2, 1013^{a}24). As we have already seen, it is preceded in time by its privation (*Phys.* 1. 8, 191^{b}15) and such an event can be given a position in both time and space. Time, space, and void are necessary conditions of motion (*Phys.* 4. 1, 208^{b}36) and coming to be is to be regarded as a kind of motion (*Phys.* 3. 1, 201^{a}10–11). Whatever becomes, comes to be, has an efficient cause which moves it from privation to existence, from possibility to actuality, and the cause is 'the primary cause of the change or coming to rest' (*Phys.* 2. 3, 194^{b}29). Now, the theological position is very different. For them the world is a miraculous event created out of nothing. Space and time are divine creations in much the same way as the objects within them. As Averroes comments in the *Faṣl al-maqāl* 'time according to them is something which accompanies motion and bodies' (*FM* 11), since it is composed of discrete atoms which last for only the instant over which God creates them. Averroes takes the theologians to argue in this sort of way.

They agree with Aristotle that whatever has no beginning has no end (*De caelo*, I. 10–12, 279^{b}5–292^{b}22), since what is finite is limited in both directions, while the infinite is not limited in any direction. If the series of events which make up the world has no beginning, it can have no end. If it is infinite, then it cannot be limited in any way, yet, since we can say that the series of events has reached an end at the present time, it appears that the infinite has been limited in some way. This implies that the series of events which makes up the world must have a beginning. They go on to argue that time is not only not a condition for the existence of the outer sphere, but is instead really contingent upon it for its own existence. The world can then be regarded as having a beginning at which the creator not only produced it but also time and space as well.

Averroes tries to get around the apparent irreconcilability of the philosophical and the theological positions by defending a subtle account of the nature of time. He concedes to the theologians that time is 'something temporally originated' but qualifies this admission 'by what is circular' (*Discourse*, p. 209). He goes on to argue that this does not imply that either the world or time itself had an absolute beginning at some point in the finite past. Time is circular in the sense of being without a beginning or an end. There is no inherent difficulty in the notion of measuring parts of a circle, of identifying starting and finishing positions, and there is consequently no problem in measuring periods of time. It does not follow that we should be in a position to measure the entire range of time up to the present moment. But 'when time is imagined correctly as a cyclical continuum, within the spheres, it is not necessary for its past to have a completion, for if it had a completion it would have had a beginning, whereas that which has no beginning has no completion' (*Discourse*, p. 209).

Averroes' argument here is that the apparent discrepancy between the views of the theologians and the philosophers on the origin of the world is not as unbridgeable as might be thought if we take a close look at the notion of what it means to come to be in time:

However, if it were to be described as temporally originated in the true sense, it would be because its existence changes and is not static. For the world which is in constant change is more truly called temporally originated than things which are in a state of occasional change, if there were existents of this description here (*Discourse*, p. 211).

The world as a whole, together with the outer sphere, are both eternal and temporally originated. They are eternal because their being and activity have no first beginning and no final end, yet they are temporally originated because they undergo constant and continuous change:

the heavens and the sublunary bodies belong to the genus of existents whose existence lies in their movement, and if this is true, they are eternally in a continual becoming. And therefore, just as the eternal existent is more truly existent than the temporal, similarly that which is eternally in becoming is more truly coming to be than that which comes to be only during a definite time. And if the substance of the world were not in this condition of continual movement, the world would not, after its existence, need the creator (*TT* 167–8).

If a precondition of time is motion, and if motion cannot take place without the existence of the world, then time can be regarded as eternal if the world is in a continual process of production and reproduction. Before this continual production, which might be identified as a process of creation, there was nothing out of which the universe could be created. In a sense, then, the world was created out of nothing without being preceded by time. Since the world is in a condition of continual change, it is in a very strong sense temporally originated. But it would be a mistake to think in terms of a period of time elapsing before the world was created. It is easy to picture to oneself such a possible state of affairs, but the picture would on closer examination not really be possible at all. We should not allow ourselves to be taken in by pictures which represent as plausible inconceivable states of affairs. Averroes insists that the tendency to use such pictures is a reflection of the notion of God as an ordinary creator, someone rather like us who wonders what he is going to do in the future, pauses for a while, and then does it. This is his interpretation of the logical conclusion of Ghazali's thesis. On the contrary, God is a unique kind of creator who cannot be sensibly thought of as acting in time at all, except in so far as he brings about the series of temporally defined alterations in the world itself. Averroes is not prepared to be defensive about his claim that this constitutes responsibility for the mutability of events in the world. From his point of view, God is the paradigmatic change agent, who brings about the context within which temporal judgements make sense. The theologians err in arguing that God's activity is as temporally defined as our activity, whereas they should acknowledge that divine activity defines temporal distinction as such, and our judgements about time are merely an aspect of what is thereby made possible. It is in this way that Averroes seeks to reconcile theological accounts of God's relationship to his creation with philosophy. God is the essential cause of the world which is kept in existence due to his continuing existence, and the events of the world are brought about accidentally by him. The world was brought into being through one eternal act, and accidentally exhibits a variety of temporal features. These latter, however, are entirely dependent upon the existence of the eternal and essential act. So God does on Averroes' account bring about the everyday events of the world, but only indirectly. It is rather like the relationship between the person who owns the freehold of a property and the leaseholders. The freeholder creates the structure within which many other people can own leases through his ownership of a building (in English law). Only one thing exists, the building, which can be seen from two different points of view, from the point of view of the owner, and from the point of view of the people who live in it. The owner is related only obliquely to the leaseholders, and yet they can only hold leases if someone owns the building and makes it available to others. God has created the world, but not in the way that we create artefacts. He created the world by giving what exists a kind of meaning, and its connection with him preserves that meaning. In just the same way, the owner creates leases by legal creation, and keeps them in force by continuing to respect them. This is certainly a far more complex view than that offered by Ghazali, and in Averroes' opinion is far more appropriate as an account of the relationship between the deity and the world.

Is God really an agent?

Ghazali is highly suspicious of the philosophers' notion of God as an agent. On his understanding of what God should be able to do, the deity is an individual who makes decisions which affect his creation, who can act and who can desist from acting whenever he wants, who can make something out of nothing and then annihilate what he has created. He explicitly attacks the view of agency and causation which Avicenna defends and which had a large influence on the philosophical curriculum at the time of Ghazali. According to Avicenna, when an agent brings about an effect, he moves it from the category of the possible to the actual. It must have been possible, since now it is actual. Had it not been possible at some stage, it could never have become actual. Not only is the resulting effect actual, it is also necessary through the action of the agent. Once the agent has acted, the effects of the action follow of necessity. The effects must come about, although the type of necessity involved here is essentially derived from the existence and potency of the agent. The precise means by which causes and effects are linked are various, with causes and effects coexisting in some cases, and not in others. The cause of the world is taken to be continuously involved in creating and recreating the universe, rather in the way that $2 + 2$ is continuously equivalent to 4.

As might be imagined, Ghazali takes great objection to this model of creation and causal connection, since it appears to exclude God's will from the picture. The normal use of the term 'agent' (*fa'il*) is taken by him to imply the existence of a desiring, willing, and choosing state of mind, not something which acts out of necessity. Averroes argues that there are serious conceptual problems with this understanding of God as an agent:

he who chooses makes a choice for himself of the better of two things, but God is in no need of a better condition. Further, when the willer has reached his object, his will ceases and, generally speaking, will is a passive quality and a change, but God is exempt from passivity and change. God is still farther distant from natural action, for the act of the natural thing is a necessity in its substance, but is not a necessity in the substance of the willer . . . In addition, natural action does not proceed from knowledge: it has, however, been proved that God's act does proceed from knowledge. The way in which God becomes an agent and a willer has not become clear in this place, since there is no counterpart to his will in the empirical world (*TT* 148–9).

Averroes goes on in the same section to point out that it is generally accepted that when we talk about God's knowledge we are talking about a way of knowing which greatly differs from our own, and it seems appropriate to treat God's will in a similar way. This sort of approach seems to Ghazali to be an evasion and a construction of a concept of the will which is a pale imitation of the full-blooded concept:

according to the philosophers the world stands in relation to God as the effect to the cause, in a necessary connection which God cannot be imagined to sever, and which is like the connection between the shadow and the man, light and the sun, but this is not an act at all. On the contrary, he who says that the lamp makes the light and the man makes the shadow uses the term vaguely, giving it a sense much wider than its definition, and uses it metaphorically . . . but the agent is not called a creative agent from the sole fact that it is a cause, but by its being a cause in a special way, namely that it causes through will and through choice (*TT* 150).

Averroes' reply to this argument is interesting because it takes an unexpected direction. One would have expected him to say that talking about God did indeed involve vague and metaphorical language, and, given the relative status of God *vis-à-vis* his creation, this is only to be expected.

But he does not take this line. He suggests that God possesses our attributes of knowledge and will, and to the point of perfection. He is not like an empirical agent or natural cause 'but rather the agent of these causes, drawing forth the universe from non-existence and conserving it' (*TT* 151). He is not limited by contingency in his knowledge and will, and is the cause of everything which exists. This sort of language does not call for a metaphorical use of our terms, however, since when we speak about God's attributes we have in mind the ultimate in accomplishment and power regarding characteristics which we too possess, albeit in weaker proportions. Now, Ghazali's point is that, if God has to create the world and has to create it in a certain way, then it is vacuous to talk of his wanting to create it in a certain way. He had no alternative. Instead of using a concept of God with well-developed personal characteristics, one would be thinking in terms of something like an abstract principle or an inanimate object. If God is not perfectly free to decide that he wants something to happen and then bring it about, he cannot really act. The will is a faculty which can differentiate between things which are exactly the same without any external interference. Ghazali also thinks of God as having precise information about individuals in existence rather than the very general and abstract information which the *falāsifa* allow him, so that God's decisions and choices are closely related to how he finds the world, and what he wants to do in it.

Ghazali gets into a long and involved discussion which seeks to prove that the philosophers do not regard God as a voluntary agent, but only as an involuntary agent with no power to choose and select alternatives. He wants to conclude that the only real type of agent is the voluntary agent, and voluntary agents produce their effects in time. Yet, according to the philosophers, God acts on an eternal world, which was not created in time (*TT* 162). Ghazali bases his attack upon Avicenna's account of causation which identifies the causal relation with necessity in the sense that the effect is inseparable from its cause. The sorts of examples which Ghazali has already given involve the effect being linked to the cause in the way in which a shadow is linked to that of which it is the shadow, light rays are linked to the sun, and the downward movement of an unimpeded stone is linked to the stone itself. Ghazali suggests that we can only talk about natural causes making things happen when we speak metaphorically, because really the only proper way in which something can be an agent is where it is a thinking, independent, and potent entity. Natural causes really only represent the instruments through which real agents operate, and we would no more accuse a knife of murder than we should blame a car for running someone down. If anyone is guilty, it is the person who operates the equipment. In his response Averroes points to the ways in which we speak about natural causes bringing effects about in very similar terms to the effects of voluntary causes. In the absence of an agent we would blame the knife for the death of the individual, not morally blame it but causally account for the death in terms of the activity and potency of the knife.

Divine acts differ from human acts due to their eternal effectiveness. Since God is eternal, his acts must be eternal too; he is constantly acting and there was no time at which he was not acting. Ghazali suggests that this account involves an inappropriate understanding of what is involved in an act, since for him an act is something which brings something from privation into existence by creating it entirely new, out of nothing. An eternal act cannot fall into this category, since it must always be working with pre-existing material. Averroes argues that there is no incompatibility between eternal creation and creating new things since within the context of an eternal world there are many parts which are changed entirely by divine action. He further points out that, since the world is the perfect creation of the perfect creator, it must represent a perfect act, and as such should be completed. The notion that God has to tinker around with his creation is rather a problem for Averroes, and, although he claims that this shows the significance of God's agency at every stage of the world's existence, he is possibly abandoning the view of the world as a perfect product which 'just as a house after being completed and finished does not need the builder's existence' (*TT* 168).

Ghazali uses a powerful example to express Avicenna's model of the causal relationship between God and the world;

> when a man moves his finger in a bowl of water, the water moves at the same time as the finger, neither before nor after . . . But if we suppose the finger eternally moving in the water, the movement of the water will be eternal too, and will be, despite its eternal character, an effect and an object . . . And such is the relation between the world and God (*TT* 169).

The philosophers whom Ghazali points to here argued that the temporal relation between true agents and their acts is one of simultaneity. Then, if the agent is temporal, its act is temporal, and if the agent is eternal, its act is also eternal. A popular example is the one just given of the hand moving in a bowl of water. If the hand or finger moves, the water moves simultaneously with it, and not before or after it. If the hand moves eternally, so does the water, and if God's activity of creating is eternal, then the whole system of celestial and sublunar cycles will also move eternally. Avicenna might expand this model to argue that, while God might not be temporally prior to his creation, he is none the less ontologically prior to it and it can only come about through his existence and consequent actions. Of course, Ghazali rejects this sort of example, pointing out that even in the ordinary case it is not the hand which moves the water, but the person who operates the hand. Only a voluntary agent can move the water, and that agent causes movement which proceeds from nothing and disappears into nothing, being continually replaced by new actions as long as he wishes to move the water. As far as the Ash'arites are concerned, the real agent can only be God, working through others to bring about the actions he chooses.

Avicenna's account of causation is radically different from the Ash'arite account. According to the former, God cannot be thought to have caused the world to exist at a particular time, and then remained apart from his creation because of his status as an essential rather than merely accidental cause. God necessitates the existence of the world, and no delay is conceivable; thus his existence is simultaneous with his creation. On the Ash'arite view, an act which comes into existence no longer has any connection with its agent. Its maintenance in existence is a matter of its continual recreation by a divine power. Although as we have seen Averroes attacks this view, he also attacks Avicenna's formulation of the relationship between God and the world. For Avicenna, when an agent brings about a state of affairs, that state of affairs exists only while the agent is connected with it. In that case the world and its contents are entirely dependent upon an agent for their existence. It would appear then that the only ontological status which things have lies in their relationship with their creator. This view in a sense encourages an Ash'arite response, since it puts so much emphasis upon the *relation* between the world and its creator to the detriment of the substances and relations which Averroes takes to exist in the world. All that the Ash'arite philosopher has to do is to change Avicenna's theory by interpreting the relationship as contingent rather than necessary. Averroes presents a model of the world which is opposed both to Ash'arism and Avicenna in that it consists of substances along with relations and a whole range of accidental rather than essential relations with other substances.

An important aspect of Averroes' defence of Aristotelianism is its emphasis upon the world as a moving being consisting of moving parts. He uses this principle a good deal in the Third Discussion of the *Tahāfut al-tahāfut*. For example:

the philosophers do not mean by the expression 'eternal' that the world is eternal through eternal constituents, for the world consists of movement. And since the

Ash'arites did not understand this, it was difficult for them to attribute eternity at the same time to God and to the world. Therefore the term 'eternal becoming' is more appropriate to the world than the term 'eternity' (*TT* 172).

God sets in motion the celestial spheres which in turn set in motion sublunar phenomena, and God is perpetually maintaining that motion by his activity. In the same way that God is eternal, that is, has no beginning and no end, so is the world eternal, since it is a correlative of the divine eternal activity. What is eternal is not anything which actually exists now in the world, but the general principles which lie behind empirical change and development. In this part of the *Tahāfut al-tahāfut* Averroes takes pains to distinguish sharply his views from those of Farabi and Avicenna on modality and the doctrine of emanation, which we shall examine in more detail later. He is not content to be on the defensive all the time, though, and briefly attacks the notion of God which Ghazali presents: 'The Ash'arites denied the existence of causes, and professed that this living, knowing, willing, hearing, seeing, powerful, speaking essence exists in continuous existence connected with everything and in everything. But this assumption may be thought to imply consequences open to criticism' (*TT* 218–9). These consequences are that there must exist an essence which exists eternally and executes divine actions, yet the Ash'arites deny the existence of eternal compound essences, and assert that there is no purposive action in the sublunar world. The first consequence follows from the thesis that all combinations of properties are combinations of accidental features of a subject, and as such must be capable of a time reference. How can an eternal being with qualities be eternal if it consists of temporally defined qualities? But the implication which Averroes thinks is more serious is that 'there is in the empirical world no life at all' (*TT* 220). Those activities in the empirical world which seem to display will, choice, and intention are mere epiphenomena; in reality the only source of these purposive characteristics lies with a supernatural being. Averroes does not produce a proof that this interpretation of natural events is invalid, but appeals to our understanding of natural events to establish its implausibility. Any philosophical theory which has as one of its implications that everything in the empirical world has the status of a dead or inorganic entity is a theory which does not have much claim to be able to describe the way things are arranged.

Averroes is successful in his approach in the Third Discussion in challenging theological accounts of the agency of God as more satisfactory than Aristotelian accounts. There are indeed problems in calling God a real agent, and these for Averroes stem from the differences which exist between God as a creator and human creatures. Given these differences, it would be surprising if the sorts of human characteristics which Ghazali proffers as essential aspects of God's nature could be unproblematically applied to the deity.

Miracles and causes

One of Ghazali's main reasons for attacking the necessity of the connection between cause and effect is his desire to preserve the intelligibility of miracles. A miracle is an event which goes against the normal run of events, and is made to do so by God. Yet on the philosophical account of causation which was current in his time, the cause cannot really exist without the effect, nor can the effect exist without the cause.[1] Avicenna is quite clear in holding that the relation between cause and effect is a logical relation, not just a matter of contingent empirical reality, and as such is completely invariable. This leaves the problem of accounting for the existence of miracles, for, if the lawlikeness of natural events is logically grounded, how can there be events in the world which contravene those laws? It is worth acknowledging here that Islam as a faith does not make great use of miracles in its doctrines or history, and yet there are well-attested reports within the religion of miraculous events, and so any philosophically orthodox doctrine must encompass these sorts of phenomena.[2] Avicenna did provide for miracles by a variety of methods. He claimed that some people can predict the future through their extraordinarily developed imaginative and/or intellectual powers. By seeing a piece of evidence now they can extrapolate from it and accurately predict what is going to happen. In another time these are presumably the sort of people who make a lot of money on the Stock Exchange. In addition, some events called miraculous are just very rare physical phenomena, as when a blind person who has been unable to see for a long time bangs his head and regains the power of sight. There is a causal explanation for both these types of phenomenon, but we do not immediately know what it is, and so we classify it as a miracle. In this way Avicenna tries to maintain both the existence of miracles and the existence

---

[1] An excellent account of this theory can be found in Barry Kogan, *Averroes and the Metaphysics of Causation* (State University of New York Press: Albany, 1985), ch. 3 (hereafter referred to as *AMC*).

[2] Leaman, *Introduction*, p. 82.

of inseparable and necessary connections between causes and their effects.[3]

In his response to the Avicennan view Ghazali is at first surprisingly mild. He does not deny anything the philosophers assert and states:

we are only opposed to their limiting themselves to this [i.e. the naturalistic account], and to their denial of the possibility that a stick might change into a serpent, and of the resurrection of the dead and other things. We must occupy ourselves with this question in order to be able to assert the existence of miracles and for still another reason, namely to give effective support to the doctrine on which the Muslims base their belief that God can do anything (TT 514).

In his account of miracles Averroes seems to transform an epistemological issue, namely, how can we discover that miracles are possible, into a political problem, what role in the community are miracles expected to play? This is a very common strategy in Averroist thinking. He claims that the ancient philosophers did not say much about miracles because they acknowledged the extreme importance of miracles for the existence of religious laws. This is intriguing, since one might have expected him to argue that the ancient philosophers did not talk about miracles due to their lack of adherence to a religion resembling Islam. He goes on to state that religious laws exist in order to assist human beings in the pursuit of virtue, and, in so far as miracles form part of these laws, they are very important for the well-being of the community. This leads him to tend to restrict miraculous events to prophets, who have a definite political role in the community in their capacity to teach the masses to obey the laws of Islam. He does not rule out miracles occurring provided that they are brought about through the presence of prophets and are logically possible. Miracles have a purpose, and ultimately this is to draw the community closer to their religion. So:

The clearest of miracles is the venerable Book of Allah, the existence of which is not an interruption of the course of nature assumed by tradition, like the changing of a rod into a serpent, but its miraculous nature is established by way of perception and consideration for every man who has been or who will be till the day of resurrection. And so this miracle is far superior to all others (TT 515–6).

In this passage he is not referring to the i'jāz al-Qur'ān, the miracle of the Koran, where this means the excellence of its style, but its supreme legislative function. Right at the start of the discussion we can see that Ghazali and Averroes have different agendas when it comes to miracles.

[3] Ibid. 79–82; Kogan, AMC, ch. 3.

The latter is interested in the political role of the miracle and the appropriate context within which the miraculous event takes place, while the former is concerned to show that the philosophers cannot allow a real sense of miracle to exist within the confines of their account of causation.

For Averroes miracles are spontaneous natural events which are perfectly possible but which contravene the laws of nature. Ordinary human beings cannot perform them, and they are designed to strengthen general adherence to religious law. He is critical of Avicenna's account of them as entirely due to the extraordinary powers of the prophet's soul (*TT* 515). Supporters of the esoteric view might think that we have an instance of dissimulation here, in that Averroes comes closer to Avicenna's view than he is prepared to admit openly. Barry Kogan, for example, refers to 'the radical divergence between this [i.e. Averroes'] view and the apparent meaning of the Qur'ān, [therefore] his project would hardly be to enlighten the ordinary believer'.[4] He also suggests elsewhere that Averroes might regard miracles as spontaneous events, apart from the rational organization of the world. After all, in his long commentary on the Physics (c. 47, fo. 66ʳA = *Phys.* 2. 4, 196ᵇ5–7), Averroes comments that Aristotle does not discuss the view that chance is a sort of divine cause. Kogan thinks that this is a hint of Averroes' belief in a connection between the problem of chance and that of miracles.[5] Before we get involved in the convoluted form of thinking which is required if we are to start to seek esoteric meanings, let us see whether we can understand Averroes' text by taking it at face value. He claims that a miracle is both logically and naturally possible, but extremely unlikely. He does not rule out divine intervention in the sublunar world, albeit in this case through appropriate intermediaries, the prophets. And while his interpretation of miracles is clearly not obviously equivalent to that of the Qur'ān, he has a theory of allegorical interpretation which allows philosophical techniques to be applied to certain scriptural texts but not necessarily to be made generally available. What is important for Averroes with respect to miracles is not the question as to whether they are natural or supernatural events, but what use is made of them in political terms. Most believers might well think of miracles as supernatural events brought into being by a personal deity who wishes to impress a group of people on a particular occasion with his power, or the credentials of his prophet. But then most believers accept a literal interpretation of Islam in any case, and there is nothing wrong with that. On the contrary, for Averroes it is very wrong to challenge their

4 *AMC* 84.
5 Ibid. 282–3.

view and introduce them to a more philosophically perspicuous account. The miracles are designed to get over a message and if they do so then they are useful. If the message can be transmitted in other ways, that is alright too, and those who understand at a deeper level what meaning the miracles encapsulate need not worry over the implications of their naturalness as opposed to supernaturalness.

As we have seen, Ghazali argued that a proof of God's omnipotence lies in the status of miracles as God's interruption and direct intervention in natural phenomena. Averroes is not challenging God's omnipotence, though, when he suggests that the Qur'ān is the best sort of miracle, since he is pointing to the nature of the law as the very best example of the excellence and power of the message of Islam. The basis of Averroes' limitation of the nature of miracles lies in his theory of causation, which is a modification of Avicenna's account. According to the latter, while we cannot actually observe the causal connection, we can over a period of time observe regular connections which lead us to make justifiable inferences about causal connections and future events. Despite the unobservability of the actual causal nexus, Avicenna argues that logically this connection is necessary rather than contingent. Effects do not just happen to be brought about by their causes, nor are they events which now and then follow other events. The effects *must* follow their causes because they are necessitated by them, and the whole of creation is a necessitated and necessitating series of events. One of the planks upon which Ghazali rests his attack on this analysis of natural events is the fact that we cannot actually observe the causal nexus, but only what comes before and what comes after. All we see is a conjunction of discrete events. An association naturally forms in our mind, but we do not actually have evidence of the nature of the connector. Ghazali wants to establish that God is the real agent in apparently natural events, the necessary and sufficient condition of those events taking place, and there is no observable or indeed unobservable causal nexus to 'compete' with him for influence in the world of change.

He points his attack directly at the notion of necessary natural connections right from the beginning of this section:

According to us, the connection between what is usually believed to be a cause and what is believed to be an effect is not a necessary connection; either of two things has its own individuality and is not the other, and neither the affirmation, negation, existence and non-existence of the other . . . it is in God's power to create satiety without eating, and death without decapitation, and to let life continue despite the decapitation, and so on with respect to all connections. The philosophers, however, deny this possibility and claim that that is impossible (*TT* 517).

It is important to become clear here about the nature of Ghazali's criticism of the philosophers. He requires a rigorous proof from them of the logical nature of the relationship between cause and effect. He does not seek to challenge the ordinary belief that many events in the world precede other events, and that our experience of such facts provides us with good grounds for believing that we can work out what is going to happen in the world. His bugbear is the thesis of causal necessity. He goes on to argue that causal relations are as they are because of God's influence over the world's organization.

He gives the example of a piece of cotton and a flame. It is possible for the flame to touch the cotton and yet for no fire to ensue, and for the cotton to be burnt without it even touching the flame. (*TT* 517–8). He employs his previous argument against calling involuntary agents agents at all when he says that the fire in itself is without power unless directed towards a certain end by God. The philosophers might respond that it is of the nature of fire to burn, and of cotton to be burnt, and when they come into contact a conflagration is inevitable. Yet Ghazali points out that 'observation proves only a simultaneity, not a causation, and, in reality, there is no other cause but God' (*TT* 518). He gives the further example of a blind man coming to see who has no understanding of the distinction between day and night. During the day he sees objects, and puts this down to the efficacy of his eyes. When night falls and he cannot see again, he realizes that it was really the sun which ultimately made him able to perceive objects. The point of this example is to suggest that we should not be taken in by proximate phenomena which themselves depend upon more powerful and yet distant things (*TT* 518–19).

In his response Averroes tries to make a sharp distinction between the empirical question of which laws are valid as empirical laws, and the logical status of the Aristotelian account of matter. If we are to talk of natural objects, we must assume that they have fixed characteristics and qualities if we are ever to be successful in knowing what we are talking about. If we take it that anything can behave in any sort of way, we should lose grip on the naming process and be unable to distinguish between phenomena in the world. The truth of this claim, if it is true, is unconnected with the truth of the particular causal claims which we might make (*TT* 520). Naturally, there are plenty of occasions on which we go awry, and other occasions on which we are unable to discover the cause. He strongly argues that:

Logic implies the existence of causes and effects, and knowledge of these effects can only be rendered perfect through knowledge of their causes. Denial of cause implies the denial of knowledge, and denial of knowledge implies that nothing in this world can be really known, and that what is supposed to be known is nothing but opinion, that neither proof nor definition exist, and that the essential attributes which compose definitions are void. The man who denies the necessity of any item of knowledge must admit that even this, his own affirmation, is not necessary knowledge (*TT* 522).

The apparent extremity of this remark is not entirely directed towards Ghazali's point that when we say that fire burns cotton, what we see is only the fire and then the burnt cotton, that is, we cannot actually see the power which causes the burning of the cotton. Ghazali's thesis is stronger than this. According to it, what we normally think of as agents and their effects are really only creations out of nothing which do not persist after their creation. They are nothing more than combinations of accidental properties consisting of atoms which exist for only a minute portion of time. The only power in the universe is to be found in the activity of God who causes things to come into existence and if he wishes recreates them so that they stay in existence. On this model it would indeed be the case that causal connection is an empty principle, since the 'agents' and their 'acts' are in existence for far too short a period of time for any significant connection to take place between them. All that experience justifies us in saying is that the effect occurs with (*ma'ahu*) the cause rather than through it (*bi-hi*). As Marmura has pointed out, Ghazali accepted Avicenna's canons of appropriate lawlikeness in nature as an adequate guide for finding out what future natural phenomena are likely to take place, without at the same time accepting the logic of the Avicennan account of the necessity of the causal relation itself.[6] Avicenna's principles of valid inductive inference are useful in so far as they fit in with God's plans for his creation, but their validity extends only as far as those plans. There is nothing more in the rules than their agreement with God's approach towards natural phenomena. In other words, causal thinking merely describes what God does; it does not prescribe what he must do.

Averroes suggests that, if we examine the nature of our experience of the world, we do appear to be confronted with stable objects which have the ability to bring about other objects and states of affairs when they change. The way in which we would describe our experience is very different from a continual creation *ex nihilo* of states of affairs and their continual annihilation and reproduction. It is just an important aspect of our

---

[6] M. Marmura, 'Ghazali and Demonstrative Science', *Journal of the History of Philosophy*, III (1965), 183–204.

experience that we acknowledge the existence of powerful objects. And of course there is nothing in this description which would upset Ghazali. He merely adds that there is no logical impropriety in affirming the cause and denying the effect, and vice versa. God could kill someone without removing his head, and God could keep someone alive despite the absence of a head. This appears to be a rather moderate claim, especially as Ghazali is prepared to accept the *de facto* utility of causal thinking in our everyday affairs. Why in that case does Averroes in the above passage accuse him of denying the possibility of knowledge? His reasoning might be that Ghazali is throwing doubt on the practice of seeking causes, and that practice is intimately connected with finding out about the world. Yet this would be an error. Not only is Ghazali not in opposition to the discovering of causes; he insists on the application of Avicenna's rule to that activity. But Averroes makes a stronger claim: that, if Ghazali's argument is valid, it results in its own refutation. The basis of this attack lies in the connection between a term and its essential properties. If the connection between a term and its causal properties is a connection of meaning, then accepting the term and denying its properties will be to contradict oneself.

Averroes' response to Ghazali's critique of the logical status of causality is to argue for a connection between how we know things, their causal properties, and what we call them. The causal properties of an entity are an essential aspect of our understanding of that entity. If we try to strip things of their causal properties to reveal the 'real' substance remaining, we shall end up with nothing at all, since the ways in which we label objects in the world are directly influenced by our grasp of their characteristics *vis-à-vis* other objects. For example, we might wonder whether to count a decapitated person who continued to act as a normal human being as a person any more. It might seem that the only thing which is different in this case from the normal case is that a particular individual is without his customary head, or indeed any head at all, and, although it is doubtless difficult to think how we might react were such a person to continue to appear to live (apart from running away from the creature, of course), Ghazali's point is that there is nothing logically impossible about that state of affairs, and any theory of causality which does not allow for it goes awry. But this case is an interesting one and provides material for Averroes to respond to the occasionalist argument. Is the decapitated person still a person? Does the decapitated person fulfil the criteria of being alive despite his apparent behaviour? Could we cope conceptually with this sort of change to our normal experience of the world without having to incorporate vast alterations in our understanding of the ways in which nature works? This rather conservative response might seem to beg the question, in that it appeals to fixed meanings which presuppose fixed natures for empirical objects. Averroes does interestingly replicate here Aristotle's arguments against the Heraclitean flux (*TT* 520), as Van den Bergh usefully points out,[7] when he claims that 'If a thing had not its specific nature, it would not have a special name nor a definition, and all things would be one—indeed, not even one.' If absolutely *anything* can happen to our everyday objects, we should not know what to call them anymore, and would no longer have any use for our language about them. If this is the implication of Ghazali's thesis, then he appears to be refuting himself, since he cannot say that a decapitated person can live, but only that a thing which resembles what we used to call a person can act in certain ways without what we used to call a head, and this is not what he wants to say at all.

Averroes' main argument is that an essential aspect of what *x* is is to be found in what *x* does, and how its activity relates to the activity of other objects around it. If divine intervention led to a vast confusion in our world, this would not just mean that we would lose all grasp of the future through the unpredictability of nature, but more importantly that we would no longer know what to call things. Our ordinary language of common-sense objects and their characteristics would fail to have purchase on anything. Now, we have to be careful here, because Averroes is not arguing that everything connected with a thing is an essential aspect of its meaning, nor indeed that we cannot be mistaken in our judgements about the causal properties of things. There are a lot of ways in which we make mistakes about our everyday objects and their properties, and many of those properties are not essentially related to our concepts of things. But some properties are part of the definition and essence of the thing, and to claim that the thing exists without its properties is an exercise in contradiction.

One of the advantages of Averroes' argument here is that it provides some sort of account of how it is possible to name things in the world of our experience. Naming is possible because we can identify relatively stable entities with regular patterns of behaviour and lawlike connections with other such entities. It is important to grasp that the point of this theory is not just to explain how it is possible for us to *know* things about the contents of the world, but primarily how it is possible to know what to *call* things in our world. It does not establish that our knowledge claims are

[7] *Notes*, p. 178.

generally true, nor that we are invariably correct in our attempts at reidentification of similar instances of a given concept. Yet were we to be totally at a loss to identify objects and to make epistemic claims about them we would inhabit a very different sort of conceptual scheme than that to which we are accustomed. Ghazali appreciates this point and provides an account of the apparent stability and utility of our conceptual scheme. God might bring about all kinds of radical changes in our expectations concerning the future, and we would be in a position of not being able to make reliable predictions or find our way about effectively in the world. Fortunately:

God has created in us the knowledge that he will not do all these possible things, and we only profess that these things are not necessary, but that they are possible . . . and protracted habit time after time fixes their occurrence in our minds according to the past habit in a fixed impression. . . . There is, therefore, no objection to admitting that a thing may be possible for God, but that he had the previous knowledge that although he might have done so he would not carry it out during a certain time, and that he has created in us the knowledge that he would not do it during that time (*TT* 530).

All that knits our perceptions together into perceptions of a unified and stable reality is the power of God to create what we take to be knowledge of the external world. In a sense this really is knowledge since it corresponds with God's creation of the regularities which we experience in nature. When God creates a miracle he both changes our state of mind and the appearance of the natural events. Normally, though, God maintains habitually the sort of lawlikeness and regularity to which he has made us accustomed.

As might be expected, Averroes reacts vigorously to this theory. His guiding principle is that 'true knowledge is the knowledge of a thing as it is in reality' (*TT* 531), not a correspondence with a state of mind which is directly created by the deity. He is particularly critical of Ghazali's use of the notion of habit to explain our expectations of the regular connection between cause and effect. Averroes suggests that this concept only has the apparent force it possesses in Ghazali's argument through its ambiguous application to a variety of different contexts. It could refer to the habit of God in determining the normal course of things, the habit of things themselves when they follow their normal course, or our own habit of passing judgement upon things. It cannot mean the habit of God. God cannot have a habit since 'habit' is equivalent to 'trait acquired by the agent and necessitating the recurrence of his activity in the generality of cases' (*TT* 523). No alteration is supposed to take place within God in

Islam (xxv. 41) and his behaviour is to be distinguished from ours in its lack of variability. It cannot be the nature of things themselves to which Ghazali refers when he uses the notion of habit, since he denies explicitly that there is a nature of things as such. Indeed, this is the whole aim of this section of his argument. Finally, it might be used to describe our own way of passing judgements upon things, but it must rid itself of the implication that this technique is an aspect of our human nature in coming to an understanding of the world, since the very notion of a fixed nature or essence is antagonistic to Ghazali's principles. Perhaps it just means that on the whole we tend to make particular judgements about regularity, and fortunately for us God normally correlates those judgements with what he brings about in the world. This is a useful piece of argument on Averroes' part in pointing to Ghazali's desire to link the notion of the habitual ordering of nature to both the habit of God in creating a certain order in events and to the habit of human beings regarding this order as having some necessary causal nature. What he wants to show here is that if we adopt Ghazali's proposals we are involved in a radically different view of knowledge and habit than we might think initially.

In opposition to the philosophers' notion of God who does not seem to do very much, Ghazali develops a concept of a God who is hyperactive, organizing both the course of events in the world and forming impressions of these events in our mind. Ghazali does not dispute the thesis that there are things which God cannot do, but he restricts this to logical impossibilities. He is able to bring about any state of affairs which is physically unlikely or novel but logically conceivable (*TT* 533–7). He is not limited by the apparently fixed nature of physical objects which he can change at any time he wishes. The notion of necessity which Ghazali uses is limited to the structure of logical rules, while a much broader notion is employed by Averroes. For Ghazali, there is no logical necessity which does not exist between propositions, and God can do anything with the objects in the world. The fact that God cannot do what is impossible (that is, logically impossible) is rightly not seen by Ghazali as a limitation of God's power, which cannot be expected to countenance contradictions and correspondingly senseless propositions. The rules of meaningful argument are specified by the logical connections which obtain between different statements, and these are unaffected by the possible changes which God could introduce into the world. Ghazali saw logic as having a useful role in establishing a rational theology which could argue in favour of orthodox statements and rule out unbelief, and challenging logic itself would be a matter of throwing out the baby with the bathwater. Ghazali is even prepared to accept aspects of the philosophers' account of natural necessity for the sake of the argument before he presents a refutation of the inability of God to change such fixed and stable natures (*TT* 535). We must hold on to the notion of the inviolability of logical rules if we are to be able to talk meaningfully about God's power and what it can and cannot be expected to encompass.[8]

But what is to prevent the extension of logical necessity in the direction of natural necessity? To take an example, he talks about the possibility of a corpse being made by God to sit up and write scholarly books in a clear script, which he accepts is not an everyday event, and yet it could be done (*TT* 535). Such an example is possible because it represents what God can do as opposed to what usually happens, or better, in Ghazali's terms, what he usually does. Might not Averroes be able to argue here that if we start talking about corpses producing books we are using a different notion of corpse and what is involved in writing books than is customary? After all, Averroes is committed to the view that there are certain kinds of natural behaviour which are constitutive of their objects, and if the behaviour suddenly alters, even just once and with supernatural influence, we would be at a loss to know how to describe what is happening. To take an example of how we might try to account for an unusual phenomenon, when a popular belief existed in the power of witches one of the criteria for being a witch was being seen in two places at once. Yet it was acknowledged that it is logically impossible for the same thing to be in two different places at once. So the solution was to claim not that one person was seen in two places at the same time, but that the sighting of one of the witches was of the real witch and the other sighting was of her familiar. This is a good example of how we might get around a discrepancy in our usual system of expectations and experiences to fit our discordant experiences into a logical framework which at the very least makes them possible.

This sort of example could be extended to the case of the scholarly corpse. If a corpse did sit up and write a theological tract we would be presented with a difficulty in understanding what was happening. This event would lead to all kinds of discord within our conceptual scheme. It is rather like looking for an object which is nowhere to be found, and which appears to have just gone out of existence without cause. We may, and do, say in frustration that it has completely disappeared without trace and explanation. But if we really think through the consequences for our conceptual scheme of something just going out of existence like that, then

---

[8] He thus falls clearly into the group of theologians who did not accept the popular slogan '*man tamanṭaqa tazandaqa*' or 'he who supports logic supports unbelief'.

we shall have to change other parts of it relating to the nature of matter. If God can just make things disappear, and the dead move in animated ways, we should have to acknowledge that whole areas of our experience had become ineffable and only a divine influence could be brought in as an explanation. There is absolutely no difficulty in imagining both these events taking place, just as in previous discussions there is no difficulty in imagining first God without the world, and then God with the world. I can think of a corpse getting up, taking up a pen and writing a scholarly article for *Mind*, and my description could be very detailed. For Averroes, however, more is required to establish the coherence of these examples than the fact that we can imagine them taking place, for 'only the masses rely on imagination, and he who is well trained in intellectual thought . . . renounces imagination' (*TT* 256–7). This is a rather formidable dialectical point given Ghazali's suggestion that nothing more than imagination lies behind the tendency to accept the necessity of the causal relation. But Averroes is making a stronger point here, namely, that the way in which Ghazali uses apparently conceivable exceptions to the normal run of things to throw doubt on the lawlikeness and necessity of nature is to adopt an invalid philosophical method. More is involved in establishing the possibility of a state of affairs than can be discovered through trying to form a picture of it in one's mind. We shall see how Averroes develops this point in the course of his work and what significance it has for his account of language and meaning.

An unalterable creator and a changing world

As we have seen, Averroes defended vigorously the idea that an eternal and unalterable agent produced an eternal world, and criticized Ghazali's theory of a world which is temporally produced and will come to an end at some point in the future. This does leave Averroes with a problem, though, of explaining how it is possible for an eternal creator in his unalterable wisdom to produce the temporal and mutable phenomenal world which we experience. After all, when discussing the nature of causal connection Averroes places great emphasis upon the fact of change and movement characterizing the essence of ordinary objects in our world. What is the relationship between this changeable system of things and its eternal creator? Averroes argues that God establishes an unalterable and stable framework within which the world of change operates. The heavens are taken to have the characteristics of animals, and their movement has an effect upon the sublunary world. The outermost heavenly sphere moves continuously and eternally, generating life and movement in the sublunar world. This is his technique for reconciling the eternal movement of the spheres with the purely temporal physical phenomena in this world. He claims that the evidence for the heavens having life and perception follows from our observation of them as purposive and rational entities, yet it would be a mistake to think of the heavens having souls in the same way that ordinary animals have souls, since, if the souls were powers in bodies, they would be a part of composite, and hence corruptible, beings. We can none the less talk about the souls of the spheres wanting things, loving, seeking, and so on. The spheres move, and cause the sublunar world to move in harmony with themselves, by seeking to reach and identify with the actuality and activity of the intelligences as their end. They seek to perfect themselves, and this is taken to explain their particular continuous movements and the corresponding movement which takes place within the world of generation and corruption.

If we are to get clearer on the account which Averroes presents of the relationship between the world and its maker, we shall need to understand Aristotle's position on this issue. Aristotle argues that motion can be continuous only so long as it is sustained by something (*Phys.* 7. 2, $243^a32-245^b2$) and his proof of the existence of a first cause establishes a first mover that continually sustains the motion of the heavenly spheres (*Phys.* 8. 5–9, $256^a42-266^a9$). He goes on to argue that the first cause of the motion of the spheres is an incorporeal being. He derives this conclusion from the principle that nothing of infinite magnitude can conceivably exist. Any thing which exists, even the universe as a totality, must be finite, and as such it can only have finite powers which in turn only produce motion for a finite period of time. Yet motion, and especially the motion of the heavenly spheres, is eternal and so must be moved by an infinite power, by an agent with infinite capacity to cause movement in other things. The ultimate cause of motion must then be non-composite and non-physical, separate from the spheres themselves or any other part of the corporeal universe. It must be incorporeal and distinct from the universe (*Phys.* 8. 10, 267^b19-26). This leads to a problem. Aristotle argues in *Physics*, 8, that a finite body can contain only finite power, and in *De caelo*, 2, he claims that the heavens possess only finite power since they are bodies (*De caelo*, 2. 12, 293^a10-11). Yet it is also a familiar Aristotelian thesis that the universe is eternal. Averroes tries to resolve this problem by making a distinction between the structure of the celestial and the sublunar bodies. The latter are composite in the sense that they comprise form and matter, where the matter is actualized only through the form, a material form which is only capable of existing in matter. The power through which a sublunar body acts originates in the form, and, since that form must be present in the matter, that power is present also in the matter. It is divisible, since it is material, and is naturally finite. The celestial bodies enjoy a different ontological status, though. The matter and the form of the spheres do not make up a compound object. Rather, they possess a separate, albeit related, existence. The substratum of the spheres exists 'through itself', as a result of its own simple nature, and it can do this because it contains no contrary capable of bringing about the destruction of the substratum.

The form of the spheres is not a material form present within a material substratum, and the substratum is not in a state of potentiality requiring a form to bring it to actuality. It cannot then not exist or cease to exist. The motion of the sphere is produced by a force originating from the immaterial form associated with the substratum. Since the form is immaterial, the power produced is not limited or finite, and the capacity to move continually through time is infinite for the spheres, although not for the sublunar world. If the celestial spheres consisted of a compound between form and matter like ordinary bodies they could contain only a finite power for movement and existence. The order of the heavens would then be variable: they might move and might stop moving, they might exist at one time and not exist at another. Given the principle of plenitude, every possibility must eventually be realized in an infinite period of time (accidentally interpreted), and the heavens would inevitably at some stage stop moving and existing. Averroes uses this argument to show that the structure of the heavens must be radically different from the structure of the sublunar bodies. The first cause is incorporeal and eternally moving the whole universe; as such it is infinite and has infinite powers to affect other bodies.

It is interesting to consider the relationship between Averroes and Aristotle on the question of the link between the heavens and the sublunar world. Aristotle was vague on the precise nature of this link, although towards the end of the *De generatione et corruptione* there are indications of a view of the heavens as an efficient cause of the events below. None the less, the general trend of Aristotle's thought is to interpret the teleology of the world as being immanent, without divine inspiration. In his long commentary on the *Metaphysics* Averroes argues, to the contrary, that nature could not produce rationally organized beings without the influence of an intelligent being (*Tafsīr*, p. 1502). The causal route which

Averroes develops is a rather indirect one, and has the prime mover communicating his intellect to the world of becoming through the mediation of the heavenly motions and the 'proportions' and 'forms' which these in turn produce in prime matter. He follows Aristotle in arguing that the prime mover must be eternal and have continual activity. Were it to start the world off and then stop operating, everything would have to come to a halt (*Tafsīr*, pp. 1567–8). The first mover moves the world through moving the heavenly spheres by being an object of love for them. In the same way that a lover is moved by the person he or she loves, so the spheres move in response to the existence of the first mover. One of the problems with using the metaphor of love is that, once one is in love, one can easily fall in love with an undesirable object. This is not an issue for celestial beings, though, since they have no sense perception and no access to the undesirable objects which tempt mortal creatures. Only material beings could confuse what is desirable and what is worth desiring.

What we seem to have here is a combination of two conflicting theories. One is Aristotelian and acknowledges the influence of the celestial bodies on the sublunary world while at the same time denying any kind of efficient or creative causality between the two. On this view the sublunary world exists eternally with the celestial spheres and the question of its origin is not even explicitly discussed. The heavenly intellects think only of themselves and what is higher than themselves, namely, the first intellect. The other approach involves a Neoplatonic model which regards the lower world as in some way the effect of and dependent upon the upper world. This leads to the problem which Averroes is constantly tackling, of how the eternal can be the principle of the transitory. And of course, once the theory of emanation is rejected, as by Averroes in his mature work, the problem deepens. Averroes is not a slavish follower of Aristotle, not even of the version of Aristotle which was mediated through Islamic culture. He was a determined opponent of the sort of Neoplatonic views then popular within the *falsafa* tradition, but had little alternative but to express his ideas using the philosophical vocabulary of Neoplatonism. We should not regard his arguments as nothing more than an attempt at reconciling two conflicting models of the relationship between the first mover and the world, but rather as an attempt at getting clear on the precise nature of that relationship.

How then does the prime mover act on the world? He uses the analogy of a man going off to the baths. The form of the baths in his soul stimulates his desire to go to the baths, and so is the efficient cause of the action, while the baths themselves are the final cause of his movement. If the object of desire is immaterial (that is, the prime mover) it can stimulate movement both as an efficient and as final cause without interfering with its absolute unity (*Tafsīr*, pp. 1594–5). After all, lack of matter in the object implies lack of multiplicity and a resulting complete unity. Why, though, should this constitute an explanation of the movement of the stars and the consequent sublunary world? If they are perfect, why do they not just stay still? Averroes uses here the example of a person walking for the sake of his health, but it is not very persuasive, since a perfect person would not need to take exercise. A more attractive line of argument is provided by the theory that, in the same way that a carpenter is enabled to make a chest by the form of the chest being present in his soul, and then bodily movement is required in order to combine it with matter (*Tafsīr*, pp. 1595–6), so the forms of the sublunary world are potentially in the celestial bodies, and their motion at the celestial level causes their transition in the sublunary world from potentiality to actuality. Celestial movement takes place because the heavenly bodies possess a perfection which consists in movement, and this leads quite accidentally to bring into being the world of generation and corruption.

The prime mover is taken to contain in some way all the individual forms of the universe. The individual differences between the motions of the various spheres may be due to differences between their intellects or to differences in the prime mover itself. He uses two interesting images here. In one the world is like a good state in which the citizenry obey and imitate the ruler, and where authority exists through the ruler. The order of the universe depends on the imitation of a transcendental ruler in the same way as the order of the state depends upon the influence of a good king. The other example describes a variety of techniques leading to a certain end, such as horse-riding. We must have a clear grasp of the nature of the end if we are to be successful in making equipment for riding horses. The end is just one, but the means to it are many and encompass different aspects of it (*Tafsīr*, pp. 1651–2). Averroes is obliged to illustrate his account of the connection in these rather picturesque ways because of his refusal to interpret the connection as either directly causal or in accordance with emanation.

Thus far it has been argued that one of the difficulties of Averroes' attempt at describing the relationship between the prime mover and what is moved is the unavoidability of using language from the doctrine of emanation to present a theory which goes against that doctrine itself. The account of emanation which Averroes had in mind was that put forward by Farabi and Avicenna. Basically, it starts with the principle that God is identified as the necessary existent which is one and simple. This being should not be seen as intending other things to be created, for then it would be acting for something lower than itself and would inevitably introduce multiplicity into the divine essence. And yet there must be some way of producing multiplicity out of the divine unity, since it is a fact of our experience that many things exist. Avicenna tries to get around this problem by arguing that the necessary existent would think about itself and thus produce a first effect, a pure intelligence. Once God thinks about himself, a first intelligence is produced which immediately introduces multiplicity into reality. The first intelligence thinks about three things: God's existence as necessary in itself, its own existence as necessitated by God, and the radical difference between the nature of its own existence and that enjoyed by God. These three acts of knowing bring about the existence of no more than three things, working on the principle that from one only one can proceed which secures the coherence of the system. The existence of another intellect, a soul, and a sphere, in this case the sphere of the heavens, are necessarily brought about, which then goes on to produce a series of triads which explains the creation of yet more things. The second intelligence replicates a similar process of thought as the first, and so leads to the production of a third intellect, another soul, and a sphere, this time the sphere of the fixed stars. The process continues through the thinking of the successive intellects and results in the spheres of the planets, the sun, and the moon, each with its intellect, soul, and body, only coming to an end with the sublunary world, the realm of generation and corruption in which we live. The tenth and last intelligence is the agent intellect, which does not possess a soul and the body of a sphere, but instead produces human souls and the four basic elements of our world.

The central problem which Avicenna thought needed solving was how to reconcile an eternally existing world and an eternally existing God without having the perfect simplicity and unity of the deity ruined by contact with the multiplicity of material things. His solution was to interpose many levels of spiritual substances, the intelligences, between God and the world of generation and corruption. This approach is essentially followed by Averroes when (or if) he wrote the epitome (rather inappropriately called a *talkhīṣ*)[9] of Aristotle's *Metaphysics* about ten years before the *Tahāfut* and the long commentary (*tafsīr*) on the *Metaphysics*. In the epitome all multiplicity is explained as deriving from the perfect unity of the first being, while the active intellect provides forms

[9] More properly called a short commentary (*jawāmi'* or *mukhtaṣar*) than a middle commentary (*talkhīṣ*).

for the species of sublunar beings from outside the natural order.[10] By the 1180s, however, he was scathing about this sort of account, and about Avicenna in particular. Some have suggested that he might have been convinced by Ghazali's arguments on this issue, and he certainly on many occasions goes along with the broad thrust of Ghazali's critique of the theory. His main grounds for complaint lie in the conjuring trick whereby the Neoplatonists tried to derive multiplicity from unity. A standard argument is that the creative process gets under way in the beginning by the first being or principle being thought about by the first intellect, where the latter's contemplation of both the former and itself brings into being the multiplicity of the universe. Averroes came to reject this axiom of the Avicennan system, arguing that, if two beings are immaterial and one thinks about the other, they will become identical (*TT* 180, 185). He denies the claim of the Neoplatonists that they do justice to the view of the Greek philosophers that final causation explains how celestial bodies move in line with their principles. By adhering to an Aristotelian view of divine being, Averroes has God both stimulating movement of the spheres by acting as their final cause and also determining the essences of things as their formal cause:

This consequence, that everything which exists is simple, is a necessary consequence for the philosophers, if they assume that the first agent is like a simple agent in the empirical world . . . . But the person who divides existents into abstract existents and material . . . existents makes the principles to which the sensible existent ascends different from the principles to which the intelligible existent ascends, for he regards as the principles of the sensible existents matter and form, and he makes some of these existents the agents of others, until the heavenly body is reached, and he makes the intelligible substances ascend to a first principle which is a principle to them, in one way analogous to a formal cause, in another analogous to a final cause, and in a third way analogous to an efficient cause (*TT* 175–6).

It is worth noting here the subtlety of the relationship between the principle (*mabda'* being a translation of the Greek *archē*) which is related to the world of generation and corruption in a way similar to a whole variety of different causal links.

   Averroes provides quite a lengthy and interesting account of an

[10] There is, it is worth noting, a controversy about the genuineness of the epitome as really by Averroes. In support of its genuineness, see B. Kogan, 'Averroes and the Theory of Emanation', *Medieval Studies*, 42 (1981), 384–404, while in opposition there is C. Genequand, *Ibn Rushd's Metaphysics* (Brill: Leiden, 1984), 10–11. For an agnostic view see my review of the latter in the *Journal of Semitic Studies*, 30/2 (1985) 324–5.

Aristotelian theory of generation (TT 211–21) in which he refers to a variety of views on the relationship between the first principle and the world. He starts off by pointing out the existence of four types of cause and the role of the form of a thing which comes about as its immediate cause, so that a man causes the production of another man, and so on. Since these causes do not form an infinite series,

they introduced a primary, permanent efficient cause. Some of them believed that the heavenly bodies are this efficient cause, some that it is an abstract principle, connected with the heavenly bodies, some that it is the first principle, some again that it is a principle inferior to it, and these philosophers thought it sufficient to regard the heavens and the principles of the heavenly bodies as the cause for the coming into being of the elements, since according to them they too need an efficient cause (TT 211–12).

What these different formulations have in common is the idea that 'they had agreed that the heavens were the principles of the perceptible bodies' (TT 212; see also *Tafsīr*, pp. 1534, 1609). Averroes' standard response to interpretations of the way in which the heavens affect the sublunar bodies is tentative rather than definite, as indeed was the case with Aristotle. Insisting on just one causal mechanism to explain all levels of production and generation is to ignore the differences which exist between sublunar bodies and celestial bodies, the latter being moved by incorporeal principles which are not finite nor are they powers in bodies (TT 214).

According to Avicenna, the intelligences form a series of successive emanations, whereby each intelligence causally affects the intelligence emanating from it. God is the only uncaused cause in existence. The series has an order in two senses, causally and in terms of excellence or nobility (what Aristotle calls *timioteron* in *Cat.* 12, 14^{b}4–5). Although Averroes rejected the Avicennan doctrine that the hierarchical order between the spheres or between the intellects was causally structured, he argued that there is indeed an order based upon nobility (*sharaf*) (*Tafsīr*, p. 1633) which increases in nobility in direct proportion to increases in abstraction:

these abstract principles depend on a unique abstract principle which is the cause of all of them, that the forms and the order and arrangement in this principle are the noblest existence which the forms, the order, and the arrangement in all reality can possess, that this order and arrangement are the cause of all the orders and arrangements in this sublunary world, and that the intellects reach their different degrees of superiority in this, according to their lesser or greater distance from this principle (TT 217).

It is interesting to see how, despite his apparent enthusiasm for strict adherence to Aristotelianism, Averroes was forced by the emanationist philosophical terminology not only to deviate from Aristotle but to express himself in language which seems to draw him closer to Avicenna. Yet his basic objections to emanationism remain, especially to the idea that the first intelligence and the first sphere are produced by a prior substance which is really the first. Since the only reason for the existence of immaterial entities is their ability to impart motion, there cannot be more such substances than there are motions observable in heaven. Secondly, the notion of a causal chain in which one intellect or sphere produces another implies an order in time, yet the immaterial entities are timeless. When we talk about production (*yaṣdura*) what we have in mind is the sublunary event whereby the object passes from potentiality into actuality. There is no potentiality in the celestial realm and this form of production cannot exist. Averroes replicates the Aristotelian vagueness in specifying the nature of the relationship between the heavens and the sublunar world.

What can God know?

It seems rather surprising to ask within the context of a religion like Islam what the limits of divine knowledge are. God is taken to know everything there is to know, both the highly abstract truths of physics and mathematics and the very particular truths of the sort of weather we are having today. But there is a longstanding problem in Islamic philosophy connected with God's knowledge of particulars. This problem takes many forms. Firstly, there is a difficulty in reconciling divine omniscience with the perfection and unity of God. God is expected to know all that there is to know, and at the same time to be immutable and eternal. If he knows today that the weather is chilly, and that it is likely to be better tomorrow, the contents of his mental state are always changing, which is far from the concept of an immutable deity. Then there is the problem of God's knowledge of the future. If he knows what is going to happen, does this not imply a total lack of human freedom to choose? If he does not know what is going to happen, then he is not omniscient. Lastly, is it really appropriate to think of God knowing absolutely everything? Perhaps it would be better to think of him concerning himself only with important things rather than trivial matters.

The *falāsifa* all addressed this issue, and presented a variety of solutions.[11] Averroes is no exception, and, while it is true to say that he

[11] Leaman, *Introduction*, pp. 108–20; 'Alfarabi on God's Knowledge of Particulars', *Journal of the School of Abbasid Studies*, 1 (1987).

steers close to Aristotle in his approach, he is by no means a slavish adherent incapable of using Aristotelianism creatively to analyse current concerns. Averroes' account of God's knowledge of particulars is interesting, and marks something of an advance on the views of his philosophical predecessors. Now, as far as the Qur'ān is concerned, there is no doubt that God has definite knowledge of particulars, even particulars which change and perish. There is the much-quoted passage 'there does not escape him the weight of an atom in the heavens or in the earth' (xxxiv. 3 = x. 62). He is aware of our thoughts (l. 15) and of everything which happens in the world: 'And with him are the keys of the secret things; none knows them but he. He knows whatever is on the land and in the sea, and no leaf falls without his noticing it. Nor is there a grain in the darkness of the earth, or a green or withered-up thing which is not noted in a distinct book' (vi. 59). Of course, it is important that God should know about these apparently petty phenomena, since among them are the actions of human beings who need to be judged and rewarded or punished. Yet the transcendence of Aristotle's God or the unmoved mover is such that it appears to be unconcerned with many everyday events ('Are there not some things about which it is incredible that it should think?' (Met. 12. 9, 1074^{b}25)) so that 'There are even some things which it is better not to see than to see' (Met. 12. 9, 1074^{b}32). Although, as we have seen, Averroes and his philosophical predecessors argued that the world of change depended in some rather convoluted way on the nature of God, that God is immutable and unaffected by matter, pure actuality without any kind of potentiality, and so presumably unconcerned about the events in the world of generation and corruption. Lastly, there is the problem of how God could find out what goes on in the world given his lack of sensory equipment, something made clear in Aristotle's De anima.

There is another problem attached to the idea of God knowing ordinary temporal events based on the principle that the object of knowledge is identified with the intellect of the knower. In that case God would be closely connected to the objects in the world of generation and corruption in the sense that his intellect would mirror the great diversity and mutability of empirical events. Yet this is foreign to the notion of a perfect and transcendent God; a deity who takes a personal interest in his creation must none the less be separate from that creation in status, and not appear to be like a very clever and well-informed natural being. Averroes in fact accused the theologians of making God out to be nothing more than an 'eternal' man (TT 425). The philosophical view which the theologians were criticizing is essentially that of Avicenna, who argued that the only sort of knowledge we can apply to God is universal and necessary knowledge, not contingent and particular knowledge. God can know the abstract principles which lie behind the construction of the world and the movements of the spheres, and everything else which comes into the category of theoretical knowledge, but it is nugatory to think of him coming to know the very minor and uninteresting facts of our everyday lives. But, as Ghazali points out, these facts are very significant from a religious perspective:

this principle implies that God cannot know whether Zaid obeys or disobeys him, since God cannot know any new occurrences that happen to Zaid, as he does not know the individual Zaid . . . he cannot know that Zaid becomes a heretic or a true believer, for he can only know the unbelief and the belief of man in general, not as instantiated into individuals. God can even not know Muhammad's proclaiming himself a prophet at the time he did (*TT* 457–8).

He rejects with similar ferocity the argument that God would only know very general principles about the world, as opposed to specific details. In his *Munqidh* he denounces the philosophers' position as heresy: 'their declaration "God most High knows universals but not particulars" . . . is out-and-out unbelief . . . the truth is that "there does not escape him the weight of an atom in the heavens or in the earth"'.[12]

Whatever problems there are in making sense of the idea of an immaterial deity observing events in our world, surely Ghazali has a point in his description of the Islamic view. God is expected to have knowledge of individuals and their behaviour. If he is detached from the world, in the sense in which someone who makes a clock is later detached from it when it is sold and taken somewhere else, what is the use of talking about divine judgement and the purpose of prayer? In his response to Ghazali's challenge, Averroes counter-attacks by suggesting that Ghazali's view of divine knowledge makes God's way of knowing similar to that of human beings. As he says:

Ghazali's objection . . . is that it is possible that God's knowledge should be like the knowledge of man, that is that the things known should be the cause of this knowledge and their occurrence the cause of the fact that he knows them, just as the objects of sight are the cause of visual perception and the intelligible the cause of intellectual apprehension (*TT* 467–8).

When we perceive material differences between things we use our sensory

---

[12] Ghazali, *al-Munqidh min al dalāl* (The Deliverer from Error), trans. R. McCarthy, *Freedom and Fulfillment* (Twayne: Boston, 1980), 76–7.

equipment; we are affected by those things and form impressions of them accordingly. We make mistakes, we are sometimes not entirely right in our judgements about objects in the world, and, most importantly, we are dependent upon their existence and visibility (and other states of sensory availability) for our knowledge of them to be possible. Surely this is not how it is for God's knowledge of them. Not only would it be fallible and limited, it would also produce change in him. Just as we change from moment to moment in response to what we apprehend, so God would alter. On top of all this, he would be in the power of things to affect him for his knowledge of them to be possible, just as we are. This is far from the normal Islamic interpretation of God's knowledge.

Thus far Averroes is content to throw back Ghazali's arguments not by proving demonstratively that the philosophers' view of God's knowledge is coherent with the God of Islam, but by dialectically pointing to religious and logical difficulties in Ghazali's account of God's knowledge. This is a very common strategy in the *Tahāfut al-tahāfut*, and highly appropriate given that his strategy there is to refute Ghazali and not establish his own position as such. When he argues with Ghazali he concentrates upon trying to make sense of the notion of a God with Aristotelian characteristics having knowledge of particulars. There is an additional problem though, which Ghazali does not raise, within the context of Aristotelianism. In the ninth chapter of the *De interpretatione* the issue of how to make sense of God's knowledge of *future* particulars and at the same time leave room for human freedom of action is articulated. Aristotle seems to be arguing that, if every proposition is either true or false, it follows that everything happens necessarily and there is no possibility of the existence of human free will. If a future-tensed proposition such as 'There will be a sea-battle tomorrow' has to have a truth value, then nothing we can do will affect its taking place or otherwise. Indeed, we have already commented on the significance of Aristotle's principle that 'nothing perishable can forever remain one and the same' (*De an.* 2. 4, 415^{b}4). Yet it seems rather harsh for religions to claim that people will be punished for their deeds when their lives and deeds come to an end if God knew all the time what they would do. We would then be in the position of not really having any say in the matter at all. On the other hand, if the future is undetermined, then God would not appear to know what is coming up in the future. This obviously presents a problem for a religion which believes in an omniscient diety.

In both his middle and long commentaries on the *De interpretatione* Averroes makes no direct reference to divine omniscience and its relevance for future contingency. While he accepts that contrary elements about the past and present are completely divisible into those that are true and those that are false, he accurately reflects Aristotle's qualms about saying the same about future contingent propositions. Of these he says 'matters existing in the future—namely, possible things—do not divide into truth and falsehood in a completely definite manner' (*Middle Comm.* 142 = *De int.* 9, 18ª33–4). If they did, they would be necessary and there would be no room for chance or probability. Two recent commentators on this and related texts, Charles Butterworth and Barry Kogan, take it that Averroes here is agreeing with the interpretation of Aristotle which represents him as adhering to the radical contingency of the future,[13] especially as Averroes goes on to make a threefold distinction between different forms of possibility, ranging from events whose occurrence is as probable as their non-occurrence, to those which are likely to occur, and finally to those which only rarely take place (*Middle Comm.* 146–7). But it is evident in these passages that we are not being presented with Averroes' own views, since virtually everything else in his thought suggests that he does not accept that the future just happens to turn out in a particular way. To adapt an Aristotelian example, a coat which has been cut up may not possess the capacity for being burnt, but it does for ever possess the negative property of not being burnt. If in the whole of time it will not be burnt, there is no time left at which a capacity to be burnt could be actualized, and so the cloak is incapable of being burnt. Averroes seems to adhere to an aspect of what Hintikka has called Aristotle's 'principle of plenitude' here, according to which what is possible has happened, or will happen at some time.[14] From God's point of view, these apparently arbitrary possible events are far from arbitrary and possible in the sense that they could have turned out differently than they did. In his defence of natural causation in the *Tahāfut*, Averroes argues against Ghazali on the grounds that the relationship between events which are causally linked is not just a matter of contingent conjunction, but represents a relationship based on meaning. That is, given our use of the terms involved, we have to accept that fire has burning properties, and cotton the property of being easily ignited, and, if on a particular occasion it does not burn when touched by fire, we have to look for (or at the very least consider)

---

[13] Butterworth, *Middle Comm.* 100; B. Kogan, 'Some Reflections on the Problem of Future Contingency in Alfarabi, Avicenna and Averroes', in T. Rudavsky (ed.), *Divine Omniscience and Omnipotence in Medieval Philosophy* (Reidel: The Hague, 1985), 95–101, p. 98.
[14] Hintikka, *Time and Necessity*, ch. 5.

explanations of this abnormal state of affairs, explanations which themselves presuppose causal links between contingent phenomena. Averroes cannot be taken simply to adhere to the view that future contingents can turn out any way at all.

In his commentaries on the *De interpretatione* Averroes accurately reflects Aristotle's hesitancy on the issue of the status of future contingents, and there is no way in which his own views on this issue can be derived from these texts. For that one has to look in other places. The issue which Averroes confronts directly in his own words is that of explaining how God can know particular changes to take place in the world without a corresponding change occurring in his knowledge. Given God's unity, he should experience no alteration, and given his omniscience, he cannot increase or decrease in what he knows, as we do. Yet if God knows all that there is to know, including the fact that today I have toothache and the cat has fleas, then did God know these facts before they came about? If not, he is not omniscient, but if he did, then there is no difference between the actualization of a possible state of affairs and its non-actualization. If God knew about my toothache today last year, then 'the existent and the non-existent would be one and the same' (*Ḍamīma* (Appendix) to the *Faṣl al-maqāl*, p. 128). That is, in 1985 he knew that I was going to have toothache on 16 June 1986, and now that it is 16 June 1986 he knows that I am having it, and, although the description of the event is identical in both cases, the dating of the event is crucial in understanding it. This leads Averroes to claim that 'it can hardly be conceived that the knowledge of a thing before it exists can be identical with the knowledge of it after it exists' (*Ḍamīma*, p. 129). It is not a solution to the difficulty, then, to argue that God's knowledge consists of a timeless proposition about my toothache, since if he is to know anything of interest it must be in terms of *when* such events take place, and this implies that he changes as his mental state changes in line with the changes in the world.

Ghazali tries to escape from this dilemma by treating knowledge as independent of the position in space and time of its objects. If knowledge is regarded as a relation between a knower and a thing known, why cannot the latter change while the former remains unchanged (*TT* 459)? Averroes argues very plausibly that the knower must also change in epistemic state if its objects alter, since otherwise it is not accurately assessing the nature of the state of affairs before it. Indeed, Averroes' reply to Ghazali here, as so often, is to criticize him for making his notion of God so similar to the everyday notion of human beings. God's knowledge is not like ours, which is irremediably dependent upon being affected by external objects, and to think of him as being dependent upon them for his knowledge to be possible is a gross misunderstanding of his relationship with the world. He knows such objects because he is their maker, and as such they derive from him, in a way which Averroes does not specify. He puts this point very clearly at the end of the Thirteenth Discussion thus:

it is impossible, according to the philosophers, that God's knowledge should be analogous to ours, for our knowledge is the effect of the existents, whereas God's knowledge is their cause, and it is not true that eternal knowledge is of the same form as temporal. He who believes this makes God an eternal man and man a mortal God, and in short, it has previously been shown that God's knowledge stands in opposition to man's, for it is his knowledge which produces the existent, and it is not the existents which produce his knowledge (*TT* 468).

But how does God actually *know*? Since Averroes claims that 'knowledge of individuals is sensation or imagination, and the knowledge of universals is intellect' (*TT* 461) and 'God thinks only himself, his essence must of necessity be intellect' (*TT* 462), one would expect him to restrict God's knowledge to universals, or perhaps to unique species in addition as Avicenna argues.[15] After all, to know individuals God would need to be rather like us, and we know that he is very different. In his long commentary on the *De anima* Averroes points out that:

Aristotle . . . posited the individual distinct powers in four orders. In the first place the common sense, then the imaginative power, then the cogitative and then the memorative . . . Although man has a cogitative power it does not follow that this power is the specifically rational power. A rational power deals with universal representations, not particulars (*Long Comm.* 415–16).

Since God possesses rationality *par excellence*, how much more true it must be in his case that he does not apprehend particulars! In an important statement of his position on the use of human imagery in descriptions of God, Averroes argues that:

The holy law ascribes hearing and seeing to God to remind us that God is not deprived of any kind of knowledge and understanding, and the masses cannot be made to grasp this meaning except by the use of the terms 'hearing' and 'seeing', and for this reason this exegesis is limited to the learned, and therefore cannot be taken as one of the dogmas of the holy law common to the masses (*TT* 454).

One would expect at this stage for the notion of God as a knower of non-unique individuals to be rejected by Averroes on philosophical grounds.

---

[15] Leaman, *Introduction*, pp. 112–13.

Yet in fact he distinguishes God's knowledge not only from our sort of knowledge of individuals, but also from our way of using universals in our knowledge claims. He makes the puzzling claim that 'since knowledge of the individual is for us knowledge in act, we know that God's knowledge is more like knowledge of the individual than knowledge of the universal, although it is neither the one nor the other' (*TT* 345), which is backed up by 'His knowledge cannot be described as universal, nor as particular' (*Tafsīr*, p. 1708). What he seems to mean here is that human knowledge involves abstraction, the use of very general concepts to order aspects of our experience, and the very generality of those concepts makes them usable time and time again to order and organize our varying experience. Universals are capacities or powers to apply general concepts, and as such are inappropriate as the objects of God's knowledge. When we receive experiences and wonder what sorts of concepts to use, we are in the position of limited and fallacious creatures trying to make sense out of what we find before us. This cannot be the case for an eternal, omniscient, and creative deity, whose knowledge is equivalent to his creation. After all, 'for the human understanding there is a limit . . . beyond which it cannot trespass, and this is our inability to understand the nature of this knowledge' (*TT* 344–5). God's knowledge is identical with what he produces, while 'our intellect is knowledge of the existents in potency, not knowledge in act, and knowledge in potency is less perfect than knowledge in act; the more our knowledge is universal, the more it comes under the heading of potential knowledge and the more its knowledge becomes imperfect' (*TT* 345).

When he says that God's knowledge is neither individual nor universal, but more like the former than the latter, Averroes is arguing that God can know particulars in so far as he knows what went into their construction. He knows this because his knowledge is not limited to a finite point of view. He has perspicuous knowledge, and does not just know what sorts of concepts *may* be applicable to certain kinds of experiences. Rather, he knows exactly which concepts apply to each and everything in the world. God's 'knowledge is superior to ours, and his knowledge is related to the existent in a way superior to our relationship to the existent. There must be two kinds of existence, a superior and an inferior, and the superior existence must be the cause of the inferior' (*TT* 463). This superior knowledge, Averroes implies, is even able to grasp the infinite as a whole (*TT* 345), which limited creatures like us find impossible. He ascribes this limitation to the fact that 'the things known to us are separated from each other, and if there exists a knowledge in which the things known are unified, then with respect to it the finite and infinite are equivalent' (*TT* 345). This very interesting claim suggests that the universal/particular dichotomy is replicated by the infinite/finite dichotomy, and provides yet more evidence of Averroes' belief in God's perspicuity. God's ability to apprehend the organization of the whole of reality enables him even to fulfil the Qur'ānic claim 'Nor shall there escape from it [i.e. God's knowledge] the weight of an atom, either in the heavens or in the earth' (*TT* 346 = xxxiv. 3).

It is clear from Averroes' work that he is none the less not in sympathy with Avicenna's view that God apprehends the variety of things in the world through a perspicuous grasp (*daf'at*) which takes everything in at once. In his commentary on *Metaphysics Lambda* he criticizes this approach for identifying God's knowledge with knowledge of universals, which as we have seen he regards as only potential rather than actual knowledge (*Tafsīr*, pp. 1706–7). He wants to distance himself from the general philosophical position that God can only know particulars in a universal way. He argues that on the contrary it is through knowing his essence that God knows the existents since his essence is the cause of their existence. He gives the example of someone who knows the connection between fires and heat, and who as a result knows what heat is, and what it means to call something hot. This sort of knowledge is neither universal nor particular. It is not empirical knowledge because it is knowledge of essences or meanings, and so it cannot be knowledge of particulars; it is not universal knowledge since it is not knowledge of how things might be (that is, what concepts might be applicable to them) but rather knowledge of how things are (that is, how they must be). We can only identify God's knowledge with our own knowledge through equivocation (*ishtirāk*) because they could not really be more distinct. Our knowledge is the effect of what he brings about, whereas his is caused by what he himself brings about (*Tafsīr*, pp. 1707–8).

It is by insisting on the *unity* of the bird's-eye view which the deity has of his creation, through his understanding of how the universe might best be regulated, that Averroes can try to elude the charge that his notion of God does not involve mutability. Emphasis on unity leads him to an uncharacteristic statement of approval for Islamic mysticism: 'this is the meaning of the ancient philosophers, when they say that God is the totality of the existents which he bestows on us in his bounty and of which he is the agent. And therefore the chiefs of the Sufis say: there is no reality besides him' (*TT* 463). Yet is he presenting a viable theory here? Kogan suggests not:

why should the process of causal knowing actualize particular potentialities which are presumably external to itself any more than a philosopher's reflections? The only capacities brought to fulfillment by such activity are presumably the thinker's own. Thus when the theory of causal knowing is recognizably epistemic, it is not causal; and when it is causal, it is not epistemic. How that difficulty can be resolved, if at all, is something that Averroes evidently leaves unanswered.[16]

This critique presents very clearly a general difficulty with Averroes' thought here which is emphasized throughout the commentary of Van den Bergh also. But the difficulty is not fatal. My reflections merely have as their objects ideas, some of which have corresponding objects in existence in the external world, and some of which do not. What really exists in the world are objects which are external to me and independent of me. For God, the reverse is the truth. What he thinks about and what he creates are identical; his epistemic state and his causal properties are the same. After all, 'true knowledge is conformity with the existent' (*TT* 463), and 'demonstration compels the conclusion that he knows things, because their issuing from him is solely due to his knowing' (*Ḍamīma*, p. 131). Averroes suggests in his long commentary on the *De anima* that: 'In this way, then, as Themistius says, man is assimilated to God, in that he is and knows, in some way, all things. For things are nothing other than his knowledge, and the course of things is nothing other than his knowledge. How marvellous that order, and how extraordinary is that mode of existence!' (*Long Comm.* 501). On an Aristotelian account of knowledge, a knower is identical with the objects of knowledge—they are not distinct from him. If God knows anything at all, he knows everything, and from an epistemic point of view he is identical with everything he knows. The rationale of the universe, its order, and structure are a reflection of God's thought. As we have seen, he provides the principle according to which the sublunary events operate. Through thinking about his own being, he will at the same time be thinking about the structure of the world which mirrors that essence. Would he not, then, be thinking about a great variety of phenomena, and so violate the principle of divine simplicity? This is only a problem if we forget that God is taken to be immaterial, which implies that he does not change, is completely independent, and cannot be acted upon.

Averroes' response to the question as to whether God has knowledge of particulars is then typically complicated. God has knowledge of essences, of the kinds of eternal things and connections which persist in the world.

---

[16] Kogan, 'Some Reflections', pp. 100–1, see also *AMC* 246.

Since his knowledge is identical with himself it could not be otherwise. He could hardly be identical with contingent and accidental phenomena. He is not unconnected with these phenomena, though, in the sense that they represent transitory instances of the necessary and essential relationships which he has laid down. These contingent instances originate in the structure of the world, and, since God clearly knows that structure, it might be said that he knows what goes into the construction of the contingent events which are made possible by it. This need not imply that they are themselves objects of his knowledge. For example, God knows the physical laws and principles which govern the universe, but it does not follow that in addition he is aware of how those laws actually work out. To understand the laws of gravity it is not necessary to observe every falling apple, or even any falling apple. The descent of a particular apple is only an appropriate object of knowledge of a sentient creature with visual faculties and is far beneath the dignity of the deity. Averroes seeks to make his view theologically acceptable by arguing that yet again it is the theologians who misrepresent the nature of God. He is far removed from the sort of knowing subject which we represent, and any attempt at interpreting him as just like us but more so, the Superman concept, is guilty of failing to acknowledge the significance of the difference between God and ourselves.

The Soul and Essence

Did Averroes deny the immortality of the individual soul?

ONE of the features of the doctrine of Averroism which made it so controversial in Christian and Jewish communities is the apparent denial of the immortality of the soul as generally understood in these religions. While it is a commonplace of the extensive literature which has accompanied Averroes studies that a rigid distinction should be drawn between the thought of the philosopher himself and the developments which others made of his work, there can be little doubt on reading his analysis of the soul that it would be difficult to reconcile that approach with standard Islamic and Christian teachings about immortality and the afterlife. Yet to say that it is difficult to reconcile two accounts is not to prove that they are irreconcilable, especially when one considers the fluidity of religious terminology. This section is intended to throw light on this controversial issue and to reconcile Averroes with Averroism, if not with religion itself.

Averroes is in a slightly more difficult position in establishing the religious acceptability of his notion of immortality than are his philosophical predecessors. The accounts of the soul and the afterlife constructed by Farabi and Avicenna, for example, did not stick closely to Aristotelian principles. Souls were interpreted much on the lines of separate substances, and an afterlife could be described as consisting of those substances.[1] Averroes' stricter adherence to Aristotelian principles ruled out this option. Aristotle's account of the soul and the body rejects the model of the latter as a temporary and destructible container for the former, an immortal and everlasting being. His description of the soul is of the form or principle of every living thing, and as such very much bound up with those things (*De an.* 2. 2, 413^{b}10–13). The soul is an aspect of the organism itself and 'is inseparable from the body' (*De an.* 2. 1, 413^{a}4–6). Bodies are combinations of form and matter, and there is no point in

---

[1] For an account of how this topic was developed in Islamic philosophy, see Leaman, *Introduction*, 87–107.

talking about matter existing without form when we are talking about organisms.

On the face of it, then, there is no point in contemplating a purely spiritual existence for the soul, bereft of its anchor in the material world. Persons just are combinations of soul and body, and in the absence of the latter there are no persons left. Interestingly, Ghazali seems to take this point when he criticizes the *falāsifa* for being

opposed to all Muslims in their affirming that men's bodies will not be assembled on the Last Day, but only disembodied spirits will be rewarded and punished, and the rewards and punishments will be spiritual, not corporal. They were indeed right in affirming the spiritual rewards and punishments, for these also are certain; but they falsely denied the corporal rewards and punishments and blasphemed the revealed Law in their stated views.[2]

If *we* are to survive into an afterlife, then our bodies (or at least some sort of body) must be present. But Aristotle does not leave the position like this. He wonders whether all the workings of the soul are dependent upon the body for their function. He points to views of the soul as just as dependent upon the sensation and the body as every other form of sensory experience. He points to the affinities between thinking and sensing (*De an.* 3. 4, 429^{a}10–430^{a}9) and to seeing (*De an.* 3. 5, 430^{a}10–432^{a}26), and treats them all as kinds of change analysable in terms of their causal properties. This leads him to hint at the existence of a type of thinking which may not be part and parcel of a physical entity. He suggests that:

Since in every class of thing, as in nature as a whole, we find two factors involved, (i) a matter which is potentially all the particulars included in the class; (ii) a cause which is productive in the sense that it makes them all (the latter related to the former as for instance an art to its material), these distinct elements must likewise be found within the soul (*De an.* 3. 5, 430^{a}10–14).

Now, he argues that if thinking has a material cause, this cause must possess certain characteristics. In so far as intellect is the material cause of thinking it must be impassible (*apathes*) or capable of receiving a form without being subject to any change (*De an.* 3. 4, 429^{a}15–16). Since the intellect is able to receive all forms it must be unmixed (*amiges*) through having no form of its own (*De an.* 3. 4, 429^{a}18–22). Its only properties are its capacity to think. It cannot for this reason be part of the body, since then it would be affected by the body, so it must be separable (*achoristos*) from the body and simple (*aplous*).

[2] Ghazālī, *Munqidh*, p. 76.

Aristotle is working from the principle that everything in the world consists of both material factors and productive or causal factors. The soul is a natural aspect of a thing, and as such must incorporate an intellect disposed to receive thought and an intellect disposed to cause those thoughts. He mentions explicitly the 'passive intellect' and only hints at the existence of an 'active intellect' which by contrast makes everything (De an. 3. 5, 430ᵃ14ff). The development of the full-blooded concept of the active or agent intellect is very much an attempt by Alexander of Aphrodisias to widen the analysis of the nature of human thinking.[3] This difficult topic is approached in a number of ways. Aristotle compares the agent intellect with light, since light is a necessary condition of the act of vision over and above the capacity to see and the visible object. Since Aristotle abandoned the Platonic approach to our abstract knowledge being based upon independent abstract entities, he requires something like the active intellect to 'illuminate' the potential intelligibles present in sense objects rather as light brings out the colours of objects hidden in the dark. The concepts are already present 'in' the objects, and the active intellect makes it possible for us to perceive them. The light metaphor brings out nicely the apparently independent nature of what makes abstract thought possible, since light is distinct both from the capacity to see and the objects of sight. Indeed, Aristotle hints at the independent and substantial existence of the active intellect as 'separate from the other and pure, being in its own essence actuality' (De an. 3. 5, 430ᵃ17–19), and 'once separated from the body this intellect is immortal, indeed, eternal' (De an. 3. 5, 430ᵃ22–3).

Aristotle is undeniably hesitant about the active intellect, claiming that: 'Our only explanation must be that mind alone enters from without and is alone the divine element. When and how and from where mind comes is a most difficult question, which we must answer carefully and as best we may' (De generatione animalium, 2. 3, 736ᵇ273). His commentators have not been so reticent. Alexander, for example, interprets the active intellect to be an external substance acting upon the individual soul, a force which is ultimately to be identified with God actualizing the human soul, forming its matter. The Neoplatonists argued that it was an emanation from God flowing into and filling the human soul.[4] The different metaphors which philosophers use in trying to clarify the use of a concept become important here. Themistius is quick to grasp the significance of

[3] Alexander of Aphrodisias, De anima, ed. I. Bruns, Supplementum Aristotelicum, ii (Berlin, 1887), 84 ff.

[4] Leaman, Introduction, 89–90.

the different imagery employed by Plato and Aristotle. Plato uses the example of the sun, which brings out strongly the idea of something transcendent making possible our application of universals to our sense data. Aristotle talks about light, which is also one phenomenon, but in addition is diffused into many things.[5] This is not the only image employed by Aristotle here, though. He relates, as we have seen, the agent intellect to the material intellect as 'an art to its material' (*De an.* 3. 5, 430ᵃ12–13). This gives rise to a more immanent interpretation of the agent intellect, whereby the agent intellect would be a condition of the material intellect which makes it possible for this intellect to receive the intelligible. On the other hand, we get a more transcendent interpretation if we take Aristotle to mean that which produces light, for then the agent intellect would be an efficient cause of thinking which brings to light the intelligible form implicit in the image, perhaps by preparing the material intellect for the reception of the intelligible form. We are, it must be remembered, dealing with something which is 'separable, impassible, unmixed, since it is in its essential nature activity' (*De an.* 3. 5, 430ᵃ17–18). When no longer dispersed among objects, light becomes once more a unitary thing: 'The soul is closely similar to light: light is divided by the division of illuminated bodies, and is unified when the bodies are annihilated, and this same relation holds between soul and bodies' (*TT* 30). This image obviously has its ultimate source in Plato's *Republic* where he persuades Glaucon 'that the sun not only makes the things we see visible, but also brings them into existence and gives them growth and nourishment, and yet it is not the same thing as existence' (*Republic*, vi. 508ᵇ). It is not the same thing as their *genesis* because it is the real and essential basis to the contingent and temporary existence.[6]

Similar sorts of problems arise when we come to analysing the material intellect. Some commentators emphasized its unity with the body and consequent corporeality, while others stressed its separability from the body and its ability to know universals. The latter approach was adopted by Theophrastus and Themistius, while Alexander and ibn Bājja adhered to the former view. Averroes discusses these different approaches in his long commentary on the *De anima* and recognizes that they each highlight an important aspect of the material intellect. He argues that the material intellect must be incorporeal, since it is a repository for abstract universals, and yet at the same time it must make possible thinking which includes a

[5] *Themistii . . . de anima paraphrasis*, ed. R. Heinze (Berlin, 1899), 103.
[6] Van den Bergh's suggestion of Plotinian influence on Averroes with respect to this point is entirely misguided—see *Notes*, p. 15 n. 2.

corporeal element, thinking about the world and its contents. He establishes the incorporeality of the material intellect on the grounds that this intellect can receive all material forms as intelligibles, and this is only possible if it is initially free from all such forms (*Long Comm.* 385–6). If it is free from all such forms, it surely cannot be a body or part of a body, nor can it be subject to growth and decay. It must be eternal. This creates a major difficulty for Averroes. If both the material intellect and the agent intellect are eternal, then the perfection of human thought which results in the speculative intellect (which Aristotle mentions at *De an.* 2. 1, 412^{a}19–27) and its subject matter, the intelligibles, must also be eternal. The reasoning here is that if both an agent and that on which the agent acts are eternal, the product must also be eternal. Yet we are talking here about the agent intellect acting, and the speculative intellect being formed, in the sense of a developmental process through which the individual perfects his thinking, and we are using terms which inevitably bring in time. We can over a period of time become more and more adept at abstract thought, and we then move closer to perfecting ourselves as rational creatures, but we could not do this if the thinking processes involved are eternal. For in that case they could not change and would be perfected right from the beginning.

It might be feasible to argue that the language of action and production is only being used equivocally, and nothing really changes throughout the process of human thought. This would be wildly counter-intuitive. In any case, if the material intellect is eternal, then the intelligibles it receives must also be eternal, as must the sense data from which they arise, and the forms of those data must also be eternal. But they are not. We are talking here about sensory forms which are of their very nature subject to alteration, and any theory which cannot handle this fact is not worth having. This approach suffers from yet another difficulty. If we are generable and corruptible through our ultimate perfection, the speculative intellect which we attain over a period of time, then we must regard the material intellect as equally generable and corruptible. After all, it is only the first stage in the process of intellectual perfection. Yet, if it is generable and corruptible, how can it be eternal? If the material intellect is not individual, but entirely general, then when the material intellect of one person is actualized, the material intellect of everyone must be affected at the same time, so that, if one person knows something, then everyone will know it at the same time.

Averroes is quite clear that this sort of approach, which he credits to Themistius, is not going to take us anywhere (*Long Comm.* 392). If we are going to start from the Aristotelian premiss that the material intellect is impassible, separable, and simple, we shall none the less have to reconcile these characteristics with the notion we have of human knowledge and how it is constituted. Alexander takes the contrary approach from Themistius, and argues that the material intellect is corporeal, but in a subtle sense. It is an ability or disposition (*epitediotes*) of a body, not a body itself, nor a physical faculty. He bases his argument here not upon the light metaphors employed by Themistius from Aristotle's text, but on the example of the ability of a writing tablet to receive written characters and the ability to walk latent in a new-born infant. This in itself leads to a variety of difficulties, in particular in reconciling Aristotle's description of the material intellect as impassible, separable, and simple with Alexander's description of a disposition as an accident inhering in a subject. Ibn Bājja takes up Alexander's analysis and develops it in a very interesting way. He tries to account for the role of the material intellect by identifying it with the imagination, which seems a useful move, since the imagination is based firmly in the body and yet consists of images which lead to more abstract intelligibles once it starts operating. Averroes objects to the precise way in which ibn Bājja describes the relationship between the images and the material intellect, yet this suggestion of ibn Bājja's is an important one. Averroes claims that this approach does not properly explain how the intelligible comes to be in the material intellect. Aristotle compares the relationship between the images to the material intellect to the relationship between the sensory forms to the sense organs, while for ibn Bājja the relationship holds between the sensibles and the sense organs. In that case the images would be produced in the material intellect, whereas for Aristotle they must act upon the intellect. In any case, if the material intellect is identified with the imagination, it would have the images as its form, and could not receive other, more abstract, forms such as the intelligibles. In itself the imagination is too closely related to perception to stand in for the role of the material intellect (*Long Comm.* 398).

Averroes argues that if we are to throw light on this difficult area we should return to Aristotelian principles. Thinking must have a material cause which is passive and receptive and an efficient cause which is active and productive. The material intellect represents the passive and receptive faculty. It cannot be corporeal like the other faculties of the soul, since it receives the material forms as intelligibles, and so cannot have a material form of its own. It must be capable of escaping dependence on the material world. If it cannot have a material form, it cannot be corporeal, grow and decay, and must be eternal. The material intellect is that 'which is potentially all the concepts of the forms belonging to the universal material forms and is not something existing before it understands them' (*Long Comm.* 387). The problem arises yet again though, that, if we accept this proof that the material intellect and the active intellects are eternal, how can the speculative intellect, which they form, and its subject matter the intelligibles, be contingent? Averroes tries to solve this difficulty by his use of the notion of imagination. In so far as we require in thought to use a particular image or picture we are operating at the level of contingent and mutable phenomena, yet we can use these specific images to establish universal and entirely general relationships between concepts, which means that we are operating, at one and the same time, at the level of eternal and intelligible concepts (Aristotle gives a useful example at *De memoria*, 1, 449^{b}30–450^{a}7). The point which the use of the particular example makes is an entirely universal and abstract point, but the example itself is specifically adapted to the way in which we can make such points clear to ourselves. In such a case the speculative intellect is eternal with respect to intelligibles, and transitory with respect to images. The model Averroes is working with here seems to be one where images are received by the imaginative faculty and converted into more general images for the cogitative faculty, which then produces intelligibles for the material intellect.[7]

This might seem to be nothing but a subtle evasion on Averroes' part of the difficulties involved in reconciling the nature of our thought with the possibility of abstraction. The argument he presents is that thinking can be regarded as neither an entirely mental nor an entirely physical phenomenon. Thinking involves the matching of the intelligible existing in the material intellect with the intelligible form existing in the image, and, while the former is universal and abstract, the latter is a predisposition of the imaginative faculty, a physical faculty which deals with individual and mutable phenomena. Averroes' main critique of the analyses offered by Themistius, Alexander, and ibn Bājja is that on their

---

[7] *Averroes' Epitome of Aristotle's Parva naturalia*, trans. and int. H. Blumberg (Medieval Academy of America: Cambridge, Mass., 1961), 25–6. There is a remarkable congruity of views among Averroes' writings on this aspect of the philosophy of mind. See, in particular, *Long Comm.; Treatise on the Possibility of Conjunction*, ed. P. Hannes (Halle: Kämmerer, 1892); *Epistola de connexione intellectus abstracti cum homine* and the first three chapters of *Tractatus de animae beatitudine*, in *Aristotelis opera . . . cum Averrois Cordubensis variis in eosdem commentariis* (Juntas: Venice, 1562–74; repr. Minerva: Frankfurt a. Main, 1962), ix (1573); and the epitome and middle commentary on the *De anima*, whose whereabouts are discussed in *Ma'amar bi-shelemut ha-nefesh le-rabbi Moshe ha-Narboni*, ed. A. Ivry (Jerusalem, 1977).

view thinking only involves material, agent, and speculative intellects. He agrees with Alexander that there is a distinction to be made between the active and the material intellect, but disagrees that the latter is perishable. He disagrees with Themistius that the intellect in action is eternal. He argues that it is partly perishable (when directed towards sensory data), and partly eternal (when directed towards abstract forms). His introduction of imagination, sometimes referred to as the passive intellect (*Long Comm.* 409) is designed to mediate between the eternity and universality of the intelligible present in the material intellect when actualized and the contingency and individuality of the image present in the imagination.

It will be recalled that Aristotle used two metaphors in talking about the agent intellect. According to one, it is an art acting on an object, while, in the other, it is like light in the activity of seeing. Averroes is suspicious of the first metaphor, since it implies the immediate application of the intelligible into the material intellect. On the contrary, thinking presupposes the existence of an image and the image must be related to a previous sense experience. The agent intellect may indeed be regarded as like an art in the sense that it plays a part in the production of the intelligible, but it does this indirectly and through a variety of mediated processes. Averroes is happier with the light analogy, arguing that the agent intellect both prepares the material intellect so that it can receive the intelligible, and also structures the intelligible in the image in such a way that it can be picked up by the material intellect (*Long Comm.* 410–11). The material intellect is a disposition for the reception of intelligible forms in the imagination when actualized by the active intellect.

This in brief is Averroes' account of how it is possible to think about things in the world. Can we also think about things which are not physical, like the agent intellect, and which are themselves part of the explanation of how we can think about things at all? Like most of his philosophical predecessors, Averroes argues that we can think not just about material forms, but about immaterial forms as well, and these constitute the most worthwhile objects of human thought. This can only come about through a process of perfection of the speculative intellect through practice in abstract thought until it becomes conjoined with the active intellect and then is known as the acquired intellect. He takes up a remark of Themistius that at this level we 'are similar to God in that to an extent we are and know all things' (*Long Comm.* 501). This point is also well made by a much later Averroist philosopher, Pomponazzi, who suggests that 'To say that the intellect has two modes of knowing, viz., one without an image at all, and one with an image, is to transform human nature into the divine'.[8] This process is described in fairly orthodox philosophical terms as not only abstracting the intelligibles from the images but also becoming aware of primary propositions which represent the axiomatic principles from which valid syllogisms describing the structure of reality may be constructed. The agent intellect works on these primary propositions to produce the speculative intellect, and constitutes the form of that intellect.[9]

Let us look in a bit more detail at the process of perfection of the human intellect. The individual intellect loses its individuality through becoming immersed in a realm of universal concepts. When we are at the level of using imaginative representations, those representations very much belong to a particular individual, and they represent aspects of the material side of the agent intellect. Once there is progress to more and more abstract thinking, these more graphic forms are put behind the individual thinker and immersion or conjunction occurs with the agent intellect itself. As human minds become more and more perfect, they become less and less human and individual. They free themselves gradually of the material body and its accompanying ideas, and become much more like the agent intellect. They lose in specificity and gain in generality, and any normal sense of person disintegrates totally. Aristotle makes some useful comments upon this prospect:

Actual knowledge is identical with its object: in the individual, potential knowledge is in time prior to actual knowledge, but in the universe as a whole it is not prior even in time. Mind is not at one time knowing and at another not. When mind is set free from its present conditions it appears as just what it is and nothing more: this alone is immortal and eternal (we do not, though, recall its former activity because, while mind in this sense is impassible, mind as passive is destructible), and without it nothing thinks (*De an.* 3. 5, 430ª20–5).

Once our mind achieves knowledge which is immortal and eternal, i.e. knowledge of universals and abstract principles, it becomes identical with those objects of knowledge to a degree. Once we reach the state of the acquired intellect and know everything there is to know about the formal structure of reality, there is no longer any 'us' around to do the knowing. What happens after our death? Since he does not think that the material

[8] Pomponazzi, *De immortalitate animae* (1516), ch. ix (my translation; partial translation is available in P. Pomponazzi, *On the Immortality of the Soul: The Renaissance Philosophy of Man*, ed. E. Cassirer, P. Kristeller, and J. Randall, Jr. (Chicago, 1948).
[9] Averroes follows Avicenna's account of perspicuous knowledge here, see Leaman, *Introduction*, pp. 116–18.

intellect is material or a power in something physical, he argues that it must be numerically one for all individuals. There cannot be more than one since multiplication within a species is inconceivable without the presence of matter. The species of the human intellect can be regarded as eternal, since the active and material intellects which constitute it are immaterial and so cannot decay. When separated from matter, individual souls are absolutely one:

Zaid and Amr are numerically different but identical in form. If, for example, the soul of Zaid were numerically different from the soul of Amr in the way Zaid is numerically different from Amr, the soul of Zaid and the soul of Amr would be numerically two, but one in their form, and the soul would possess another soul. The necessary conclusion is therefore that the soul of Zaid and the soul of Amr are identical in their form. An identical form inheres in a numerical i.e. a divisible multiplicity, only through the multiplicity of matter. If then the soul does not die when the body dies, or if it possesses an immortal element, it must, when it has left the bodies, form a numerical unity (*TT* 28–9).

The notion that, if anything survives after death, it is the species and not the individual is one which Averroes supports in a variety of contexts. For example, he comments:

The question which still needs to be examined is whether the temporal particulars which proceed from the heavenly movement are intended for their own sake or only for the preservation of the species . . . it certainly seems that there exists a providence as concerns individuals . . . however, in reality this is a providence which concerns the species (*TT* 504).

Human beings are temporal particulars proceeding from heavenly motion, in accordance with Averroes' cosmology, and as such temporary and destructible. Only the species is preserved from annihilation. Since 'the numerical plurality of individuals arises only through matter' (*TT* 577) whatever it is that survives the death of the body is not the individual person.

But Averroes does not leave the discussion at this stage. He goes on to make some intriguing suggestions about the nature of survival after death. The body may well not survive death, but it does not follow that nothing material nor spiritual is left. One notable aspect of his writing here is that he tends to give a *political* reference to the issue. He wonders how to present this issue to the masses. One suggestion is to relate death to sleep:

the comparison of death with sleep in this question is an evident proof that the soul survives, since the activity of the soul ceases in sleep through the inactivity of its organ, but the existence of the soul does not cease, and therefore it is necessary that its condition in death should be like its condition in sleep . . . And this is a proof which all can understand and which is suitable to be believed by the masses, and will show the learned the way in which the survival of the soul is ascertained. And this is evident from the divine words: 'God takes to Himself souls at the time of their death; and those who do not die in their sleep' (*TT* 557).

By 'evident proof' here Averroes is surely being ironical, since there is nothing in the comparison between death and sleep which provides demonstrative proof. Indeed, the very fact that what we have here is an analogy is proof in itself of a lack of logical rigour. When he takes up this Qur'ānic passage in a theological work ((*Kitāb al-kashf 'an manāhij al-adilla* (Exposition of the Methods of Argument concerning the Doctrine of Faith)), to ask 'Does scripture contain an indication of the immortality of the soul or a hint of it?' (*Manāhij*, p. 78), one might feel that this is a very strange question to put. However, what he is pointing to here is the fact that Islam, in common with many other religions, insists on the survival of persons after death, and not just of their souls, and the question of precisely what from the person continues into the afterlife is not one decisively settled either by religion or by philosophy.

There are hints in Aristotle of something spiritual surviving death. He quotes Aristotle: 'Death is a cessation; it must therefore be of the organ, as is the case in sleep. As the Philosopher says, "If the old man were to find an eye like the young man's eye, he would see as the young man sees"' (*Manāhij*, p. 78).[10] The reference is to *De an.* I. 4, 408^b21 where Aristotle makes some hesitant remarks about the lack of resemblance between the mind and the senses. He follows this comment thus: 'Thus senility results from an affection not of the soul but of the body that contains it, like drunkenness and disease. So too thought or contemplation decays through the destruction of some other part within, but is itself unchangeable. Mind is probably something more divine and immutable' (*De an.* I. 4, 408^b22-9). The example implies that bad eyesight in the old is not due to any decay in the power of sight but just in the instrument, with the suggestion that parts of the instrument or the instrument itself may be destroyed or decay without the accompanying capacities being similarly damaged. This probing by Aristotle to see how far the soul can be prised away from the body is very tentative, and does little to combat the central Aristotelian thesis that body and soul are conjoined within the individual person.

[10] See also *Long Comm.* 88 and *TT* 556.

Averroes is also rather hesitant in his account of the relationship between the body and the soul (see in particular *TT* 567), but he does acknowledge a form of immortality:

it must be admitted that the soul is immortal, as is proved by rational and religious proofs, and it must be assumed that what arises from the dead are simulacra of those earthly bodies, not those bodies themselves, for that which has perished does not return individually, and a thing can only return as an image of that which has perished, not as a being identical with what has perished . . . what perished and became anew can only be specifically, not numerically, one (*TT* 586).

But what matter will be available to individuate these new persons? Averroes has a suggestion here:

He who claims the survival and the numerical plurality of souls should say that they are in a subtle matter, namely the animal warmth which emanates from the heavenly bodies, and this is a warmth which is not fire, and in which there is not a principle of fire; in this warmth there are the souls which create the sublunary bodies and those which inhere in these bodies (*TT* 577).

This form of heavenly warmth can be taken to constitute bodies for the distinct souls to inhabit, although these bodies will not closely resemble our own. Some commentators, George Hourani among them, think that Averroes here is offering an account which he regards as philosophically respectable of how personal immortality is conceivable.[11] Another suggestion is that Averroes is offering a *reductio ad absurdum* of the whole idea of a future material embodiment. The gap of unconsciousness between our death and 'our' reawakening might be linked by the soul uniting with the heavenly warmth or spiritual matter, and the analogy of sleep for death would have some point given that in both cases there exists a degree of material and mental continuity. Averroes may well be throwing this out to those who argue for a numerical plurality of souls as a way of supporting the possibility of their account. He does after all consider a considerable variety of views of the relationship between the soul and the body without explicitly ruling out very un-Aristotelian theories (*TT* 114).

The metaphor of light is clearly an important one:

I do not know any philosopher who said that the soul has a beginning in the true sense of the word and is therefore everlasting except—as Ghazali relates—Avicenna. All other philosophers agree that in their temporal existence they are

---

[11] G. Hourani, 'Averroès musulman', in *Multiple Averroès* (Les Belles Lettres: Paris, 1978), 29–30.

related to and connected with the bodily possibilities, which receive this connection like the possibilities which subsist in mirrors for their connection with the rays of the sun (*TT* 107).

Light gives a mirror its very being as a mirror and could be regarded as its form. Light brings the mirror to life, as it were, and, although the source of light, the agent intellect, may be regarded as eternal and immortal, once there is no longer a living physical recipient for the light, there is no need to think of it existing any more in any form whatsoever. Of course, if we have some other reason for believing in the existence of immortal individuals, perhaps based upon a revelation, then Averroes can provide an account of matter appropriately organized for those individuals. Whether we should take this to be an admission by him that there are, and indeed must be, such individuals, is surely highly questionable. By far the best defence of the compatibility of Averroes' thought and individual survival into the afterlife is provided by Ovey Mohammed in a recent book. He suggests that Averroes does not defend the possibility of the immortal soul, but rather the embodied individual who develops his intellect and is provided in the next life with a different body to live in. As he concludes: 'Averroes acknowledges that continuity between this life and the next is through the soul, while maintaining that, as the perfection of an organic body, the soul can have no activity apart from a body. Man will enter into "eternal life" when the resurrection body takes the place of his earthly body at the new creation.'[12] This is indeed how Averroes puts it, but the emphasis which Mohammed places on his views is misleading. The whole style of Averroes' remarks is hypothetical, not categorical. He is not saying that this is what happens to the person after death; rather, he argues that, if you want to say that after death persons are reconstituted, this can only take place given the points about intervening matter and different bodies which have been mentioned. There may be good religious grounds for accepting bodily resurrection, and there are no philosophical grounds for ruling out such an afterlife. Averroes' acceptance of this option is rather grudging.

To give yet another example of this lack of enthusiasm one need only look at the very last section of the *Tahāfut al-tahāfut* where Averroes deals with Ghazali's charge that the philosophers reject bodily resurrection (*TT* 580–8). He points out that the earliest philosophers did not discuss the topic, and that bodily resurrection is common to a number of religions, not

---

[12] O. Mohammed, *Averroes' Doctrine of Immortality* (Wilfrid Laurier University Press: Ontario, 1984), 113.

just Islam. Then he points to a political rationale for adhering to such a doctrine:

> In short, the philosophers believe that religious laws are necessary political arts, the principles of which are taken from natural reason and inspiration . . . the philosophers further hold that one must not object . . . to any of the general religious principles . . . for instance bliss in the beyond and its possibility; for all religions agree in the acceptance of another existence after death . . . all religions agree also about the acts conducive to bliss in the next world (*TT* 582).

He goes on to argue that all religions must be followed, but at each period human beings are obliged to follow the best:

> the doctrine of the beyond in our religion . . . is more conducive to virtuous actions that what is said in others. Thus to represent the beyond in material images is more appropriate than entirely spiritual representations . . . And Ibn Abbas said: 'There is no relation in the other world to this world but the names.' And he meant by this that the beyond is another creation of a higher order than this world, and another phase superior to our earthly . . . Those who are in doubt about this and object to it and try to explain it are those who seek to destroy the religious prescriptions and to undo the virtues (*TT* 585).

Yet, although he goes on in the next page to say that 'it must be admitted that the soul is immortal, as is proved by rational and religious proofs' (*TT* 586), it is not clear what these rational proofs are. Are they the political justification for this religious doctrine, with their assurance of bringing the majority of the community to virtuous action by their adherence to the doctrine of bodily resurrection? There is no other possibility, since the philosophical proofs which Averroes produces show that bodily resurrection is feasible in the sense of logically possible, but not necessary and undeniable.

Averroes' position here is a very subtle one. One of the best ways of approaching it is to look at the analysis of the much-derided Averroists. It has for a long time been fashionable to decry the ability of the Averroists to understand the source of their inspiration. Yet on the whole they accurately derived the implications of his thought. On the question of immortality, for example, Pomponazzi argues in common with most Averroists that reason alone cannot establish the immortality of the soul, and that, given the thesis shared by Aristotle and Averroes that the soul is the form of the body, the soul is mortal. None the less, immortality of the soul is an article of faith and so must not be denied. This is a reasonable analysis of Averroes' position, namely, that an account can be provided to establish the possibility of the immortality of the individual soul. Then the religious belief in the existence of such an entity will not be ruled out from the beginning by its inconceivability. So we are not offending reason if we adhere to such a notion, and indeed from a political point of view we have no alternative if we wish to live in a stable state which permits intellectual and moral progress to perfection. Yet there is no rational proof of the existence of such an individual afterlife, and a great deal of rational proof which points in the contrary direction.

The active intellect and human thought

What is radical in Averroes' account of human thinking is his notion of the relationship between the agent intellect and individual thinkers. According to him, the material or possible intellect is individual and a separate entity, so that there is only one for the whole of humanity. The agent intellect is also unique and a separate entity, and only one exists for all thinkers. The material intellect is not a separate substance distinct from the active intellect, as we have seen. The contact of the active intellect with the imagination of individual thinkers makes it possible for those thinkers to receive abstract notions. This receptivity can be seen as just another way of describing the material intellect becoming individualized in each human mind, in just the same way as the sun's light becomes individualized in every body it illuminates. If we take this analogy seriously we can see why there can only be one material intellect, for the light produced by the sun does not belong to any particular body, and the material intellect does not belong to any particular human mind. The agent intellect is not part of the human mind, but rather a separate thing. When it is in contact with the material intellect there must be some cause of its conjunction, and the cause is to be found in the agent intellect itself. The latter is one for everyone, since it is a separate intelligence which efficiently produces knowledge in the individual minds of people by producing the abstract and intelligible forms in their minds. If we wish to use the language of faculty psychology, we can talk about the existence of a faculty which is designed to receive the intelligible forms from the active intellect. This faculty, or disposition, is referred to as the passive intellect or the imagination, and, since it is partially constituted by the body, it necessarily perishes with it. The material intellect is nothing more than an aspect of the potentiality of the active intellect, a potentiality which exists because the active intellect is not always active. When it does connect with the imagination, though, it produces the material or possible intellect, which represents the possibility of receiving intelligibles. This possibility is not a separate entity, but only the instantiation by the active intellect of an aspect of itself in individual human minds.

For Averroes, if an individual person is to understand something, the active intellect must be connected with his mind in some way. He sometimes ascribes the cause of this connecting to the speculative intellect, which represents the ability to receive intelligibles, and is an aspect of the material intellect. The active intellect is rather like the form of the speculative intellect, and the latter is rather like the active intellect's matter in that it requires actualization in the material intellect. The light of the active intellect actualizes our ability to speculate abstractly, that is, use abstract concepts, as form actualizes its matter. When we use such abstract ideas our material intellect is being perfected by the active intellect, and in a sense the abstract ideas themselves are a cause of the conjunction which brings about that increase in perfection. The sequence of events, which should not be interpreted temporally, goes something like this: abstract notions are potentially present in the products of the imagination, in the sense that our images represent not just sensations but images of things. As we refine and increase the purity of our abstract ideas, we reach a stage of being actualized by the active intellect, which constitutes a state of the material intellect that may be said to be in a sense in us. The agent intellect is then at one with the material intellect, and with each individual mind. The active intellect is the efficient cause of the forms in the imagination, and is the form of human beings in that it specifies for them as their proper function the production of abstract ideas and contemplation.

Many philosophers were strongly influenced by Averroes in their accounts of human thinking, but in addition rejected a crucial aspect of his account to provide a version which they felt to be both philosophically and theologically more palatable. Albert the Great, for instance, accepted the doctrine of the internal senses so popular among the *falāsifa* which specified an increasing range of abstraction. It starts with the common sense, which permits us to be aware of the workings of our basic sensory equipment. Then we get imagination, which enables us to work with the images of sensible objects even when these are no longer present, although it does not succeed in abstracting those images from the sensible nature of those objects. When we perfect our thinking more fully we think in terms of ideas which have been separated from all material conditions and which are thus purely general and universal. Yet the account which Albert provides is very different ultimately from that of Averroes. For the former, both the material and the active intellects are parts of the human mind, and must be so if we are to be able to talk about individual people thinking (this objection is also put firmly by Aquinas).[13] There are obvious individual differences in knowing between people, and this appears difficult to reconcile with the existence of only one material intellect for everyone. We would all have to know the same thing at the same time. Again, it is a familiar Aristotelian thesis that if A is to actualize B in the sense of provide B with a particular property, A must not only already have that property but must be distinct from that which it actualizes (*Phys.* 3. 2–3, 201^b16–202^b29). Yet the active intellect is equivalent to the material intellect when embodied in human individuals, and so would end up actualizing itself. There exists a whole host of additional difficulties with the idea of the existence of just one active intellect within an Aristotelian epistemology and metaphysics, and the theological difficulties are of course legion. It would seem that there is no difference in the distribution of immortality to individuals after death, which vitiates the idea that happiness in the next life has to be earned and deserved. Given the identity of the material and active intellect, everyone will achieve immortality, since immortality results from the conjunction or union with the active intellect in such a way that all individual differences dissolve.

There have been attempts within the context of Averroes' philosophy at rescuing the notion of individual immortality. Both Albert and Aquinas accept a good deal of the Averroistic conceptual apparatus without taking the last step and concluding that the active and material intellect are one and the same. It is this last step which produces the range of difficulties to which we have referred, and it seems a useful move to try to detach that step from the premises which led up to it. One argument against taking the last step which is particularly popular with Aquinas takes the line that Aristotle did not hold Averoes' view of the active intellect, and thus it must be abandoned.[14] A more compelling approach is to suggest that the active and material intellects can retain their characteristic qualities of explaining our thinking and knowing and yet be individualized and parts of individual human beings. In his critique of Alexander Averroes set himself deliberately against this sort of approach. He argued that it depends on interpreting the material intellect as a preparedness (*epitediotes*), a disposition, or capacity. Since it is a characteristic of us which may or may not be realized, it is far from being an essential property

[13] St Thomas Aquinas, *On the Unity of the Intellect against the Averroists (De unitate intellectus contra Averroistas)*, trans. B. Zedler (Marquette University Press: Wisconsin, 1968).
[14] Ibid., ch. 1.

which we possess. When it is actualized it is affected by 'the active intellect . . . a being coming from without, not a part or a force of our own mind, but something in us which comes from without'.[15] Since it is brought to life by something external to itself, Alexander concludes that it must be corruptible. Averroes' attack on this notion is not so much directed at the mortality of the material intellect, but at its apparently contingent relationship with respect to the agent intellect. He interprets Alexander as holding that we have a bundle of capacities which we might realize or not, as the case may be, and if they are realized, then this comes about through the influence of the active intellect. Averroes' own view is that this is far too loose a formulation, in that the character of the material intellect is essentially related to the individual of which it is an aspect.

Indeed, as Averroes argues:

there are three types of intellect in the soul. One of these is the receiving intellect, the second is the producing intellect, and the third is the produced intellect. Two of these intellects are eternal, namely the agent and receiving intellects, but the third is generable and corruptible in one sense, eternal in another sense (*Long Comm.* 406).

He seeks to stress the objectivity of knowledge in his account of human thinking, so that when we know that p is true, we are affected by a mechanism which communicates to ourselves the truth of p. As Aristotle puts it: 'Actual knowledge is identical with its object; in the individual, potential knowledge is in time prior to actual knowledge, but in the universe as a whole it is not even prior in time' (*De an.* 3. 5, 430ª20–5). If something is true, then it is true, and the fact that we may come to appreciate its truth at some time does not show that it became true at that time. On the contrary, it always was true, and we have just at that time come to appreciate it. Once we come to know it, there is nothing standing in the way of ourselves and the object of knowledge. Indeed, if there is some item of knowledge which is knowable, then at some point in the eternal species of humanity it will be known. The active intellect provides the formal aspects of this knowledge while our individual sense data constitute the matter, and in this way we can rest assured that what we seem to know in a formal sense, that is, the formal concepts we use, are accurate and have their source in something paradigmatically objective, the very general principles which express the organization of both the universe and the thinking beings in it. Through the unity of the active and

[15] Alexander, *De anima*, p. 108.

material intellects he is noting that what makes our knowledge true is independent of our personal judgements. The identity of the knower and the object of knowledge is emphasized in order to highlight an important feature of knowledge.

What is this important feature? It is the contrast between our thinking that p is the case, and p actually being the case. Averroes is so concerned at the gap between our view of the world and the world itself that he insists that in cases of knowledge the formal principles which make up the world structure our particular sense data in such a way as to give us some sort of a metaphysical assurance of the truth and accuracy of those knowledge claims. The assurance comes about through the identity of the active and material intellect. Were these to be distinct, it would always be open to us to wonder whether in general the concepts we apply to order our experience are appropriately applied in those cases, since there exists a gap between our use of those concepts and the question of whether they are rightly so used. If, on the other hand, our application of such concepts is nothing more than the individualization of some of the formal principles which regulate the universe, the gap disappears. Although in particular cases we might well doubt whether our attempts at discovering the truth about the world are well founded, we can have no general doubts about the conceptual machinery we employ, since this comes from the world itself and accurately describes the way in which that world is structured and organized. As Gersonides puts it: 'If . . . the agent intellect is understood according to our own theory knowledge will be of a stable and subsistent object outside the mind, and this is the order in the mind of the agent intellect.'[16]

Given the close interest which Gersonides took in Averroes' work, it might be useful to look at the former's explanation of how one can move from Averroistic premises to derive different conclusions. He argues that the basis for the proof that the material intellect is immortal is to be found in these four premises stemming from Alexander, namely:

1. The objects of knowledge pertaining to the sublunar world are generated and originated in the material intellect.
2. Everything that is generated is corruptible.
3. Apprehension of the agent intellect is possible for us.
4. In apprehending the agent intellect, the material intellect becomes immortal.[17]

[16] Gersonides, *The Wars of the Lord. Book 1: Immortality of the soul*, trans. S. Feldman (Jewish Publication Society of America: Philadelphia, 1984), 160.
[17] Ibid. 170.

Although the material intellect is corruptible and so mortal, when it is in conjunction with the active intellect it becomes immortal. This sort of approach shows how the material intellect can despite its corruptible and generable character become incorruptible and independent of matter. In the view of Alexander and Averroes, this immortality comes about through the apprehension of the agent intellect by the material intellect whereby a link is established between something material and potential with something immaterial and eternal. Gersonides objects to this approach. He argues that the notion of such a conjunction does not make sense, and that a better place to seek immortality is in the nature of the material intellect itself. He has a large number of arguments against the notion of conjunction or union, but they come down in the main to the impossibility of an identity coming to exist between our minds and that of the agent intellect. As Averroes puts it: 'According to Aristotle the ultimate happiness for men as men is their conjunction with this intellect, which has been explained in his book the *De anima* to be the moving and efficient principle of all of us.'[18] How can our intellects be compared with this all-encompassing principle which lies behind the whole direction and structure of the world? We can never know everything that is known by the agent intellect, and so there is no point in talking about a union or conjunction taking place.

Does this criticism present a serious problem for Averroes? It is only a problem if by union or conjunction he means complete apprehension of the active intellect. There is no reason to think that he wanted to assert anything so strong. Grasping the active intellect is not necessarily a matter of grasping it all, but rather it involves participation in an aspect of the set of principles which direct the universe. Gersonides argues that we can find immortality in the most abstract and scientific subject matter becoming the content of our thought. Although our bodies decay and perish over time, our acquisition of scientific information implies that part at least of our minds is occupied with a content which is immaterial and eternally valid. That part, the acquired intellect, must be capable of surviving the death of the body since it is not dependent upon the body for its contents, the scientific and universal knowledge which it contains. This theory also accounts for different kinds of people retaining different amounts of universal knowledge after death, and thus enjoying a more or less stimulating intellectual afterlife. For Gersonides, with the death of the body there is no further opportunity to gain knowledge, and one is left

---

[18] *Talkhīs kitāb al-nafs*, ed. F. Ahwāni (Maktabat al Nahḍah al Miṣrīyah: Cairo, 1950), 57 (my translation).

with what one possessed at death. Yet with the breaking of the link with the material world one is in a position to unify and grasp as a whole what one has intellectually, since the empirical conditions which underlie even universal knowledge have now dissolved.[19]

Within the context of medieval philosophy this approach is unsatisfactory. When Averroes speaks of conjunction with the active intellect he uses the term *ittiṣāl*, which is to be distinguished from the much stronger notion of *ittiḥād* or union. Clearly he has in mind an identification of our perfected intellect with the agent intellect, but not a complete unification. This is a relationship which Averroes was determined to represent clearly—he did after all produce five works on the nature of the relationship between our thinking and the agent intellect. And it is important to emphasize that for Averroes the relationship holds between the active intellect and human beings as a species rather than as individuals.[20] When we concentrate upon the individual thinker we can see that he loses in individuality as he increases in knowledge. The more we refine our thought, the more abstract and universal it becomes, the less it depends upon the imaginative forms which are in the beginning so important a part of our coming to know and understand. The imagination represents the way in which we are personally differentiated from other people, since we all have different ways of summoning up memories and images, and we all see the world from a slightly different and individual point of view. Once our intellect has become perfected and concentrates upon purely theoretical and rational subjects without interpreting them in figurative language or imaginative form, we lose whatever individuality exists or seems to exist. As he says:

there must be an active intellect to extract the universals from their material and sensible elements in order to make them actually intelligible, so that the material and potential intellect can receive and understand them . . . the nature of the active intellect is in one sense "form" for us, and in another sense it actualizes the intelligibles, so the material intellect can receive and understand them . . . the active intellect is always superior to the passive or material intellect.[21]

Once conjunction has been achieved, the form of the active intellect becomes our form entirely, not in the sense that we then know everything

[19] *The Wars of the Lord*, p. 170.
[20] This point is emphasized in two of his short essays on the nature of conjunction which have been translated into Latin as the *Epistola de connexione intellectus abstracti cum homine* and the *Tractatus de animae beatitudine*, part of *Aristotelis opera*, ix.
[21] *Talkhīs Kitāb al-nafs*, pp. 88–9 (my translation).

that there is to be known about the world, but in the sense that we abandon all the contingent aspects of our knowledge and thinking and concentrate entirely upon the formal aspects of those activities. Since that form is provided for us by the active intellect, it dominates our thought to the detriment of our individual personalities.

It is interesting to note that this discussion is one of the very few areas concerning which Averroes admits that he changed his mind. In his summary of the *De anima* he largely adheres to ibn Bājja's view of the material intellect as a disposition which exists independently and can achieve immortality and immateriality through the perfection of its thought.[22] In his later work on the *De anima* he replaces this account with the doctrine of the essential identity of the material and active intellects. Averroes' problem in his later work is to reconcile a series of contrary notions in his account of human thought, the accidental with the essential, the material with the immaterial, the contingent with the necessary, the particular with the universal, the corruptible with the eternal, and the complex with the simple. He is seriously in need of an intermediary here to resolve these dichotomies, and he finds it in the notion of imagination. We cannot use sensation alone as the object of our thought, but must also employ imagination to detach ourselves sufficiently from the sense data themselves for their objectivity to be possible. Imagination links our sense experience with our notion of the world as consisting of changing relationships between relatively stable objects. In an obvious dig at Plato he suggests that: 'If the intelligible forms possessed an independent existence, then we would all share the same intelligible forms together with the same knowledge, so that science and knowledge need not be acquired but could just be a matter of recollection or memory'.[23] The intelligibles do not enjoy an independent existence, though, but are aspects of our imaginative forms, the more abstract end of the continuum of abstraction along which our imaginative forms are structured. Averroes emphasizes this point in his *Tahāfut*, where he claims that 'What is universal does not exist independently of our thought' (*TT* 499). Objects are objective in the sense that they exist independently of our thought, and, when our judgements about them are true, this means that our claim about them corresponds to the way they really are, independently of us. The objectivity of the universals we employ is to be established by their origin in the active intellect, as parts of the structure of our world.

[22] But not completely. see ibid. 90.
[23] *Talkhīṣ ma baʿd al-ṭabīʿah*, ed. U. Amin (Muṣṭafā al Bābī al Ḥalabī: Cairo, 1958), ii. 1004 (my translation).

Essence and existence

It is important to emphasize that Averroes does more in his *Tahāfut al-tahāfut* than defend Peripatetic philosophy from the ravages of Ghazali. Ghazali's critique is levelled at Avicenna, and Averroes does not intend to defend Avicenna at all times. On the contrary, Averroes seeks to establish a form of Aristotelianism which is secure against both the assaults of Ghazali and the elaboration of Avicenna. The nature of the distinction between essence and existence is a good example of the way in which Averroes attempted and succeeded in interpreting the two Persian philosophers as representing a common position despite their apparent differences. There has been a good deal of controversy in the literature as to whether the discussion of the distinction between essence and existence in the philosophy of the Christian and Jewish communities after the death of Averroes was accurate. It will be argued here, and indeed throughout the book, that both Averroism and the reaction to it in the medieval and Renaissance world provided a broadly accurate reflection of the central issues in Averroes' thought.

There are a large number of issues on which Averroes bitterly criticized Avicenna, and these are usually on points where Avicenna developed views on Aristotle which contradicted Averroes' interpretation. Perhaps the most important of these issues is that of the relationship between essence and existence. Not only is this dispute interesting in itself, but it has been widely argued recently that Averroes' critique of Avicenna is misguided, his arguments unsuccessful, and as a consequence the later medieval debate is founded on error.[24] I want to argue here that this is not the case, that Averroes did understand his predecessor's point of view and produced telling objections against it, and that the later debate in Christian Europe was accurately based upon an issue of real philosophical significance.

Let us take Averroes' objections in order. Firstly, there is a terminological point. Avicenna's key error is taken to be his thesis that existence is an accident. This is partly because of his interpretation of the

---

[24] See in particular F. Rahman, 'Essence and Existence in Avicenna', *Medieval and Renaissance Studies*, 4 (1958), 1–16; F. Shehadi, *Metaphysics in Islamic Philosophy*, (Delmar, Caravan: New York, 1982); F. Cunningham, 'Averroes vs. Avicenna on Being', *New Scholasticism*, 48 (1974), 184–218; P. Morewedge, 'Philosophical Analysis and ibn Sina's "essence–existence" Distinction', *Journal of American Oriental Society*, 92 (1972), 425–35. For a particularly confused view see N. Rescher, 'The Concept of Existence in Arabic Logic and Philosophy', in his *Studies in Arabic Philosophy* (University of Pittsburgh Press: Pittsburgh, 1966), 69–80.

SOUL AND ESSENCE

105

Arabic term *al-mawjūd* (literally 'what is found') for 'existence'. Avicenna is said not to realize that this term was used by the translators of Greek philosophy into Arabic to refer not to an accident of something, but to its essence (*dhāt*) (*TT* 372). This term used to represent 'existence' can be used in (at least) two ways, either as meaning 'the true' and thus having a copulative function, or as meaning a 'thing' or 'entity' (*TT* 302). According to Avicenna, existence is an element excluded from the analysis of the nature of anything other than God. Existence is an aspect of the typewriter upon which I am working now, the typewriter as a substantiated object, but it is not part of the essence of the typewriter, of the typewriter *qua* typewriter. This is because the typewriter, like everything else other than God, is contingent and only possible in itself because necessary through another, and is dependent for its existence on a necessary being.[25]. The necessary being itself, though, is obviously not limited in this way, and its existence is part of its essence unlike everything else in the universe.

The claim which Avicenna seems to be making that existence is an addition to essence implies that existence is logically distinct from essence, that existence is not part of the nature of a thing. This is an eminently sensible position to adopt. Ghazali puts this point very well when he says that:

Man has an essence prior to existence, and existence occurs to it and is added to it. In the same way, a triangle has an essence, i.e. it is a figure with three connected sides, and existence is not a part of its essence, and so we can grasp the essence of man and the essence of a triangle without knowing whether they exist in the external world or not (*TT* 303).

Averroes follows this argument with a detailed refutation. He argues that knowledge which is objective must involve an apprehension of the essence of its object, since otherwise it is not objective. Knowledge that *p* is objective knowledge if it is knowledge that *p* exists, and so existence is far from accidental to a thing, but it is rather the essence of a thing: 'Essences which come before knowledge of their instantiation in our minds are not really essences but only nominal definitions, and it is only when we know that they have meaning outside our minds that we can say that they are [really] essences and definitions' (*TT* 304). A thing does not exist by virtue of a property added to its essence but because of its essence—existence is not an attribute which can be added to the essence of a thing. It is a quality which is the very essence itself (*TT* 331).

[25] More detail can be found in Leaman, *Introduction*, pp. 28–37.

Averroes is not in any sense denying that existence can be an attribute when used in a logical sense. That is, in sentences of the form '*p* is true' and '*p* exists', the predicate 'exists' is obviously an accident. Yet he at the same time insists that when *mawjūd* is used to mean 'entity' and 'thing', then it is used as a name for the existing thing and not for a property of it. As Van den Bergh comments: 'For Averroes existence is the existent, *to on*, the individual, *tode ti*, it is the substance, *ousia*, it is the subject . . . of a sentence; for Avicenna existence is to exist, *to einai*, it is added to the subject as a predicate in such sentences as "Socrates exists", and as "a predicate is an accident"'.[26] This might seem to be a rather trivial argument over the primary sense of existence, with Avicenna selecting the predicative sense as his paradigm of the concept itself, while Averroes prefers to identify essence and existence, to use existence to characterize substance. Many of the commentators on this dispute have claimed that the real difference between Avicenna and Averroes is nothing more than a matter of emphasis[27] or a misunderstanding on Averroes' part of Avicenna's thesis.[28]

If we examine Aristotle's analysis of individuality and essence, though, it will become evident that Averroes is quite accurately trying to defend the Aristotelian position. Aristotle spends a great deal of time on the analysis of what it is that makes up a particular individual. Although matter is obviously an important aspect of individuality, it is not matter alone which makes a thing that particular thing, but matter taking a particular form. If it were only matter that was involved in individuation, and not form, then it would be possible to draw a clear distinction between the form in Avicenna—his status as a human being—and all his specific features, and lump the latter together under the label of matter. Avicenna would then consist in matter which was made up of a bundle of accidents. This is far from Aristotle's view. For him, if Avicenna is libidinous and Averroes is puritanical, these are not just accidents in matter, but different directions that rationality has taken, rationality being part of the essence of human beings. Aristotle even occasionally flirts with the view that the essence of the individual and the individual itself are one and the same, when he says that 'a particular thing is thought to be nothing other than its own substance, and the essence is said to be the substance of each thing' (*Met.* 7. 6, 1031ª17). It is this notion of the individual as consisting of a fusion of form and matter, of the actual and the potential, which gives rise

[26] *Notes*, p. 131 nn. 224–5.
[27] Shehadi, *Metaphysics*.
[28] Rahman, 'Essence and Existence', and Cunningham, 'Averroes vs. Avicenna'.

to so much difficulty among the Islamic philosophers in making sense of the notion of individual survival of the soul after death.[29].

Aristotle is quite clear in maintaining the primacy of substance and the interrelatedness of existence and essence in his account of ontology and the nature of individuality. But, as so often with Aristotle, his comments are probing and hesitant rather than dogmatic and completed, and the Islamic philosophers extended his arguments and tried to fill in the gaps in his exposition. Avicenna wrote extensively on topics such as the nature of existence and essence, yet without explicitly setting out to confute Aristotle, and indeed some commentators have suggested that the distinction between existence and essence itself originated with Aristotle.[30] Most commentators have taken Averroes' side in the dispute with Avicenna, and have accepted his criticisms of the latter as being powerful. However, there is now a trend to change this attitude and to regard Averroes' critique as misguided and based upon a false understanding of Avicenna's point. This trend has recently been supported at length by Fadlou Shehadi, and was initiated by Fazlur Rahman in his influential article 'Essence and Existence in Avicenna'. Rahman argues that Avicenna's critics have misunderstood the different context in which Avicenna uses the concepts of essence and existence. There is a logical sense in which a predicate is called accidental in just those cases where it is not part of the essence of the subject, and in those cases 'is happy' and 'exists' are logically equivalent. Yet it is an interpretative error to regard him as holding that in the metaphysical analysis of substance existence is equally an accident either of the notion of substance or of a particular piece of substance. Were it true that Avicenna confused the logical and metaphysical senses of 'accident' then he might well hold that the Aristotelian concept of substance, the actually existing individual thing, would consist of a prior essence which at some point becomes actualized. Avicenna is concerned to stress the contingency of existing things, their dependency ultimately on God, and so he attempts to bring out the accidental nature of existence. He does this by stressing on a number of occasions the difference between the idea of something, its essence, and its distinct reason for existing, namely, its ultimate cause, God.

Yet it is worth noting that on the many citations of the distinction

---

[29] See Leaman, *Introduction*, pp. 87–108.

[30] A. M. Goichon, *La Distinction de l'essence et de l'existence d'après Ibn Sīnā (Avicenne)* (Desclée de Brouwer: Paris, 1937), 132 n. 1; N. Rescher, *Studies in the History of Arabic Logic* (University of Pittsburgh Press: Pittsburgh, 1963), 41.

between existence and essence, Avicenna does not seem to extend the
logical distinction into a real or ontological distinction. In the *Ilāhiyyāt*
(Metaphysics) of his *al-shifā'* (Book of Healing), he distinguishes between
existence (*anniyya*) and essence (*māhiyya*) at 2. 344, while at 2. 347 he uses
the contrast between instantiation (*wujūd*) and essence. At 3. 15 he
distinguishes between the concept or notion (*ma'nā*) of a triangle and its
instantiation.[31] The distinction is commonly found in his *Dānish Nāma-i
'alā'ī* (Book of Scientific Knowledge) and in the *Kitāb al-ishārāt wal-
tanbīhāt* (Book of Remarks and Admonitions).[32] Sometimes the distinction which is made is an accurate representation of the complexity of the
term 'existence', as in this passage from 1. 5 of the *Ilāhiyyāt*:

to every thing there is a reality by virtue of which it is what it is. Thus the triangle
has a reality in that it is a triangle and whiteness has a reality in that it is a whiteness.
It is that which we should perhaps call 'proper existence' (*al-wujūd al-khāṣṣ*), not
giving this the meaning of affirmative existence, since the term 'existence' is also
used to refer to a variety of meanings, one of which is the reality a thing happens to
have. . . . It is obvious that each thing has a reality proper to it, i.e. its essence. It is
known that the reality proper to each thing is something other than the existence
corresponding to what is affirmed.[33]

Avicenna's distinction between affirmative and proper existence is
interesting. The former represents the use of 'existence' when we say that
something exists either in our minds or in the world. Proper existence, on
the other hand, is identical with a thing's essence. It seems to come down
to an acknowledgement of the existence of a particular concept, and no
more than that. In the *Isagoge* of the *Shifā'* he makes the same point when
he claims that 'the triangle has as a necessary concomitant that the sum of
its three angles should equal two right angles, not by reason of the two
[affirmative kinds] of existence, but because it is a triangle'.[34] This

---

[31] Ibn Sīnā, *Kitāb al-shifā': al-ilāhiyyāt* (The Book of Healing: Metaphysics) ed. M.
Musa, S. Dunya, and S. Zayid (Organisation Générales des Imprimeries Gouvernementales:
Cairo, 1960).

[32] Ibn Sīnā, *Danish Nāma-i 'alā'ī* (Book of Scientific Knowledge), trans. P. Morewedge,
The Metaphysics of Avicenna (Columbia University Press: New York, 1973), *Kitāb al-ishārāt
wal-tanbīhāt* (Book of Remarks and Admonitions), ed. S. Dunya (Dār al-Ma'ārif: Cairo,
1956–60), trans. S. Inati, *Remarks and Admonitions*, Part One: Logic (Pontifical Institute of
Medieval Studies: Toronto, 1984), 55–8.

[33] *Ilāhiyyat*, p. 21; discussed in detail in M. Marmura, 'Avicenna on Primary Concepts in
the Metaphysics of his *al-shifā'*', in R. Savory and D. Agius (eds.), *Logos Islamikos: Studia
Islamica in honorem Georgii Michaelis Wickens* (Pontifical Institute of Medieval Studies:
Toronto, 1984), 219–39; translation, p. 226.

[34] Ibn Sīnā, *Kitāb al-shifā': Isagoge (al-madkhal)* (Healing) ed. M. Khudayri, G.
Anawati, and A. Ahwani (al-Maṭba'a al-Amrīyya: Cairo, 1953), 34 (I have modified
Marmura's translation).

distinction between affirmative and proper existence is just another way of
representing the distinction between essence and existence. The argument
is that the notion of the existence of a thing is distinct from its essence.
Existence cannot be called a genus, species, difference or property of the
species, and it cannot even be an accident of the non-concomitant kind by
which a thing is occasionally but not necessarily described. He makes it
clear in his *Kitāb al-ishārāt wal-tanbīhāt* that existence is nothing more
than a concomitant accident which may on occasion characterize the
essence.[35]

From the account so far given of Avicenna's theory, there do not seem
good grounds for holding him guilty of any logical confusion about the
relationship between existence and essence, or for accusing him of
elevating a logical distinction to the ontological level in an objectionable
manner. After all, he just seems to be saying that essences may exist either
in our minds or in the world, and that the notion of some non-divine
essence which exists in our thought tells us nothing of its existence in the
external world. Essence is entirely indifferent with respect to existence;
the essence of a thing, regarded in itself and without its cause, would not
exist, and so existence cannot be included within the essence of a thing.
What is there in this distinction between existence and essence which
could possibly give rise to objection? The objections lie not so much in the
doctrine itself, but in what it is said to imply. This comes out most clearly
in the arguments of Aquinas against Avicenna for his 'essentialism'. In his
De potentia Dei Aquinas suggests that, since existence is the very act of the
essence of a thing, it is inconceivable that essence could in any sense exist
(unless it is God) without its existence. The idea that existence is an
accident implies that existence is related to essence as merely an additional
aspect of a thing, whereas it is really the very act of essence. If when we talk
about things we are talking about the medium-sized dry goods which make
up our world, then the existence of such things cannot be regarded as
accidents, but rather as the acts of their essences.[36] Both Averroes and
Aquinas suggest that, believing existence and essence to be distinct
concepts, Avicenna meant that they are materially distinct entities, which
then require some force or principle to bring them together in the world of
objects that we know and inhabit. As al-Shahrastānī puts it:

The essential qualities of substance and accidents belong to them in themselves,

[35] Ibn Sīnā, *Kitāb al-ishārāt wal-tanbīhāt*, i. 158–73.
[36] St Thomas Aquinas, *Quaestiones disputatae de potentia Dei*, ed. Marietti (Taurini:
Rome, 1931), *passim*.

not because of any connection with the creator. He only enters . . . in connection
with existence because he tipped the scales in favour of existence. What a thing is
essentially precedes its existence, i.e. the basic qualities which make it a particular
thing. What a thing has through omnipotence is its existence and actual
instantiation.[37]

The interesting question which arises at this stage is to wonder what is
wrong with the Avicennan distinction between *what* a thing is and *that* it
is. Why do Averroes and Aquinas regard this approach as objectionably
essentialist? What objections can there be to distinguishing between two
kinds of proposition, one which consists of assertions with a truth-value in
the external world and one which merely consists of assertions which
could be true or false in the external world, but which requires something
to move it into the domain of external reality?

The opposition to this Avicennan distinction is not based so much on
the distinction itself, but on where it leads. To give one example, it leads to
difficulties in establishing Aristotelian doctrines such as the existence of an
eternal matter whose entire rationale is the impossibility of something
being produced from nothing. Ghazali attacked this doctrine by arguing
that something can come from nothing if God wants it to. Ghazali argues
in his *Tahāfut al-falāsifa* that, if we can accept that the idea of something
coming from nothing is a possible thought-experiment, then there is no
obstacle to God's making it actual. As he argues, 'possibility . . . is a
judgement of the intellect, and anything whose existence the intellect
supposes, provided no obstacle presents itself to the supposition, we call
possible. . . . These are rational judgements which need no real existent
which they might qualify' (*TT* 102). Ghazali is trying to prove that we can
think of things as possible without their being actual by showing that we
can conceive of things independently of their instantiation in the world.
Using Avicenna's distinction between essence and existence, he could
then claim that the notion of possibility is logically independent of the
notion of actuality or existence, and so the eternal existence of matter as a
substratum is not a necessary condition of our notion of possible change in
the world. Ghazali stresses this point when he argues:

the philosophers are certainly right in saying that universals exist only in the mind,
not in the external world, and that in the external world there are only particular
individuals, which are apprehended by the senses, not by reason . . . now, in the
same way, it can be said that possibility is a form which exists in the mind, not in

[37] al-Shahrastānī, *Kitāb nihāyat al iqdām fī 'ilm al kalām* (The Summa Philosophiae of al-
Shahrastānī) ed. and trans. A. Guillaume (Oxford University Press: London, 1934), 155.

the external world, and if this is not impossible for other concepts, there is no impossibility in what we have said (*TT* 110).

This ingenious move is designed to show that, just as universals are subjective and 'in our minds', so is the notion of possibility. If Ghazali is right here, then the link between possibility and actuality would be totally severed.[38]

Averroes responds at length to this Avicennan approach by arguing that what is important about the notion of possibility is its identification of states of affairs which are potentially actual, which might take place in the external world. He is defending here what has been called Aristotle's principle of plenitude according to which 'It is not allowable that it is true to say "this is possible, but it will not be"' (*Met.* 10. 4, 1047ᵇ3).[39] According to this principle, what is possible has happened or will happen at some time. If it were not possible to use the universal 'red' in the external world to pick out individuals, then there would be no point in having a concept of red:

it cannot be doubted that the judgements of the mind have value only in regard to the nature of things outside the soul. If there were outside the soul nothing possible or impossible, the judgement of the mind that things are possible or impossible would be of as much value as no judgement at all, and there would be no difference between reason and illusion (*TT* 113).

Like universals, possibility as a concept has external relevance in so far as we can use that concept in picking out phenomena in the external world. We can talk about possible states of affairs in terms of their eventual transformation into actual states of affairs, and in terms of nothing else. The notion, then, of essences which we can usefully discuss and which have no relation to the external world is an empty one. Of course, we can imagine a state of affairs in which nothing exists, and then a subsequent state of affairs in which God has brought something about, without the prior existence of matter as the Aristotelians would insist is a necessary presupposition of all physical change. That is, we can hold in our minds two sets of images which purport to represent these states of affairs, two different kinds of essence. Averroes would argue that this is not enough to prove that there are no conceptual links between change and matter, between an essence and its existence. To show that there is such a conceptual nexus one must argue that it is impossible to make sense of the

---

[38] For further discussion see Leaman, *Introduction*, pp. 50–6.
[39] Hintikka, *Time and Necessity*, ch. 5.

claim that something has changed without the prior existence of matter as a substratum, and to disprove the existence of such a nexus it is necessary to show that we can make sense of the idea of material change without the presupposition of already existing matter. More is required than just the holding of certain pictures in one's mind in a certain order.

The dispute is beginning to look as though it is not so much a dispute about the analysis of essence and existence, but about how to do philosophy. Although Averroes is critical of Avicenna's distinction between essence and existence, his real target is the interpretation of modal concepts which Avicenna introduces. Avicenna is enough of an Aristotelian to seek to avoid the occasionalism of the Ash'arites. The Ash'arites stressed the influence of God in the world by arguing that all existence and change in the universe was brought about by God's actions, so that a continually acting deity is keeping the apparently natural processes going. Avicenna argues that there are necessary causal relationships between states of affairs in the world, and what can take place can only take place if something else necessitates it. The possible is that those essence does not include its existence and so must depend upon a cause which then makes its instantiation necessary, but only necessary relative to that cause. The Necessary Being from which all existence emanates is necessary in itself, it has no cause, and its essence entails its existence. It has been pointed out that in Avicenna's modal system there are really only two kinds of being, those necessary through another and that necessary in itself, and the domain of the possible becomes conflated into those of the actual and the necessary.[40] Given the significance of the principle of plenitude, it is not difficult to see why this is the case. When Avicenna talks about the status of a thing which is not necessary in itself he comments:

It remains then that that thing, regarded with respect to its essence, is possible, but regarded with respect to its actual relation to its cause, it is necessary. If we think of that connection no longer holding, then it is impossible. But when one considers the essence of the thing itself, unrelated to anything else, the thing itself is possible in itself.[41]

The argument here is that it is possible at least to *think* about something, say, about this typewriter, without thinking about how it was made or

[40] Leaman, *Introduction*, p. 31.
[41] Ibn Sīnā, *Kitāb al-najāt* (Book of Salvation), ed. M. Kurdi (Cairo, 1938), 226; trans. G. Hourani, 'Ibn Sina on Necessary and Possible Existence', *Philosophical Forum*, 6 (1974), 74–86; p. 76.

what it is constructed from, or where it came from. But it is not possible to think of this typewriter as having no relation whatsoever to what preceded it in existence. Every contingent thing is related to something else which brings it about; the only thing which is not thus related and which can be thought of as completely independent is God who is necessary in himself.

What Avicenna is doing in interpreting modal concepts in this way is to produce a form of modified occasionalism. Occasionalism is the doctrine that apparently natural laws and states of affairs are only made possible by the direct intervention of God. According to Avicenna, a state of affairs is only possible if *something else* brings it about (except for God, of course). Averroes points out that this implies that we have to think of possible states of affairs as being non-existent by themselves, until their existence is brought about by their cause (*TT* 119). Defining possibility in terms of an external condition rather than through its inherent characteristics deprives the concept of any objective reference in the external world, while concentrating entirely on the relationships which things have with each other. He attacks Avicenna's account again in his long commentary on the *Metaphysics*, where he argues that 'It is not possible that there should be something contingent by its essence but necessary on account of something else, because the same thing cannot have a contingent existence on account of its essence and receive a necessary existence from something else, unless it were possible for its nature to be completely reversed' (*Tafsīr*, p. 1632).[42] He is arguing that it is not possible for something which is possible in itself to become necessary through its cause and yet not at the same time change its essence. There can of course be no change in essence, since on Avicenna's account existence, possibility, and necessity are accidental and only externally related to a thing and its essence or nature.

The main defenders of Avicenna among contemporary commentators, in particular Rahman and Shehadi, accept that he makes a logical distinction between existence and essence, a distinction with which Averroes would concur. They argue, though, that Avicenna does not extend this distinction to the metaphysical or ontological level where it would result in the advocacy of the priority of essences. When Avicenna talks about the accidental nature of existence in metaphysics he is merely emphasizing the contingency of the created beings in the world, the fact that they do not have to exist. In so far as it goes, Avicenna's distinction has no undesirable metaphysical consequences, and is not justifiably

---

[42] Translation taken from *Ibn Rushd's Metaphysics*, trans. C. Genequand (Brill: Leiden, 1984).

criticized by Averroes and Aquinas for its essentialism. This line of defence is alright as far as it goes, but it does not go very far, since for both Averroes and Aquinas the existence/essence distinction which Avicenna made is more of a symptom of a disease than the disease itself. That distinction is part and parcel of Avicenna's model of the relationship which exists between God and the world, and is very much part of what his successors found objectionable in that model.

According to Averroes, the source of Avicenna's position on essence and existence lies in a confusion between the essence of a thing and our thought of the thing. When the former stressed the need to distinguish two meanings of existence, one referring to the true and the other to the opposite of non-existence, he was pointing out that the first is something in the mind, whereas the second refers to things in the real world which exist outside the mind (*TT* 302). Does Avicenna really conflate the order of thought and the order of things, the logical and ontological orders? He does start with a logical analysis of the relation of essence and existence and then proceed via his theory of emanation to show how existence comes to essence from the necessarily acting Necessary Existent. In this way he is indeed stressing the contingency of the created beings, yet in a particularly distinctive way. The relationship between God and his creation is complex on Avicenna's version of emanation, and must be taken into account in this present discussion. God is a unique and completely simple being, and his activity must be in accordance with his nature. This leads to the problem of explaining the diversity of being issuing from something unique and simple. Avicenna tried to get around this problem by arguing that the world did not issue from God directly, but via a series of intermediaries which causally affect each other and eventually result in the diversity and complexity of our world. This is not ordinary causality, though, in the sense of lawlikeness or constant conjunction. Avicenna's terms for causal relations include procession (*ṣudūr*), overflow (*fayḍ*), and necessary consequence (*luzūm*), which brings out his view that the activity of a thing will affect other things and not stop within its own bounds. The overflow of causes and effects are simultaneous with its ultimate source both temporally and ontologically. It must be coeternal with God's contemplative activity, just as that activity is eternal, and the causal chain persists as long as does that activity. The universe is eternal because of the unceasing nature of God's thought and the resulting overflow which eventually constitutes our world. Ontologically, the causal series is inseparable from God because it is his overflow. Emanation provides the ontological glue which binds cause and effect, it provides the essences which are to be instantiated with their existence and with their power to actualize other essences in their turn.

There are three things worth noticing about Avicenna's use of emanation as a model of creation and causation. Firstly, it represents a very un-Aristotelian position. For Aristotle it is not really correct to talk about the first unmoved mover as having brought about the collection of things in the universe. If God is regarded as a formal and final cause, then there is no reason to insist on one thing proceeding from only one other thing, or on things being produced by an overflow from the deity to the world below. Rather, the main things in existence would depend upon the deity by regarding it as the object of desire, in their varying ways, and attempting to imitate it. And of course many things can try to imitate one thing without any problem whatsoever, so the difficulty of explaining how one thing can eventually produce many others no longer arises. In opposing the Avicennan position of existence and essence, then, Averroes was attacking the influence of Neoplatonism in philosophy.

Secondly, the theory of emanation does encourage the move from the logical distinction between existence and essence to the ontological distinction. Avicenna outlines a situation in which essences are apparently activated by their causal predecessors, where the essences lie in wait for the nudge towards existence. Ghazali criticized this view because he thought it diminished God's power, since God is then obliged (only) to actualize those essences available, rather than being able to create the essence and their existence together. This is quite clearly the approach which Aquinas also puts forward. It puts God in what might be regarded as the rather inappropriate position of being limited in his ability to create. This did not prevent Averroes from accusing Avicenna of steering too close to the theologians' understanding of how creation takes place. Using the theory of emanation to make sense of creation does do justice to the view that the contingent things of the world are dependent for their existence upon God, but it overemphasizes that dependence. It suggests that an outside factor is a vital aspect in the explanation of the existence of objects in the world, which is why I have called this position one of modified occasionalism. It seems to be a rather apologetic reaction to Ash'arite occasionalism, more of a reinterpretation of what is meant by God's influence on the world than a rigorous philosophical alternative. It also leaves plenty of room for proponents of orthodoxy such as Ghazali to run rings around the emanation theory, thus drawing fire on philosophy which is difficult to repel. In his *Tahāfut al-tahāfut* Averroes has to reply to Ghazali's onslaught on Avicenna while at the same time accepting that

Avicenna's approach is frequently misguided. The existence/essence distinction put forward by Avicenna is perfectly acceptable to Ghazali, with the modification that direct divine intervention is required to bring existence to the essences. Throughout the *Tahāfut al-falāsifa* he presupposes that we can divide up existence and essence in the way Avicenna specifies, and then uses that distinction to attack other aspects of Avicenna's thought, and Greek philosophy in Arabic, *falsafa*, in general.

The last thing worth noting about Avicenna's use of emanation and the existence–essence distinction is its radically anti-Aristotelian approach to how to do philosophy. Although Averroes certainly did not have a perspicuous grasp of Aristotle's thought, he did manage to adopt certain aspects of Aristotle's approach to philosophical problems. Aristotle approached the world as one entity, as a single order of nature with no insuperable barriers to human understanding and investigation. The sorts of dichotomies which have become so prevalent in post-Cartesian philosophy, between mind and matter, man from nature, civil law from moral law, and so on are on the whole absent in Aristotle. This was an approach which Averroes heartily adopted, and whatever else may be said about Averroes' thought, it can hardly be denied that it is extremely unified, in its maturer years at least. In the dispute with Avicenna this difference of approach comes to the fore. Avicenna is involved in dividing up things into existence and essence, into what we can think about and what really exists, into things which are necessary through another and possible in themselves. All these distinctions are used by Avicenna to go against the sort of realism and emphasis upon the notion of substance which is so important for Aristotle and his followers. In attacking Avicenna's distinction between existence and essence, Averroes and Aquinas are attacking his approach to doing philosophy and trying to replace it with a more Aristotelian approach. I think it can be seen, then, that, despite the arguments of 'revisionists' such as Rahman, Shehadi, and Cunningham, Avicenna did make a 'real' distinction between existence and essence, a distinction which was meant to take on ontological and metaphysical significance. He did give essences priority to his model of the creation of the world and causality. The Aristotelian onslaught on his distinction is appropriate and not based upon a misunderstanding of what he meant. Not only did Averroes and Aquinas identify correctly the target of their criticism; they were aware of the broader implications of Avicenna's existence–essence distinction, and in order to understand this dispute we must be aware of them also.

PART II
Practical Philosophy

Divine Law and Human Wishes

AVERROES' discussion of Plato's *Republic* is an unusual aspect of his corpus. It is his only known treatment of Plato, and is difficult to classify as a text. It shares some of the characteristics of a paraphrase, since there is quite a lot of material which merely replicates and abbreviates Plato's text (as represented in Arabic), and there are many changes in the text to relate more easily the discussion to contemporary social and political conditions. On the other hand, the text seems also to be rather like a middle commentary, with some analysis of Plato's arguments and a very definite selection of passages and exclusion of others on philosophical grounds. There is also the problem that there is no decent Arabic manuscript extant, and there are arguments about the reliability and integrity of the surviving Hebrew translations. The difficulties of the text and the consequent problems with translation have led to scholarly debates over the nature of Averroes' intentions which have reached heights of acerbity rare even within the restricted community of those concerned with *falsafa*.[1]

There is no lack of unity in Averroes' work. He begins his book by declaring as his intention the separation of demonstrative from dialectical arguments in Plato's text, and he finishes off on the same sort of note. In between he lays down his view of the nature of practical philosophy. Political science is part of practical philosophy, and regulates the appropriate behaviour of human beings in communities. The objects of political science are volitional acts which are produced by our free will and chosen after rational thought. By way of contrast with the theoretical sciences, political science does not have abstract knowledge as its goal, but practical action. This is not to say that reason does not enter into the working out of political science. Averroes produces within this context the well-worn example of medicine, which involves both a theoretical and a practical aspect. The theoretical aspect of political science involves the analysis of human conduct as such, and is, according to Averroes, covered in Aristotle's *Nicomachean Ethics*. The practical aspect can be found in his *Politics*, but, since this was not available to him, Plato's *Republic* had to do instead.

[1] A prime example of orientalist waspishness is the review of Rosenthal's edition by J. Teicher, *Journal of Semitic Studies*, 5 (1960), 176-95.

The first and theoretical part of this science proves that the human perfections are really of four kinds—speculative, intellectual, ethical, and practical—but these are not equal in status. The speculative virtues are the most important, and the others are steps on the ladder to their attainment. It is more or less impossible for an individual to excell in all the perfections, but it is possible for a combination of individuals to produce jointly all the perfections. Averroes makes the Aristotelian point that human beings are political animals in that they require others in order to acquire even one of the perfections. We need society not just in order to reach human perfections, but also to satisfy the necessities of life, and the very varied activities of different citizens constructs a social whole in which an acceptable life style is possible. Plato compares the parts of the state to the parts of the soul, so that the state is run wisely if the speculative citizens are in charge of the other less rational individuals, just as a person is wise if his rational faculties are in control of his other personality traits.

Averroes understands Plato to be arguing that justice is a state of affairs where each citizen follows the activity for which he or she is most fitted by nature. But this is only possible if such citizens are under the authority of those most skilled in the speculative sciences, just as justice in a single person is dependent upon control by the intellect of the other aspects of personality. Wisdom and courage are restricted to particular groups in society, while justice and temperance (or prudence) are present in all classes of people. Some virtues are found more in some groups of people than in others, and the Greeks are credited with strength in the speculative sciences, while the Kurds and Galicians are predominantly courageous. Nature is important here, since Plato argues that everyone is provided by nature with a tendency to be skilful in only one form of activity. Those who are in charge of the security of the state, the guardians, should be chosen from those who are physically strong and quick and shrewd; they must be naturally courageous and brought up from childhood to prepare for their martial role. Averroes runs through Plato's arguments here, as he does through his remarks on education, on the danger of listening to poetry and stories which excite physical desires and on the use of music pedagogically. Some of the Platonic arguments in favour of the abolition of private property, the desirable disappearance of gold and silver, the appropriate size of cities, not to mention the communal living arrangements for women and children, are very different from Islamic forms of life, and yet Averroes produces summaries of Plato's ideas for such social arrangements without much in the way of personal comment.

In the second book of his discussion, Averroes starts by looking at the nature of the philosophers and the sort of education they ought to receive. The philosopher is intent on examining the truth without its material trappings, the pure forms or ideas which lie behind our use of concepts in the empirical world. The philosopher has to combine all the theoretical and practical virtues, and have the ability to teach both through the use of demonstrative reason and through rhetorical and poetic methods. The ruler of the state must combine a number of qualities of king, lawgiver, and philosopher, all aspects of the nature of the *imām*. The ruler is expected to have the following natural traits: (1) he must be naturally disposed to the study of the theoretical sciences, thus enabling him to distinguish the essential from the accidental; (2) he must have good powers of retention of information; (3) he must be interested in all forms of theoretical enquiry; (4) he must love the truth and hate the false; (5) he must turn his appetites away from sensual pleasures; (6) he must not love money; (7) he must have noble sentiments; (8) he must be brave; and (9) he must always seek to attain the good and the beautiful. On top of all this, he should be a good orator, quick-witted in the sense of being able to seize rapidly the middle term of a syllogism,[2] and able to present his arguments in a simplified and accessible form. Yet, although kings ought to be philosophers, in existing cities they are not, as both Plato and Averroes admit. These states do not follow the example of those who are really wise, thinking that they can be governed by people who are not philosophers. In any case it is very difficult to find a philosopher who has the qualities appropriate for a leading political role in the state. Few philosophers possess the glowing list of attributes listed above.

In the third and last section Averroes discusses Plato's account of the constitutions of different states. The best kind of state is that which is ruled by the sort of ideal politician described in the second section. Next step down is timocracy, a state based upon the ideology of honour. Then comes oligarchy, rule by the few, and a few dominated by the desire for wealth. Fourth is democracy and fifth tyranny. The best kind of government can be either a monarchy or an aristocracy, while Averroes adds two other forms of regime, government by someone who only seeks to please himself, and government formed out of necessity. He repeats Plato's explanation of the transformation of one form of government into another, and analyses in some depth the nature of different kinds of state and the personalities of their citizens and rulers. Towards the end of his

[2] For more on this characteristic, see *Avicenna's Psychology*, ed. and trans. F. Rahman (Oxford University Press: Oxford, 1952), 36.

third section he makes some rather critical remarks about Plato's putative fondness for non-demonstrative arguments, and refuses to discuss the tenth book of the *Republic* or the first book due to their high dialectical content. He seems to think that everything else which Plato discusses is worth considering, albeit not necessarily to be accepted as valid. There are points in the discussion in which he actually intervenes by correcting Plato by reference to Aristotle, but on the whole he does not do this. As we suggested initially, it is difficult to define the precise nature of this text, especially, as we shall see, since Averroes regarded it as a propaedeutic to the *Nicomachean Ethics*.

Those parts of the *Republic* which Averroes ignores are especially significant for the esotericists, given that they believe that what is omitted is just as, or even more, revealing than what is mentioned. I have argued that this approach is no more rewarding when dealing with this text than with other works of *falsafa*.[3] The stories and myths which Plato includes in the *Republic* are viewed by Averroes as just that, stories and myths, and not only are they stories and myths, but they also relate to theologically sensitive subjects such as the immortality of the individual soul and the nature of divine retribution. He makes it clear that, while stories have a part to play in directing human action, and there is nothing inappropriate in the use of rhetoric, poetry, and dialectic as such, as part of a philosophical text such as the *Republic* these stories have no place. For they will not convince the philosopher, and may draw upon his head the wrath of the literalist who thinks he is being presented with an un-Qur'ānic view of the nature of the afterlife. Averroes claims that what is wrong with Plato's stories is that they do not succeed in their purpose. They are 'not . . . necessary to a man's becoming virtuous, nor will it be better and easier for a man to become virtuous through it. For we see here many people who,' in adhering to their nomoi and their laws, albeit devoid of those stories, are not less well off than those possessing [those] stories' (*APR* 105. 19–23) Why should we not take him at his word here? The virtues which may arise as a result of these stories are not real virtues, but only imitations of virtues. Averroes is here reminding the reader of the Platonic critique of imitation and dealing at second hand with reality. If the stories are only haphazardly connected with virtuous behaviour, then we can well do without them. If they are not then logically connected with such behaviour, they have no role in a rational argument.

---

[3] Leaman, 'Ibn Rushd on Happiness and Philosophy', *Studia Islamica*, 52 (1980), 167–81.

Of course, to the esotericist like Lerner, a careful reading of the text is replete with all manner of stylistic complexities and evasions:

for in truth it is no simple matter to tell in every instance whether Averroes is speaking in his own name. The gentle glidings from 'he says' to 'we say' and back again (with variations on route) lull the senses of the good-natured reader who nods along as Averroes repeats whatever Plato 'says' or 'asserts' or 'holds' or 'explains'. Every once in a while, however, that good-natured reader is jolted by various devices into wondering where Averroes himself stands on these matters. Sometimes Averroes tells him directly; sometimes he tells him indirectly. Sometimes Averroes merely plants the question. In all cases, however, Averroes moves with boldness and determination in setting before the attentive reader the problems that matter, the problems posed by the confrontation of classical political philosophy and the *sharīʿa*.[4]

It is worth quoting this passage at some length because it typifies the esotericist approach in its apparent subtlety and manifest cunning. Lerner argues plausibly in his Introduction that Averroes is giving his personal view when he adds the personal pronoun to descriptions of Plato's reasoning. Yet is he justified in suggesting that when Averroes refers to a topic or problem as one worth investigating, Averroes is also giving his opinion concerning the *subject* of the issue, and not just its formal status as part of an interesting argument? He gives the example of the question whether the bringer of the *sharīʿa* ought in addition to be a prophet. Interestingly, though hardly surprisingly given its subject, Averroes does not discuss prophecy to any significant extent in his book. He does say that he will 'investigate it in the first part of this science, God willing' (*APR* 61, 17–18). Now, as Lerner rightly says, Averroes identifies the characteristics of the legislator with those of the philosopher, that is, mastery of the theoretical and practical sciences along with moral and intellectual perfection (*CPR* 60, 22–61, 7; 61, 11–13). What role does prophecy have to play in this kind of model? Averroes seems to use a non-religious sense of prophecy when he describes it as a means by which the future is made known (*CPR* 41, 1–2) and as common among different kinds of states, and by implication, among different kinds of religions. Lerner comments 'Further, by equating the philosopher and the bringer of the *sharīʿa* (*APR* 61, 14), Averroes in effect denies that the *sharīʿa* has any decisive superiority.'[5] Lerner implies here that Averroes is involved in a very devious activity, merely hinting to the alert reader that the *sharīʿa* does not

---

[4] *APR*, p. xv.
[5] Ibid., p. xvii.

have the unique status which it appears to have. Yet Averroes is quite open in his views of the relationship between prophecy, philosophy, and legislation. He asserts:

What the laws existing in this time of ours assert . . . is [that the end of man is doing] what God, may he be exalted, wills, but that the only way of knowing this matter of what it is God wills of them is prophecy. And this [what God wills], if you reflect on the laws, is divided into abstract knowledge alone . . . and action—such as what it forewarns concerning the [moral] qualities. Its intention regarding this purpose is identical with the intention of philosophy in genus and purpose. That is why humans assert that these laws only follow ancient wisdom (APR 66, 11–18).

It is very clear what Averroes wants to say about prophecy and sharīʿa here, that it provides exactly the same information as philosophy, albeit in a different form. Sharīʿa does have decisive superiority, he makes it clear elsewhere (TT 582) in that it is available to a far wider cross-section of the community than is philosophy, yet there is nothing in sharīʿa which contradicts 'ancient wisdom', ʿby which he means Greek thought. Averroes' position is quite clear here, and Lerner's suspicion about his essays into dissimulation is misplaced.

Not surprisingly, Averroes challenges Plato's opinion that the Greeks are the people most suited by nature to receive the human perfections, and especially the human perfections:

even if we accept that they are the most disposed by nature to receive wisdom, we cannot disregard the fact that individuals like these, i.e. those disposed to wisdom—are frequently to be found. You find this in the land of the Greeks and its vicinity, such as this land of ours, namely Andalus, and Syria and Iraq and Egypt, albeit this exists more frequently in the land of the Greeks (APR 27, 3–7).

Averroes agrees that living within the more equable climatic zones may well lead to a fairly high distribution of intellectual activity, yet he rather grudgingly admits that other groups of people are capable of reasoning at the level of the Greeks. In his medical work, the Kitāb al-kulliyāt (General Principles of Medicine), he quotes approvingly the view of Galen that the most temperate climate is the fifth, which contains both Greece and Spain.[6] In his middle commentary on Aristotle's Meteorology he again relates the geographical position of Greece and Andalusia 'scilicet quod ipsi conversi sunt ad naturam gentis propriae illi terrae, ideo multiplicatae

---

[6] Kitāb al-kulliyāt (General Principles of Medicine), Biblioteca Nacional de Madrid, MS 5013, fo. 42 n. 42.

sunt in eis scientiae'.[7] Averroes seems to be expressing here a tentative Andalusian nationalism against the part of the world from which the Arabs in Spain originated. Although Averroes is eager to line up with the Greeks (about whom, it must be said, he knew virtually nothing in common with the rest of the *falāsifa*), he disagrees with Plato on the subject of war. Plato is disparaging of the necessity for war, arguing that it only exists in cases of necessity, and relating it to the desire for wealth in the warlike city. There is little motive for war in the virtuous city according to Plato except when it is necessary to defend the city itself from external aggression. Aristotle criticized this view, arguing that on the contrary war and preparation for war are valuable in the sense of training the disposition to be courageous.[8] Averroes seems to adopt a more pacific view than Aristotle here, accepting that the disposition to be courageous is important and can be developed by preparation for war, and yet agreeing with Plato that war as a coercive measure to change people's beliefs has very limited value, especially when it is directed against people who have some rational ability of their own (*CPR* 27, 19–23).

Lerner sees this as a radical departure from the Islamic doctrine of *jihād*, whereby the territory of Islam is in continual armed struggle with the territory of disbelief. As he says, 'Where the Koran sees the just war as leading to the conversion of all mankind to the true religion, Averroes views the just war as a mode of bringing wisdom to those who have the natural potentiality for it'.[9] Again, the implication is that Averroes is presenting un-Islamic views here. Hourani makes a milder accusation against Averroes' orthodoxy on the topic of *jihād* when he refers to Averroes' claim in his commentary on the *Nicomachean Ethics* that 'peace is preferable, and war only occasionally relevant'.[10] Islam specifies a total and unending struggle between the land of Islam (*dār al-Islam*) and the land of the infidels (*dār al ḥarb*) until the final victory of Islam is assured. But is this really the case? Did not Islam recognize the inadvisability of war in some circumstances, and possibility of success through peaceful methods? For example, the ninth-century-AD writer ibn al-Faqīh al-Hamaḍānī describes in his *K. al-buldān* the earth as having the shape of a bird, the head being China, and the left wing Central Asia, the

[7] *Aristotelis opera*, fos. 435ᵛ–436ᵛ n. 42. Sabra, 'The Andalusian Revolt', p. 153.

[8] This point is stressed by M. Mahdi, 'Alfarabi et Averroes: Remarques sur le commentaire d'Averroès sur la République de Platon', *Multiple Averroès*, pp. 91–102.

[9] *APR*, p. xviii.

[10] *Aristotelis opera*, fo. 248ʳ. The commentary is discussed in G. Hourani, 'Averroes on Good and Evil', *Studia Islamica*, 16 (1962), 13–40; p. 39, repr. in G. Hourani, *Reason and Tradition in Islamic Ethics* (Cambridge University Press: Cambridge, 1985), 249–69.

right wing Hindustan, the breast the Islamic world, the tail the Maghreb. The breast (*ṣadr*) represents the seat of faith, and pervades the whole world. To succeed in its mission, it is not necessary to wage ceaseless war against the non-Islamic world.[11] The Islamic doctrine of *jihād* is not without possibilities of development and interpretation to specify why in certain situations wars are more likely to be effective than in other contexts. Averroes relates a warring country to its potential victims on the lines of the head of the household towards his children, being obliged to teach them correct opinions by force only where there is no viable alternative course of action available (*CPR* 26, 8–24). This suggests an entirely reasonable interpretation of the doctrine of *jihād*, whereby war would only be unleashed against the infidel if it is likely to succeed in defeating them, and if it is the only way to change their opinions. Islam does after all portray itself as an eminently *reasonable* faith, accessible to those who are capable of following their own rational faculty.

Does Averroes' discussion of the *Republic* contradict the universalism which is explicit in the teachings of Islam? After all, in a well-known *ḥadīth* which Averroes quotes, the prophet Muḥammad is taken to have said 'I have been sent to the Red and the Black' (*APR* 46, 20), whereas Plato seems to argue that nations are variously endowed by nature with the virtues, and so any general religious mission would be misguided. Averroes signals his agreement with the Islamic position by pointing to Aristotle's critique of Plato on this and other topics, but there is no need to think that he is correcting Plato by the use of Islam when we can interpret him just as easily disagreeing with Plato for Aristotelian reasons. We must recall that for Averroes the *Republic* is the prolegomenon to the *Nicomachean Ethics*. He does sometimes just compare Plato's view with the Islamic view and leave it at that, as when he outlines Plato's condemnation of total warfare against people of the same culture as oneself. Averroes comments, 'These are to be called ones who have gone astray, not unbelievers. What Plato asserts differs from what many legislators assert' (*APR* 59, 20–60, 5). Lerner highlights Averroes' reluctance to comment 'on one of the great points of contention between philosophy and the *sharīʿa*; whether racial and linguistic unity ought to prevail over religious diversity'.[12] But it is worth noticing in this context that one of the things which Averroes is doing is providing a reading of the *Republic* which helps Muslims to understand what the contemporary

---

[11] Ed. M. J. de Goeje (Bibliotheca Geographorum Arabicorum:) Leiden, (1885), v. 3.
[12] *APR*, p. xxiii.

relevance of that text is. The relationship between the Greek cities in the
Republic is rather like the relationship between different communities in
the Islamic world at Averroes' time, who shared many of the cultural and
religious characteristics of orthodox Islam but differed on some aspects of
doctrinal definition. The implication that Averroes is refusing to discuss a
controversial issue pertinent to the clash between Islam and philosophy is
superfluous. Surely what he is doing here, and in so much of his work, is
trying to naturalize Plato, make his arguments appear relevant to very
different political and cultural conditions, and this is done by translating
Plato's language into concepts more amenable to Averroes' audience.

This would explain the use of contemporary political events in his
commentary to illustrate Plato's points in relevant terms. For instance,
there is little point in talking about the Delphic Apollo (*Republic*, 427^b)
when one can talk instead of the phenomenon of prophecy (*CPR* 47, 24–6)
to make a similar point. What can we say about all those passages which
Averroes reports in the *Republic* which represent arguments very distant
from an Islamic conception of a virtuous society? There are, for example,
the common holding of women and children, not to mention property, and
the greatly enhanced view of the capabilities and duties of women.
Averroes just reports on these views, but should this be taken to be
agreement or endorsement? The answer is clearly negative. All that he is
doing is presenting aspects of Plato's arguments, and leaving it to the
reader to work out how acceptable they are and how closely connected to
the notion of the just society and the just citizen.

Lerner's interpretation of Averroes as a challenger of traditional
religious values is very much a response to the interpretation offered by
Erwin Rosenthal. Both Lerner and Rosenthal believe that the religion–
philosophy relationship is very important for Averroes, with the former
holding that Averroes took pains to disguise his opinion that philosophy
was suspect from a religious point of view, while the latter argues that
Averroes consistently regarded philosophy as inferior to *sharī̔a*. For
Rosenthal, Averroes 'was a Muslim first and a disciple of Plato, Aristotle
and their commentators second'.[13] His arguments for this interpretation
are not compelling, though. Averroes consistently tries to show that
philosophy and law are both teachers of the same truth, but the law
contains the whole truth available to everyone, philosopher or no, and a
truth moreover which stems from an infallible God and not from the

---

[13] E. I. J. Rosenthal, *Political Thought in Medieval Islam* (Cambridge University Press:
Cambridge, 1958, 177.

frailties of human reason. After all, Averroes does argue that revelation sets limits to what is acceptable as an object of philosophical investigation, and topics such as God's providence, reward and punishment in the afterlife, and the ceremonial laws are said to be beyond speculation (*TT* 580–8). Rosenthal comments that 'By this limitation, medieval philosophy forfeits sovereign independence, since it is *under* the law, and it becomes religious philosophy.'[14]

The implication is that philosophers must be restricted in their investigation by the answers provided by religion, and they must not even consider certain issues since they have been settled once and for all by the teachings of Islam. This is far from being Averroes' position, though. He does, it is true, regard ceremonial laws as inaccessible to demonstration, but this is not evidence of the limitations of reason. It is rather an acknowledgement that details of religious law such as rituals differ from region to region and from religion to religion, while their central rationale remains the same. Averroes claims:

> But as for the *nomos* to be laid down concerning temples, prayers, sacrifices, and offerings, which will imprint in the souls humility and the extolling of God and the angels, why he would leave them to what God . . . commands through prophecy. It is as though he asserts that these are divine things, and that whatever of these there is in cities we ought to acknowledge as such, for they are, as it were, common to all the laws and conventions of the *nomoi* (*APR* 47, 24–9).

Particular religions will be left to work out the precise form of the rules and laws designed to induce humility and love of God, but the necessity for such rules and their general character is derivable philosophically. Averroes is really echoing Aristotle's distinction between natural and conventional rules of justice, where the former are quite general and a shared necessary aspect of political organization as such. The latter are variable, and the ceremonial laws, that is, the rules concerning prayer, fasts, festivals, sacrifices, ritual cleanliness, and so on depend upon the nature of the people to whom they apply and the sort of environment in which they live. Aristotle argued that these rather minor exemplifications of more general laws differ from place to place and time to time, and Averroes has no problems in accepting this conclusion. Does it then follow that philosophy is restricted in its scope by religion? There is no reason to think so. Religion will select the most appropriate rituals and ceremonies for a particular context, but philosophy will still be free to determine the most general laws. Indeed, Averroes explains:

[14] Ibid. 180.

This is evident from the case of those people who, having grown up with such general *nomoi* and general laws, are able, by themselves, to arrive at many partial *nomoi* and good disciplines, such as honouring parents, remaining silent before elders, and other such practical *nomoi* . . . the general laws, when firmly established, will lead the citizens to these partial *nomoi* easily and by themselves (*APR* 47, 5–10).

Rosenthal argues that Averroes is 'in a class apart' among the *falāsifa* due to his insistence upon the absolute truth and universality of *sharīʿa*, and in particular due to his interpretation of the notion of prophecy. Rosenthal suggests that 'the *khilāfa* is not simply the *Politeia* of Plato transferred and adapted to Islamic conditions. Although both are based on law, the *sharīʿa*, as revealed prophetic law, is superior to the *nomos*, as revelation is superior to myth'.[15] There is something in Rosenthal's claim here, in that revelation is taken to be superior to philosophy in the sense that it makes its message more widely available than is possible for philosophy. There are things which the prophet can do which are unattainable by the philosopher. The former can teach the masses, know about the future, establish religious laws and determine the happiness of the whole of humanity (*TT* 516). Averroes makes it clear in his *Manāhij* that through divine revelation or inspiration the prophet establishes laws which make it possible for people to attain perfect happiness, understanding of God, the universe, reward and punishment, the next life, the nature of good actions and evil deeds (*Manāhij*, p. 98). For Averroes the credentials of the prophet are to be established by his political skill and knowledge of the direction in which to employ it. Miracles do not prove the credentials of the prophet; only his legislative function can do that. There are plenty of things in this list of capacities which the philosopher does not possess. Although he would be able to answer the theoretical questions about the nature of human happiness, ethical value, and the structure of the universe, he would not necessarily have the skills (1) to embody this knowledge into a law, and (2) to persuade the general public that this is a law which must be obeyed. The point which Averroes wishes to make is that one can be a perfectly adequate, indeed, even skilful, philosopher and yet not be skilled in legislating in its widest sense, in the political context of establishing laws which embody one's philosophical understanding of how people ought to live in order to live well. What the prophet has is *practical* knowledge in addition to the theoretical knowledge which he shares with the philosopher, so that the content of the prophetic

---

[15] Ibid. 185.

law (*sharī'a*) is no different from the content of philosophical law (*nomos/nāmūs*). The prophet is far better at putting this content over to his community, and succeeds in transforming abstract ideas about human happiness into political directives and social norms which then regulate the life of the community. Thus far, then, we cannot justify separating Averroes from the rest of the *falāsifa* on the relationship between philosophy and prophecy. We cannot derive from his political writings the thesis that religion is inferior to philosophy, nor the reverse, except in a practical sense.

What is the relationship between Averroes' discussion of Plato and his views on contemporary political events? Averroes was by no means a dispassionate observer of political life. His personal well-being was intimately connected with the attitude of the authorities towards him, and towards philosophical enquiry in general. Right at the end of his text he refers to the 'troubles of the time', and throughout the work there are references to instances of contemporary relevance. Averroes accepts the problems in arriving at the ideal state, but refuses to agree that it is so unlikely an event as to be virtually inconceivable. It is not clear whether he thinks of the ideal state as precisely that, an ideal which can serve as a criterion of the value of any state considered, but whose existence at any time in the past or future is irrelevant to its role as an ideal, or whether he thinks of it as a live political possibility. Since the same ambiguity exists in Plato, he is perhaps just reflecting original Platonic doubts in his account. An example of how he uses Plato's terminology to make sense of political events can be found in his critique of what he calls 'priestly states' as in: 'the similarity between the priestly and the tyrannical states often leads the priestly parts that exist in these states to be transformed into tyrannical ones, thus bringing into disrepute him whose aim is priestly. This is the case with the priestly parts that exist in the states to be found in our time' (*CPR* 86, 6–7; I have omitted the quotation marks around 'priestly'). Rosenthal argues convincingly that this refers to the administration of the Almohad regime under Caliph Abū Ya'qūb Yūsuf as *imām* in succession to his father 'Abd al-Mu'min who had restored a strict *sunnī* Muslim ideology. The *imām* in the priestly state tries to rule in strict accordance with the *sharī'a*, but local political and economic factors might well serve to 'bring him into disrepute'.[16] Averroes even manages to identify the Platonic account of the succession of imperfect states with the early history of Islam, leading to the charge that the present regime is timocratic:

[16] Ibid. 193–4.

You may understand what Plato states concerning the transformation of the ideal constitution into the timocratic, and that of the excellent into the timocratic man, from the case of the government of the Arabs in the earliest period. For they used to imitate the ideal constitution, and then were transformed in the days of Muʿāwiya into timocratic men. It seems to be the case with the constitution that exists now in these islands (*CPR* 89, 27–32).

He is even blunter concerning the forerunners of the Almohads, the Almoravids, saying:

We often see kings being corrupted to the likes of these. An example in this time is the kingdom of people known as the Almoravids. At first they imitated the government based upon the nomos; this was under the first of them. Then they changed under his son into the timocratic, though there also was mixed in him the love of wealth. Then it changed under his grandson into the hedonistic (*APR* 92. 4–7; Lerner's notes on p. 125 should be regarded with suspicion here).

One of the attractions of the *Republic* is its identification of political changes with changes in the character of the citizens in the changing states. Despite the religious enthusiasm with which a regime may start, the human desire for wealth, pleasure, and comfort leads to a transition of regime along a steadily more undesirable path. He illustrates the move from democracy into tyranny by placing it within a local context thus:

You can discern this in the qualities and morals that have sprung up among us since the year 540 among the rulers and dignitaries. For because the timocratic constitution in which they had grown up was weakened, they came by those vile character-traits which they now [exhibit]. He only among them perseveres in the excellent virtues who is excellent in accordance with the religious laws, and this is rare with them (*CPR* 103. 5–10).

The decline is very much one from a law-abiding citizenry to a more amorphous and independent group of social agents. There are two interpretations of the decline. According to Rosenthal, it is a decline from 'the *khilāfa* and not the *Politeia* [which] serves as the ideal pattern, as his example of the Almoravids and their inevitable replacement by the Almohads clearly shows'.[17] But on Lerner's argument, 'To follow in the ways of the *sharīʿa* is to move in the direction of recovering the earlier resemblance or imitation'.[18] The contemporary rule of the Almohads has declined from a level of excellence *not* based upon the *sharīʿa* but upon an

[17] Ibid. 197.
[18] *APR*, p. xxi.

imitation of Plato's ideal constitution. Lerner implies that Averroes considers the *shari̓ a* to be a mere imitation of the ideal constitution. There is no evidence for this view, though, but Rosenthal's position is also unconvincing. Averroes' account of the transformation of one state into another does not depend upon any specifically Islamic concepts to work. Rosenthal suggests that Averroes identifies the process of change and decline in the character of the state with a lessening of the authority of Islam and a consequent weakening of the rule of law. What is significant in Averroes' description of political transformation, however, is not the decline of Islamic authority as such, but the decline of law as a controlling and generally acceptable mechanism for regulating society. Greed, selfishness, desire for luxury, and power start to have an influence on the nature of law, and on its defence and support, and this leads to a progressive decline in the character of the citizens in the state, and in the nature of the state itself. Averroes illustrates this process in terms of relatively contemporary events, and rather courageously so given his acerbic comments upon past and present rulers, but there is no specifically Islamic explanatory factor in the political analysis.

We have seen how Averroes uses Aristotle to help make some of the criticisms he had of Plato in his commentary on the *Republic*, which he regarded as the practical part of the study of politics. Hence the use of political examples taken from the practice in the Islamic world. The more theoretical part is to be found in his commentary on Aristotle's *Nicomachean Ethics*. Averroes is reasonably faithful to Aristotle in his work, but there is a definite orientation towards the discussion of politics. He takes up Aristotle's argument that, if the political process organizes all the activities carried out in the state, and if all these activities are directed towards some end, then the political organization must affect all the other activities in such a way as to reach a greater and more beneficial end than any individual activity might achieve. Aristotle's emphasis was then upon the nature of the most desirable end, while Averroes concentrates upon the good which is to be found in the appropriate organization of government in the state. When Aristotle famously expresses doubts concerning the possibility of determinate answers to normative questions (*NE* I. 3, 1094^{b}12–18), Averroes dissipates the Aristotelian vagueness and argues that the answers to ethical questions are to be found in a radically different kind of book, in a study of metaphysics, which could determinately relate the study of the nature of the most desirable end for human beings to the nature of those human beings and their position in the structure of things in the universe. He suggests that the *Nicomachean Ethics* is too practically orientated for such theoretical issues to be appropriately tackled there.

Butterworth expresses surprise that Averroes does not seek to 'correct' Aristotle by importing Islamic answers to philosophical questions about the nature of happiness, the afterlife, the role of religion in the state, and so on.[19] This would have been a crass thing to do, though, and Averroes makes no attempt at bringing in contemporary illustrations of philosophical issues in this work. Indeed, in some of the discussion of the nature of happiness he concentrates upon the notion of happiness available to the largest number of people, that is, happiness which is not dependent upon intellectual striving and excellence. There is scope in the *Nicomachean Ethics* for the Muslim commentator to identify issues in Greek philosophy with apparently similar issues in Islamic life, yet Averroes tends to ignore these. For example, he might have taken up Aristotle's suggestion that divine justice is always and everywhere the same while human justice is variable. But a central problem in the *Nicomachean Ethics*, that prudence is the basis to political skill and none the less is subordinate as a perfection to intellectual skill, is faithfully reflected in Averroes' commentary. If the best way to live is closely related to a life of contemplation, if such a life is an aim only possible to a limited number of citizens, then it seems as though the majority of citizens must aim for an inferior kind of life, one based upon prudence. It seems, then, that political understanding leads the state as a whole and the people in it to a second-class version of social and personal existence.

Averroes might well argue that, since the mass of the population can only at best expect to perfect the civil virtues, and live prudent and relatively satisfactory lives, then it is the task of politics to inculcate in them the relevant moral dispositions. This leads Averroes to an emphasis yet again upon law and legislation as aspects of social control which can lead people to behave as well as can be expected given their intellectual and moral limitations. He certainly transforms aspects of the *Nicomachean Ethics* through his reading of the text as a specifically *political* work. He argues in a most un-Aristotelian manner that the main differences between theoretical and practical enquiries are based on the nature of the objects of those enquiries, and not on the reasoning process involved in their methodologies. That is, theoretical reason is just as relevant an instrument for investigating issues concerning civic legislation, where the happiness of

---

[19] C. Butterworth, 'New Light on the Political Philosophy of Averroes', in G. Hourani (ed.), *Essays on Islamic Philosophy and Science* (State University of New York: Albany, 1975), 118–27; p. 121.

the group as a whole is the object of the enterprise, as it is in operating at the level of contemplation. Averroes wants to avoid the conclusion that the principle involved in the choice and establishment of legislation is practical reasoning; rather, the best kind of ruler is the person who has theoretical knowledge of practical affairs and who then goes on to teach the masses by speaking to them in appropriate ways. He paraphrases Aristotle thus: 'General political government, that is, the art of governing states, is the ruling disposition over all dispositions in the state, I mean the arts which are under this art because it commands its subordinate arts what they should do' (*NE* Heb. fo. 46^a). The ruler tries to encourage virtue in the citizenry, through inducing them to be 'good, excellent and submissively bent under the laws' (*NE* Heb. fo. 17^b) so that political justice exists when 'there is naturally a law between them. Justice then exists when there are rulers and others accept rule, and really justice only holds between people who are either rulers and ruled' (*NE* Heb. fo. 70^b–71^a). What is meant by this is that relative inequalities in society will be an acceptable part of political justice if they are based upon law, upon stable and fair social systems of exchange. Law is a vital aspect of the process of helping people learn how to behave well, and Averroes sees the notion of law as linking the very start of the *Nicomachean Ethics*, where Aristotle identifies the study of virtue with politics, to the end where legislation is said to be required if human well-being is to be attainable (*NE* 10. 9, 1179^{b}32–1181^{b}24).

Referring to Averroes' interpretation of Plato's *Republic*, Butterworth comments:

> It also seems to be a natural sequel to Aristotle's *Nicomachean Ethics*, if Averroes' argument about theoretical wisdom guiding practical wisdom can really be attributed to Aristotle. But since it is generally known that Aristotle did not accept that argument in the *Politics*, Averroes' attempted substitution must be rejected. Such a rejection . . . poses an important question for all students of Averroes' political teaching: in what way does it make sense to say that theoretical wisdom can guide practical matters.[20]

Butterworth asks a very interesting question here, one which is linked closely to a basic difficulty in Aristotle's account of *eudaimonia* or well-being (sometimes loosely translated as 'happiness') which survives as a difficulty for Averroes. Sometimes Aristotle makes *sophia*, theoretical wisdom, the sole constituent of *eudaimonia*, while sometimes he claims that it consists in the exercise of a more broadly based basket of virtues.[21] These two positions are clearly incompatible. They also have very different implications. The identification of a more social notion of happiness as living in accordance with a general combination of virtues would serve to make it available to everyone, yet would seem to relegate theoretical thinking to an ordinary position in the collection of virtues which make up our lives. The identification of *eudaimonia* with *sophia* would imply that the vast majority of the human population, unable or disinclined to concentrate entirely on intellectual thought, is deprived of any possibility of living well.

It could easily be argued that Aristotle has little time for the view that *sophia* is to be identified with *eudaimonia*.[22] When he compares the wise person with the person who lives a life which is only secondarily *eudaimon*, he is comparing abstractions, not real people with real lives, and he is developing an acceptable view of what it is to be a person. An important passage in this respect is this:

The wise man has no need for any such things [external goods]—with a view to his activity, that is; in fact, they are rather obstacles—with a view to *theoria*, that is; but in so far as he is a man and lives together with others, he choose to act in accordance with virtue; then he will need such things in order to live a human life (*NE* 10. 8, 1178[b]3–7).

What this seems to suggest is that *theoria* and moral behaviour cannot be regarded separately. Since we are combinations of minds and bodies we require not just the bare necessities of life in order to live as persons but also the ability to act morally. Moral behaviour can be seen as a necessary condition for the life of the *sophos*, since as a human being he or she must organize their lives to take account of moral questions and decisions. Even on the view, then, that the only really worthwhile activity is that of *theoria*, the *sophos* must involve himself in moral action as a means to spending as much time as possible in the exercise of *sophia*. The wise person may require a smaller amount of possessions than the morally good person in order to carry out his specific function, but he needs them in order to live as a human being. The wise person cannot sensibly neglect his links with other people if he lives in a world which has other people in it. Human beings do not live solitary lives (*NE* 2. 7, 1097[b]9) but are basically human beings in the sense that they must carry out their moral duties and develop

[21] Leaman, 'Ibn Rushd on Happiness and Philosophy'.
[22] T. Engberg-Pedersen, *Aristotle's Theory of Moral Insight* (Clarendon Press: Oxford, 1983).

their virtues. *Theoria* is none the less the most worthwhile activity, and beings who can spend all their time indulging in it are undoubtedly superior to the human beings which are to be distinguished from them.

It is worth reminding ourselves at this stage of the emphasis which Averroes places on moral standing when discussing the role of philosophy and its appropriate audience:

it is evident that the study of the books of the ancients is obligatory by Law . . . and that whoever forbids the study of them to anyone who is fit to study them, i.e. anyone who unites two qualities, (1) natural intelligence, and (2) religious integrity and moral virtue, is blocking people from the door by which the law summons them to knowledge of God, the door of theoretical study which leads to the truest knowledge of him (*FM* 5).

Later on he refers to one of the causes of the deleterious effects on people who read philosophy as being their 'lack of practical virtue' (*FM* 18). There can be little doubt that in his work the notion of a human being, and especially a citizen, includes moral characteristics. His argument that the place to seek an answer to questions surrounding the nature of human beings is not to be found in the *Nicomachean Ethics* is not obviously valid. Aristotle did provide an account of what human beings are and what form of life is appropriate to them. He also provided an account of the importance of education, since for people to behave well they need to be trained in virtue from infancy, and this is most attainable if they grow up under good laws (*NE* 10. 9, 1179^b31-2). Arguments by themselves cannot make people morally better. All they can do is encourage and stimulate those people who are already disposed to behave in virtuous ways (*NE* 10. 9, 1179^b31). Argument can have an effect upon the character if the person involved is of a certain kind, that is, if his passions are in a prepared state to make change possible. If one is to argue with one's audience that it should act in a certain way, there is only a chance of success if the audience already has the appropriate desires. Whatever knowledge we communicate to the audience will have no effect whatsoever upon its behaviour if it is ruled by its passions, if it cannot be induced to have the desires which it must have if it is to act and put the knowledge about ethical behaviour which is being imparted into practice. A vital aspect of this process, then, is training the passions so that, although one does not really want to do x, one does x in order to avoid a consequence of x which is more unwelcome than x itself. This is typical of the way in which the law works: by restraining our immediate desires for illegal ends it transforms those desires into different desires to behave legally, through the implicit threat of punishment for failing to do so. Of course, when we examine the phenomenology of these sorts of desires we do not generally find an internal struggle going on in the individual every time he is confronted with psychological pressures to conform to social norms, since we are brought up and accustomed to denying certain inappropriate desires until we reach the stage 'when they have become customary' (*NE* 10. 9, 1179^{b}35–6; *Rhet.* 1. 10, 1369^{b}16–18). So in the last section of the *Nicomachean Ethics* Aristotle discusses the significance of the law in the state as a mechanism which habituates the population to have the appropriate frame of mind to receive information and argument about how they should behave. So we can see that there is a ready answer to Butterworth's question of how far theoretical wisdom can guide practical issues. According to Aristotle and Averroes, before we can see our way to a useful analysis of practical matters, we have to possess as clear a view as possible of the nature of human beings. Only then will we know what particular ends and what sorts of behaviour apply to those kinds of creatures. This is theoretical knowledge, knowledge which is acquired through the application of reason on the facts of human behaviour. Human beings consist of a variety of traits and interests, and this bundle is very much part of their nature. Any description of their nature which fails to take account of this fact will go awry.

Once we know what concept of human nature is appropriate, we have important indications of how human beings ought to live and what constitutes their well-being. It has to be acknowledged by Aristotelians, though, that people themselves may not know what it is in their interests as people to do, or how they ought to behave, or there may be obstacles to their correct behaviour arising from within them or through an external source. We have seen how significant law then is in working gradually but surely on human character to encourage virtuous behaviour and discourage evil. Both Aristotle and Averroes write fulsomely on the benefits involved in being brought up from infancy in a state well organized through a system of skilfully devised laws. It is hardly surprising, then, that they should also emphasize education as an important accompaniment to legislation, and public persuasion as a political process. Averroes produced two sorts of commentaries on Aristotle's *Rhetoric*, one being a middle commentary (*talkhīṣ*) while the other is a brief summary.[23] As one would expect, the summary is far more free in its interpretation than the middle commentary, and concentrates upon the structure of rhetorical argument itself. He makes it clear that

---

[23] Translated by C. Butterworth in *Short Comm.*

rhetoric is of considerable political significance, and has a key position in the community. He sees Aristotle as being concerned with techniques of persuasion for logical as well as political reasons. After all, there are degrees of persuasiveness in speeches which can be analysed and put in order. The relative success of such speeches is useful because the public is brought to action through them, and in so far as we are social beings we have to use rhetorical techniques in our political dealings. Not just anything at all will do to bring about a change in mind in one's audience, though, and Averroes criticizes sharply the theologians he usually holds up to scorn, Abū al-Maʿālī and Ghazali, and the philosopher he normally attacks, Galen, for their fallacious attempts at the use of rhetorical argument, the enthymeme. He argues that persuasive arguments which do not work are positively dangerous, in that, not only do they mislead their audience, but they also establish as orthodox belief propositions which are reached as conclusions of fallacious reasoning. The trouble with using inappropriate logical methods of persuasion is that one ends up on different occasions with different conclusions, and this serves to confuse the public and sow doubt in its mind about the validity of religious principles as such.

Averroes goes rather further in his approach to the logical status of the certainty of the sending of the Prophet and the existence of God. Since certainty can only be achieved through a combination of sense experience and valid reasoning, these beliefs cannot be called certain. Reports which relate to such events may well be accepted and may persuade the community, but it still remains the case that certainty is not here a possibility, only persuasion. Interestingly, Averroes repeats his dislike of the use of miracles as evidence when he claims that such miraculous reports may improve public confidence in the miracle-worker but can do nothing to strengthen the validity of his claims. One recalls here his critique of basing legislation on a miracle-working prophet; legislation must have a satisfactory structure to be effective, and its miraculous basis is irrelevant to its essential character as successful legislation. This is sometimes taken by commentators to be a suspiciously un-Islamic assertion, but it needs to be emphasized that Islam is a religion which is based (at least in its own terms) on reason and not miracles. In addition, although miracles have a part to play in establishing the status of a person, it is only the carrying out of the legislative function which really establishes that status. It is after all often possible to be taken in by tricks and *coups de main*, and if one thinks that such efforts are miracles and then finds one was wrong, it might serve to weaken faith. Yet, if someone genuinely carries out a legislative task and helps institute a regime which stimulates the attainment of happiness among the general community along with an understanding of the religious roots of that happiness and the organization which leads to it, then one is not at the mercy of possible tricksters and illusionists, but one is justified in believing in the divine nature of the message, and consequently the divine inspiration of the messenger.

It might be felt that rhetoric is an unsatisfactory technique for the transmission of information as important as that relating to religion and the conduct of life, but when one sees how Averroes defines it one can see that it represents a respectable, although not unchallengeable, reasoning scheme: 'The enthymeme is a syllogism leading to a conclusion which corresponds to unexamined opinion previously existing among all or most people. Unexamined previously existing opinion is opinion which strikes a person as a probable supposition and which he trusts as soon as it occurs to him, even before he has examined it' (*Short Comm.* 63–4). The idea is that rhetoric might hit at the truth, but its chances of doing so are rather haphazard: 'the premisses employed in these two arts [rhetoric and dialectic] are not grasped in the mind in the same way as they exist outside the mind. Rather, a predicate is always asserted to apply to a subject because of what is generally accepted, either according to unexamined opinion or according to the truth' (*Short Comm.* 70). As examples of rhetorical arguments which do not hit the truth he relishes in Abū al-Maʿālī's 'proof' that creation is not possible for the elements (*Short Comm.* 66) and attacks the theologian's view that 'it is possible for everything to be created out of any chanced-upon thing' (*Short Comm.* 70). Similarly, lack of interest in the logical conditions of certainty might lead people to think that the heavens are created 'due to their similarity to created bodies with respect to extension, alteration, connectedness and other things' (*Short Comm.* 71). Complete certainty on these issues is unattainable by rhetorical means. He also pokes fun at the knots which Ghazali ties himself up in when specifying the role of consensus in Islam in establishing criteria of heresy.

Butterworth makes two powerful claims about Averroes' writings on rhetoric. He calls the summary 'this astonishing teaching in a booklet that was presented as a simple summary of Aristotle's views on rhetoric',[24] and, dealing with his work on rhetoric in general, states: 'Averroes . . .

---

[24] C. Butterworth, 'Rhetoric and Islamic Political Philosophy', *International Journal of Mid Eastern Studies*, 3 (1972), 186–98, p. 193.

appears to hold a view of rhetoric which must ultimately lead to doubt about the merits of Muḥammad's rhetoric.'[25] Just because Averroes uses theological examples to make his points in the summary of the *Rhetoric* does not show that he is challenging the theology itself. He is illustrating his account of Aristotle by bringing in contemporary examples of theological arguments of which he disapproves. Why this should be thought of as 'astonishing' defeats understanding. It is common policy for Averroes, and indeed for any commentator trying to show the relevance to his audience of philosophy from a remote and distant past. Butterworth claims that in his middle commentary Averroes is presenting a new teaching about rhetoric through his invention of Aristotelian speeches. In that work Averroes argues that rhetoric is closely connected with the structure of the syllogism, and the best way to understand rhetorical arguments or enthymemes is to compare and contrast them with demonstrative and dialectical syllogisms. This is clearly a logical enterprise, since rhetoric provides a similitude of truth along similar lines to the ways in which logic provides certainty of truth. The ways in which some theologians misuse rhetoric and fail to grasp its logical connections lead to their problems in satisfactorily establishing persuasive lines of discourse. Since most people are not really up to appreciating the logical reasons why they should behave in certain ways, or the theoretical principles behind those forms of behaviour, rhetoric is important in providing an appearance of logical necessity and rigour in arguments to correct opinions and actions.

Butterworth tries to deepen the sense that Averroes is doing something very dubious theologically when he comments: 'although Averroes pretended to agree with Aristotle's view that rhetoric is limited in that it cannot provide a sufficient treatment of the subject of legislation or of different kinds of political régimes, he actually opened his rhetoric to a broad discussion of both subjects.'[26] This is a misleading assertion. To an extent it is true that rhetoric on Averroes' account cannot really provide an adequate (that is, logically adequate) account of these issues, but it can and must provide a satisfactory account for the benefit of the majority of the citizens. Indeed, Averroes argued that not only rhetoric and dialectic may be used to persuade the community, but all kinds of other and logically even weaker techniques may be used if they are the only or best effective

---

[25] C. Butterworth, 'The Rhetorician and His Relationship to the Community: Three Accounts of Aristotle's *Rhetoric*', in Marmura (ed.) *Islamic Theology and Philosophy*, pp. 111–36, p. 134.

[26] Butterworth, 'Rhetoric and Islamic Political Philosophy', p. 195.

means of persuasion (see, for example, *CPR* sections 25, 29, 105). Averroes clearly thinks that even sophistry is acceptable provided that the ends for which it is employed are those which are designed to establish the welfare of the audience, and this is certainly not a part of Aristotle's text. Averroes' approach obliges the philosopher who has a solid grasp of logic to trim his speech when speaking politically to the sort of audience in front of him. This does not mean that the audience is denied the truth where this truth cannot be presented to them in such a way as to be generally acceptable unless it is dressed up in a non-demonstrative form. It is the truth which must be communicated, and in a way appropriate to the context and the perceived receptivity of the audience. Butterworth implies throughout his work on these texts that Averroes is dubious about the fit between the basic principles of Islam and the laws of logic. There is nothing in these texts themselves to suggest that this is in fact the case. He has mistaken the philosophical technique whereby one illustrates fallacies by using pieces of reasoning which are not only fallacious but also expressive of a dubious proposition to throw doubt on both the argument form and the conclusions as an attack on the nature of the conclusions as such. This is itself a fallacy. Additional arguments would be necessary to show that the subject of those arguments is itself invalidly used as a proper subject. For example, when Averroes is suspicious of the demonstrative status of miracles in prophecy, he is not challenging miracles or prophecy as such. He is merely suggesting that the role of miracles in prophecy is primarily to persuade those who are not susceptible to more subtle means of persuasion, by logical proof. The miracles and the prophecy are all still important, but they are there for a particular purpose which is to broadcast more widely religious truths. When Averroes refers to rhetoric as the medium through which the message is transmitted he wishes to throw suspicion on neither the message nor the medium. He is concerned only in putting that technique in its logical place.

The logical nature of Averroes' treatment of rhetoric cannot be over-emphasized. It is part of the interpretation of Aristotle's works in the Islamic world as consisting of a spectrum of demonstrative rigour, ranging from the two *Analytics*, the *Categories* and *Interpretation* down to the progressively less valid *Topics*, *Sophists*, *Rhetoric*, and *Poetics*. Poetry is by far the weakest form of argument which is available for the communication process. With it

one strives for an imaginary representation or exemplification of something in speech so as to move the soul to flee from the thing, or to long for it, or simply to wonder because of the delightfulness which issues from the imaginary repre-

sentation. They are set down in a rhythmically balanced way because they thereby
become more complete in imaginary representativeness . . . speeches which cause
something to be imagined are not speeches which make its essence understood
(*Short Comm.* 83).

Averroes does not take seriously the view that the way in which one should
examine the phenomenon of poetry is essentially dependent upon
understanding the cultural context within which that product emerged.
There was almost no knowledge or even interest in the Islamic world in the
Greek language and aspects of Greek culture such as poetry, drama, and
music. Even the distinguished tenth-century grammarian ibn Fāris was of
the opinion that 'some have pretended that that people had poetry, but we
have read that poetry and have ascertained that it lacks vigour and
agreement and possesses a false metre'.[27] Despite his assertion, there is
every reason to think that he did not in fact ever read Greek poetry, but his
claim is typical of the atmosphere of cultural superiority which ruled out as
unnecessary any profound investigation of the cultural, as opposed to
logical, work produced by the Greeks. In some ways it is remarkable that
even a thinker like Averroes who is in general very enthusiastic about
Aristotle and highly critical of the Islamic *kalām* should also ignore the
phenomenon of Greek poetry and concentrate upon its logical characteristics as a surreptitious argument form. On the other hand, it is entirely
consistent with his general approach to Greek philosophy, which is to
'naturalize' the references to Greek culture and emphasize the philosophical issues involved which concern him.

Averroes' stress on the rational qualities of poetry led him to argue that

Aristotle came to the opinion that this art was highly useful, because by means of it
the souls of the multitude could be moved to believe in or not believe in a certain
thing and towards doing or abandoning a certain thing. For that reason he
enumerated the matters which enable a man to devise an imaginative
representation . . . the art of poetics is that which enables a man to devise an
imaginative representation of each particular thing in the most complete manner
possible for it. However, these are perfections external to the primary human
perfection (*Short Comm.* 84).

So even a successful imaginative representation goes a long way away from
presenting a clear argument, and the audience which is impressed by
poetry and which stays at that level is restricted to a poor imitation of a
valid reasoning. In his commentary on Plato's *Republic*, Averroes accepts

with alacrity Plato's critique of poetry, and argues that it is most appropriate as a means of instruction for children (*CPR* 29. 21) which they should outgrow with maturity. He criticizes in particular the characteristic of Arabic poetry to concentrate on themes which have no clear moral purpose or intention (*CPR* 34. 14–28), and recommends a thoroughgoing didacticism. Like Plato, he criticizes the imitative character of poetry, and, although he recognizes its role in persuading some intellectually weak people to behave well and hold correct beliefs, this has the danger of making them feel that the imitations are accurate representations of the way things really are as opposed to mere heuristic devices. This not only results in people going awry in their judgements about reality, but it prevents them from developing their intellectual capacities to their highest degree, which as we have seen is a prime requirement on Averroes' view for success in perfecting oneself as a human being.

The attack upon poetry and rhetoric from a demonstrative point of view can also be seen as emphasis on Averroes' part for the importance of restricting the role of imagination in philosophical enquiry. Both these argument forms embody a thin thread of validity generously covered by a thick wrapping of imaginative language. The presence of the valid argument means that when ordinary people are persuaded or moved by the rhetorical or poetical language they are not misled. It is just that they have to be addressed in a particular sort of way, a way which only indirectly depends upon the truth, yet which depends upon it none the less. We must beware of being taken in by the imaginative language in which these truths are all but hidden and of using this language as though it could establish logical connections between concepts. The imaginative language would really mislead us if we thought it was more than just imaginative and appropriate for demonstrative reasoning. It will be recalled how Averroes used this principle to attack Ghazali's critique of Aristotelian metaphysics, and it is a significant aspect of his approach to practical philosophy too.

Philosophy and sharīʿa

LET us examine more closely this implication that Averroes really believed that *falsafa* and *sharīʿa* are different forms of thought with different conclusions, and that he pretended to believe that they in fact lead to the same conclusions. The issue is directly faced in his *Fasl al-maqāl*. Averroes faces the question of the relationship between Islam and philosophy and provides a legal discussion of whether the study of philosophy and logic (and it is interesting that like the other *falāsifa* he separates them clearly as different enterprises) is acceptable according to Islamic jurisprudence. We know from the outset that the answer is going to be positive, but there is scope for an ambitious or a more restricted claim, that law allows the study of philosophy, or that law insists on its study. It is an intriguing feature of Averroes' text that he takes the latter path.

How does he arrive at this position? He argues that philosophy is the teleological analysis of the world, and that as such it must involve attaining knowledge of the creator of the world. This is also, as it happens, the purpose of the law, which has the aim of regulating conduct by showing Muslims how that form of behaviour connects with the way in which God has created the world and how he wants us to live. Averroes produces several Qur'ānic passages to establish the theological basis to enquiry into the organization and direction of natural things, and there are indeed many other passages which he might have quoted to emphasize the way in which the Qur'ān calls upon the rational faculties of its audience to judge the truth of the religious narrative. This reasoning might well seem rather forced, since surely more is meant by philosophy than just teleological enquiry, and, as Hourani points out, when the Qur'ān instructs its readers to investigate how nature is organized in a purposive way, there is no obvious implication that this calls for a philosophical, and specifically Aristotelian, investigation.[1] It is, though, entirely appropriate for an Aristotelian philosopher to stress the teleological nature of philosophy, since an important aspect of Aristotelianism lies in its concentration upon the ends which human beings and other organisms seek, and it is plausible to relate this form of enquiry to grasping the nature of the creator and his

[1] G. Hourani, Introduction to *Decisive Treatise*, in *Averroes on the Harmony of Religion and Philosophy* (Luzac: London, 1961; repr. 1976), i. 10–14 and note: 'Notes et commentaries' *Studia Islamica*, 56 (1982), 184–5.

creation, in so far as this is possible. Naturally, the Qur'ānic passages which stress the desirability of extending knowledge do not insist on the study of philosophy as a necessary condition of the understanding of God's creation, and it seems rather an imposition to have this form of interpretation placed on fairly clear texts which just call for reflection on how the world is arranged. But Averroes' point is that what is involved in these sorts of cases is precisely reflection, and, if that is to be a rational activity, it requires the rules of sound philosophical reasoning.

When one looks at the verses he quotes, though, it is difficult to be convinced of Averroes' thesis. They are 'Reflect, you have vision' (lix. 2), 'Have they not studied the kingdom of the heavens and the earth, and whatever things God has created?' (viii. 185), 'Do they not observe the camels, how they have been created, and sky, how it has been raised up' (lxxxviii. 17–18), 'and they give thought to the creation of the heavens and the earth' (iii. 191), together with a reference to Abraham observing the kingdom of the heavens and the earth (vi. 75). From these rather vague verses he manages to derive the very strong conclusion that:

Since it has now been established that the law has rendered obligatory the study of beings by the intellect, and reflection on them, and since reflection is nothing more than inference and drawing out of the unknown from the known, and since this is reasoning or at any rate done by reasoning, therefore we are under an obligation to carry out our study of beings by intellectual reasoning (*FM* 2).

Hourani is surely expressing a reasonable view when he queries the aggression involved in Averroes' claim here. Why should intellectual enquiry be called obligatory when he could easily have limited himself to trying to establish the acceptability of philosophy? The thesis would then be that anyone who wants to pursue philosophical enquiry could do so, but need not. This is very different from his actual strategy which is directed towards a very uncompromising conclusion (although he does weaken it slightly later on when he distinguishes between different sorts of people with different capacities for philosophical work). Is the strong position which he adopts tenable?

A defence of Averroes' position is available. If Islam is a rational faith, and if it compels adherence by the use of rationally persuasive arguments, then it will indeed oblige its audience to use their reason to work out their view of the world and its maker. But what sort of reasoning is at issue here? Averroes has no hesitation in claiming that 'anyone who wants to understand God the exalted and the other beings demonstratively [must] have first understood the kinds of demonstration and their conditions and in what respects demonstrative reasoning differs from dialectical, rhetorical and fallacious reasoning' (*FM* 2). So an education in reasoning is a vital part of any expertise in approaching Islam, in just the same way as it is a prerequisite for a lawyer to understand the different kinds of legal reasoning before he can acquire much understanding of the law itself. This is a significant comparison, given the high status of law in the Muslim world. He points out that law, like philosophy, has developed since the start of Islam, and so should not be accused of innovation (*bidʿa*) just because it was not contemporaneous with Muḥammad and the four righteous caliphs. He also points out that most of the traditions of Qurʾānic interpretation accept that there is a necessity to approach the text and traditions from the point of view of intellectual reason, and thereby work out the sense of the text. If we have to use our intellect in making sense of Islam, then we must also (and first of all) ensure that our intellect is in first-rate working order through understanding the differences between distinct approaches to obtaining conclusions. It is necessary to listen to the understanding of reasoning which is already in existence, and to pay attention to thinkers even if they are not Muslims, or even predate Islam (which presumably gives them a good excuse for not being Muslims). He gives the splendid example that, 'when one performs a valid sacrifice with a certain instrument, no account is taken, in deciding the validity of the sacrifice, of whether the instrument belongs to one who shares our religion or to one who does not, so long as it fulfills the conditions of validity' (*FM* 4). The implication is that, if the Greeks had something useful to say on the issue of reasoning, and indeed what was said is said 'in the most perfect manner by the ancients' (*FM* 4), then we must study it. The example of the sacrificial instrument is a useful one in this context since it emphasizes the view generally held by the *falāsifa* that logic is an instrument of philosophy rather than a part of philosophy itself.[2]

One might of course accept that it is obligatory to study and learn from logic, and still wonder whether philosophy is really necessary to find out how the world is designed and what its structure is. That is, we might use our understanding of valid reasoning to try to work out from our knowledge of the world and our understanding of religion what physical principles govern the universe. On the other hand, were we to be disinclined to carry out this sort of investigation, we could just not bother with it. Now, Averroes has no objection to those people who are not

[2] For an excellent account of this distinction see A. Sabra, 'Avicenna on the Subject Matter of Logic', *Journal of Philosophy*, 77 (1980), 746–63.

capable of philosophy, or uninterested in it, forebearing from involving themselves in it. On the contrary, he recommends a policy of benign neglect as in the joint interests of those people and the philosophers. Yet for those who are capable of philosophical work and wish to pursue it, he claims that they must investigate the thought of the Greeks if they are to achieve reliable knowledge of the universe, as the Qur'ān may be taken to insist. He brings in again the comparison with the development of law. We could not expect to establish all at once a valid view of law using nothing but the basic Islamic texts. For centuries there has been controversy and discussion among jurisprudents, as a result of which in the twelfth century there existed a body of arguments, doctrines, cases, judgements, and so on which embody different approaches and ideas of how to live in accordance with *sharī'a*. This diversity is valuable in helping us work out which legal principles are valid and which are not in contemporary conditions. It is clear that Averroes holds a view of the development of valid legal hypotheses which is similar to his view of the development of valid scientific and philosophical hypotheses, that over a period of time of questioning, searching, and experimenting the right answer will emerge and put the Islamic community in a much better position to know what to accept. If the philosophical works of the Greeks and their successors contain demonstrative argument, it would be churlish to reject them just because they are pre-Islamic or not directly based upon Islamic doctrine. What is valid argument should be accepted, and what is not rejected, and we will then be in a better position to know in which direction contemporary philosophical enquiry might proceed.

It is worth considering briefly here how this approach is followed up in Averroes' jurisprudence. His *Bidāyat al-mujtahid* appears to be a fairly basic Malikite text where he gives the sorts of comments on legal problems which are to be expected of a lawyer from that school of thought. Indeed, the very orthodoxy of the book has led some commentators to doubt that Averroes even wrote it![3] Despite Averroes' defence of the use of analogy and reason (*qiyās*) in his *Faṣl al-maqāl* in appropriate cases, in his *Bidāyat* he generally recommends referring to a tradition rather than employing analogy to settle difficult cases. On the other hand, he gently pokes fun at justifying practice by the application to custom rather than rational principle (*ma'nā 'aqlī*) in legal decisions. He argues that consensus is an important cornerstone of legal justification, but not always crystal clear in

---

[3] See M. A. Badawi's comments in A.–M. Turki's 'La Place d'Averroès juriste dans l'histoire du Malikisme et de l'Espagne musulmane', in his *Théologiens et juristes de l'Espagne musulmane*, (Maisonneuve and Larose: Paris, 1982), 283–93; p. 292.

its implications for practice, and that analogy is a vital legal tool given the lack of possible reference to the Prophet's Companions and other authentic legal sources. What is important about the *Bidāyat*, though, is its general air of liberalism about valid legal decisions. Averroes does not take an uncompromisingly Malikite line throughout the book, although his heart is definitely fixed within that school of interpretation.[4] He explains how the differences between the different legal schools have arisen and why the different schools (*madhab*) were led to contrasting conclusions. The answers which he himself gives to legal problems are undoubtedly Malikite, but the general air of tolerance and liberalism throughout the book gives the impression that he does not think that those who follow other legal schools have irretrievably condemned themselves to error. The significance of this attitude will emerge when we investigate further the argument provided in the *Faṣl al-maqāl*.

As we have seen, Averroes was not an advocate of philosophy for all. It is worth quoting again his claim:

that whoever forbids the study of them to anyone who is fit to study them, i.e. anyone who unites two qualities, (1) natural intelligence and (2) religious integrity and moral virtue, is blocking people from the door by which the law summons them to knowledge of God, the door of theoretical study which leads to the truest knowledge of him (*FM* 5).

If some people have gone astray through the study of philosophy, it is not the fault of philosophy, but due to their lack of suitable qualities for its study. The problem of people working within an intellectual discipline and then behaving improperly is not specifically limited to philosophy, but can occur in any area, even in the law and medicine. Does Averroes' claim here suggest inappropriate restrictions on the study of philosophy and knowledge of God? The idea that immoral people will not benefit from the study of philosophy is justified provided that philosophy is interpreted as the theological investigation of the nature of God and his creation, since there is little point in their finding out about such things given their lack of moral concern with the implications of such findings. But the claim that unintelligent people will not be able to have the very best sort of knowledge of God might be felt to be arrogant and problematic. After all, any religion should provide a path to knowledge of its deity for even the most unsophisticated of its adherents. God is surely not unimplicated in the differences in natural intelligence which exist, and it would be harsh

[4] See the brilliant article by R. Brunschvig, 'Averroès juriste', in *Études dédiés à la mémoire de Lévi-Provençal* (Maisonneuve et Larose: Paris, 1962), 35–68.

indeed were he not to provide a route to knowledge of himself for those less gifted intellectually. It is worth noting here Averroes' apparent contempt for the notion of mysticism as a path to the knowledge of God, which other *falāsifa*, and Ghazali in particular, thought of as an important route for the sincere believer.

Averroes tries to answer this point by arguing that there are different approaches to understanding God, and an appropriate

method of assent which his temperament and nature require. For the natures of men are on different levels with respect to assent. One of them comes through demonstration; another comes to assent through dialectical arguments, just as firmly as the demonstrative man through demonstration, since his nature does not contain any greater capacity; while another comes to assent through rhetorical arguments, again just as firmly as the demonstrative man through demonstrative arguments (*FM* 6).

Averroes even claims Qur'ānic support for his position, quoting 'Summon to the way of your Lord by wisdom and by good preaching, and debate with them in the most effective manner' (xvi. 125). Any religion should be expected to present its message in a suitable form for the particular audience it is addressing. There are some people who will be attracted to and strengthened in their faith if the logical arguments for being a Muslim are pursued and explained. A lesser breed will not really be able to follow this sort of approach, but they can appreciate arguments which serve to disprove other religious tendencies. They can appreciate what is wrong with other religions, and innovatory doctrines within their own religions, and they assume that this shows that their own faith is vindicated. Of course, more is required to prove one's own religion than disproofs of other religions, but at least this is one step on the path to understanding how arguments work and provides something of a rational basis to one's thinking. In the last category are people who are drawn to adherence through rhetoric, through persuasive arguments which are based upon the use of example (*mathal*) whose logical rigour can be very thin, and yet which do preserve a tenuous connection with the rules of argumentative validity. Although this is the last category in Averroes' list in the *Faṣl al-maqāl*, it should be recalled that there are even worse methods of proof, poetical arguments for instance, which do not even go as far down the road of validity as rhetoric. As was seen when examining the discussion of rhetoric, Averroes argued that rhetoric has an important part to play in any approach to teaching the general community how to behave and what to believe. Interestingly, although Averroes clearly values the demonstrative approach far more than the other two approaches, he does not even hint that the former is the only way to acquire real knowledge and understanding of the creation and its maker. After all, there are a variety of ways of coming to know something, some of which are surer than others, and yet once the object is known it is part of one's knowledge even though the evidence which exists for it may differ from someone else's. To give an example, I may be informed that the weather is wet today by being shown the rain, examining the ground for moisture, checking the glass in the window for distortion, consulting weather reports, consulting a fir cone or a piece of seaweed, and so on. I may be informed it is wet by being told that if it was not wet then why are people coming into the house with wet umbrellas and raincoats? I may be informed that it is wet because it is invariably wet in late March in England, and it is now late March in England. All these evidences have different logical standing, and yet if it is wet today I can be taken to know it however I have arrived at my conclusion. So for Averroes we know religious truths in different ways, but we really do know exactly the same thing in the end.

Averroes develops this point to argue that there is no way in which demonstrative reasoning can clash with the principles of religion, since both religion and the conclusions of demonstrative reasoning are true. If the truth of demonstrative reasoning is not mentioned in Islam, then its existence must be inferred from something else in religion which is explicitly mentioned. If it is mentioned in Islam, but in a different way from its use in philosophy, then there is a need to go in for allegorical interpretation to account for the discrepancy. Averroes points out that lawyers do this all the time, and they only have a rather confused ragbag of legal principle, common usage, and less than demonstrative reasoning at their disposal. Philosophers understand the very best forms of reasoning, and they can use this to extract clearly the allegorical interpretation which an apparently clear passage in the Islamic canon may warrant. There is after all no requirement in Islam to take all the religious statements which can be found at their face value. There is frequently dispute among theologians and jurisprudents about the appropriate interpretation of particular passages, especially the anthropomorphic ones. The fact that interpretation is necessary here is not just a problem for philosophy, since it exists for law and theology too, and has been a problem ever since Islam commenced as a religion.

At this point one might become suspicious about the whole enterprise. What need is there to import all sorts of more sophisticated meanings into scripture when it seems perfectly clear that what is meant is a *literal* meaning? The answer Averroes provides 'lies in the diversity of people's natural capacities and the difference in their innate dispositions with regard to assent' (*FM* 8). Evident contradictions between an apparent meaning and what demonstrative reason would understand the meaning to be are designed to make philosophers note the contradiction and revise the literal meaning of the text. He even refers to this Qur'ānic passage in support of his view:

It is He who sent down upon thee the Book, wherein are verses clear that are the essence of the Book, and others ambiguous. As for those in whose hearts is swerving, they follow the ambiguous part, desiring dissension, and desiring its interpretation; and none knows its interpretation, save only God. And those firmly rooted in knowledge say, 'We believe in it; all is from our Lord'; yet none remembers, but men possessed of minds (iii. 5–7).

In addition, he claims support in his position from Ghazali and Juwaynī, in that they held that there are passages about which uncertainty of interpretation is acceptable even though the great majority of the community thinks only one meaning appropriate. That is, there is room for doubt in some cases, and there has always existed controversy about some cases where a question of theoretical interpretation arises, and it is permissible to raise doubts on the existence of only a literal interpretation in such cases. Averroes makes an interesting distinction between theoretical issues, on which claims of unanimity should not be taken as decisive, and practical matters, where it should be accepted as the last word. But why is it 'enough to establish the occurrence of unanimity on matters of practice but on matters of doctrine the case is different' (*FM* 9)? The argument here seems to be that, when we come to matters of practice there is no point in thinking that the truth of the question how we should behave is hidden or difficult to grasp, since this would make it useless as a principle of action. A decision on how to act which is taken by consensus cannot then be wrong, for the community knows everything that there is to know about moral behaviour from the teachings of religion. The theoretical conditions which lie behind that form of behaviour are less perspicuous, though, and the community as a whole may well go awry in its understanding of how a text is to be interpreted.

He uses this point concerning unanimity and theoretical doctrine to argue against Ghazali for calling the *falāsifa* unbelievers (*kāfir*). He even asserts that Ghazali himself has argued in the past that one can only be tentative in accusing people of unbelief through their violation of the principle of unanimity. Of course, this is rather a caricature of Ghazali's views here, since he does not on the whole think that what is wrong with the philosophers' basic principles needs to be revealed by their violation of unanimity, but can be seen directly by their clear contradiction of very basic and literal Islamic principles (to which must be added Ghazali's thesis that the philosophers' conclusions are reached by philosophically invalid processes). Averroes expresses his scepticism concerning the nature of the scholars who made up the community of people who pronounce on the nature of beliefs in the past. Were they really qualified to decide whether certain statements are to be interpreted allegorically or not? According to Averroes, it is only those who are skilled in demonstration who are really capable of deciding on questions of interpretation involving allegory. If demonstration conflicts with the apparent sense of scriptural passages, then those capable of demonstration know that the passages must be interpreted allegorically so as to cohere with the demonstrative truths, and 'That being the case, it is not possible for genuine unanimity to be established about allegorical interpretations, which God has made peculiar to scholars' (*FM* 10). This is a reiteration of another very powerful claim which Averroes makes in this book, namely, that the only people qualified to decide on the sense of scriptural passages are philosophers. Philosophers know the difference between the demonstrative use of analogy (*qiyās yaqīnī*) and mere legal analogy (*qiyās ẓannī*). Averroes also seems to be arguing that there is no other route to comprehension of such passages except rational thought. Even if the philosophers make mistakes in their interpretation they can be excused, since they are after all dealing with difficult matters. But the same excuse cannot be provided for people who are not skilled in interpretation. A skilful doctor or lawyer can make mistakes, and still be called skilful and a believer, but someone who merely dabbles in these areas cannot be so excused. He can have no likelihood of success in any case, and should steer clear of such topics. For people like this God 'has coined . . . images and likenesses of these things, and called them to assent to those images, since it is possible for assent to those images to come about through the indications common to all men, i.e. the dialectical and rhetorical indications' (*FM* 15). He even implies that Ghazali shares his view!

There are some texts which are obvious to anyone regardless of intellectual ability. He gives the interesting example here of happiness and misery in the next life. Anyone who thinks that this doctrine is just practical stratagem to promote social harmony is using allegory inappropriately, and is quite correctly accused of heresy or unbelief. But there are also texts which require allegorical interpretation, which must be limited to the philosophers. If the unsophisticated go in for this intellectual activity, they will end up with heresy and unbelief. They must remain satisfied with the imagery involved in the language of religious topics, since otherwise they could have no grasp of these important issues. Between these two types of texts Averroes inserts a third class, where it is not clear what to say with respect to the appropriateness of allegorical interpretation. He gives the example of the language associated with the notion of a future life. Should this be accepted as literally true, that is, does the Qur'ānic account of a corporeal future life represent a literal reading of what this life really is, or is it an allegory to be interpreted differently by different kinds of thinkers?

This question is never really answered, except in so far as Averroes claims that a scholar could commit an excusable error in his interpretation 'of the mode of the future life [but] not of its existence' (*FM* 17). The existence of the future life must not be questioned, but precisely how it exists is an issue which can and does arise for the philosopher. This gives rise to the question, which Averroes does not raise directly, of how meaningful it is to talk about a future life if there is no definite sense provided for that concept. All that we are told is that those incapable of allegory should not meddle with the concept, since this would indeed lead to unbelief, and it is an error, an error which classifies one as a *kāfir*, to discuss possible allegorical interpretation with those incapable of really understanding it. This is a subtle dig at Ghazali for allegedly doing just that, making the issue of interpretation available to others in his popular writings. This has resulted in some people attacking philosophy (for unbelief) and others attacking religion itself. Averroes felt that he must address this issue because it has already, unwisely, been raised, and it would have been better had nothing been said about it.

Religion is an attempt at communicating 'true science and right practice' (*FM* 18; also 19). There are a variety of ways of communicating, demonstrative, dialectical, and rhetorical, as we have seen. This leads to a bifurcation of concepts. Some concepts are accurate concepts of objects; others are only symbols of objects. On the whole, religion is presented for the easy comprehension of the masses: 'since the primary purpose of scripture is to take care of the majority (without neglecting to stimulate the élite), the prevailing methods of expression in religion are the common methods by which the majority comes to form concepts and judgement' (*FM* 19–20). Where there is an inner and hidden meaning, it is up to the demonstrative class, the philosophers, to discover it and keep it to themselves, and for the rest of the community to accept the literalness of scripture. Most people are best approached by rhetoric; these people use

PRACTICAL PHILOSOPHY

their opinion (*ẓann*) to apprehend the truth, and are easily persuaded by clever speeches and attractive imagery. There is nothing wrong with this state of affairs, but it is not likely to produce certain results, the sort of results available to philosophy and philosophers.

It is clear that for Averroes there exists for certain texts a definite hidden meaning which the philosophers can get at, and which ordinary people do not need to reach in any case, since the apparent meaning will be sufficient to move them in appropriate directions. What makes the action *right* is its connection, ultimately, with its hidden meaning, and the rightness of the action does not presuppose knowledge of that connection by the community as a whole. This position is directly contrary to the most influential doctrine on the meaning of ethical terms in Islam, namely, that rightness or wrongness is definable completely in terms of conformity and disobedience to the commands of God. This doctrine was shared by the four main Sunni legal schools and is vigorously defended by the leading theological movement, Ash'arism. The motive of what Hourani so accurately calls the 'ethical subjectivists' is to emphasize the power and authority of God over all things, even the meanings of ethical terms. If ethical terms are equivalent in meaning to God's commands, then once we know those commands we know everything that there is to know about how to behave virtuously, and need seek no further basis to moral action. This would strike a mortal blow at the notion that there is any point in justifying moral rules on rational as opposed to religious grounds, and at the whole enterprise of philosophy.[5] It is hardly surprising, then, that Averroes was very opposed to it.

In his commentary on Plato's *Republic* he puts the subjectivist thesis in these words, namely, 'neither good nor evil would have a fixed nature in itself, but would be good or evil by fiat' (*APR* 30. 29–30). The subjectivist view has the advantage, such as it is, of not needing to bother with the problem of explaining how a benevolent God can bring about evil in his world, since nothing in the world brought about by God can be called evil. Evil, after all, is defined in terms of disobedience to God's commands, and he has commanded the world to take its particular form, so whatever form it takes cannot subsequently be called evil. God cannot disobey his own commands and so he cannot be called evil either. Averroes' arguments against this position occur largely in the *Manāhij* (p. 113) and comprise pointing to the difficulty involved in identifying very basic religious duties with conventional ones. He suggests that if we examine our most

---

[5] This theme is comprehensively discussed in Hourani, *Reason and Tradition*. See also Leaman, *Introduction*, pp. 123–48.

important moral principles we can see that they are based upon the way in which the world (including ourselves) is constructed and are thus objective. They are not the imposition of a law which comes to us through a religion or system of legal thought. This leaves him with the problem of accounting for the evil which exists in the world. One interpretation of his solution is to relate it to the Platonic view that evil is due to the nature of matter.[6] Indeed, in his short commentary on Aristotle's *Metaphysics* he comments:

As for evils such as decay, age, etc., their existence is due to the necessity of matter. That is so because this existence is only possible on one of two conditions, either that these things to whose existence some evil is attached should not exist, or that they should exist in this condition, since more than that is not possible in their existence. An example of that is that fire is of evident use in the world, and it happens incidentally that it ruins many animals and plants. But look at providence for an animal, how it has given it the sense of touch, but that could not be in its nature without bringing it near to sensible things damaging to it.[7]

He refers to this necessity of matter again in his long commentary on the *Metaphysics* (*Tafsīr*, p. 1715). In spite of Hourani's subtle argument on this aspect of Averroes, we do not have to accept that he was committed to the view that the nature of matter made any other sort of existence impossible. The argument which Averroes presents is more interesting than that.

Hourani is not happy with Averroes' 'solution' to the problem of evil. This solution is based upon the necessity of nature and the idea that composition is a cause of corruption, so that God could not really be expected to do any better given the materials out of which he was obliged to create. This approach is indeed highly unsatisfactory, but it should not be ascribed to Averroes. If he really did think that the world was created out of a sort of stuff which made certain sorts of things impossible for God to bring about, he would be offending basic Aristotelian principles. According to Averroes, the organization of the world reveals perfect planning and an underlying rationality. Fire could not have the characteristics it has without the power to harm living things, and the sense of touch which is so useful to animals cannot exist without the possibility of being the cause of suffering in certain situations. Averroes relates the denial of these propositions to the denial of necessary

[6] Hourani, *Reason and Tradition*, p. 255.
[7] Summary (*Jāmi'*) of Aristotle's *Metaphysics*, in *Rasā'il ibn Rushd* (Dā'irat āl-Ma'ārif al-'Uthmānīyah: Hyderabad, 1947), 170; translation Hourani, *Reason and Tradition*, p. 255.

propositions,[8] and claims that God cannot be expected to accomplish the impossible. Hourani wonders whether all these alleged impossibilities are really on the same logical level. Could not an omnipotent being have created a sort of fire which did not harm living creatures, and creatures with the sense of touch who were not harmed by anything with which they came into contact? The answer which Averroes would give is that he could not accomplish these tasks, since we would then not be talking about fire and sensitive limbs, but something else. Fire is not fire if it does not burn, and occasionally it will harm us. Its harming us is incidental (*bil-'araḍ*) in that it is not specifically designed to harm us, but that potentiality exists within it and within the nature of flammable substances, and, while we could have a world without fire, we could not have a world with fire which did not burn things when in contact with them if those things are capable of being burnt. Similarly, Averroes' suggestion that composition is a cause of corruption is not, as Hourani argues, a specifically Platonic doctrine,[9] with little to be said for it. It is based upon the idea that whatever has a material content is corruptible; and whatever is corruptible will at some point be corrupted. For Aristotle the generation of one substance involves the destruction of another, so that the matter which was in the thing which was destroyed moves to the thing which is created. This is not to be taken as an empirical generalization, but a theory which explains how it is possible to talk about something changing into another thing, and Averroes is quite justified given his Aristotelian framework to relate the workings of nature to the level of necessity. As we have seen when looking at his views on causality, the relationship between a substance and its powers is not an empirical relationship primarily, but a necessary relationship, and a substance which did not possess those powers would not be that substance. The account which Averroes provides to reconcile God's goodness with the evil in the world does not, then, presuppose some sort of Platonic belief in the necessity of an evil nature, but rather an Aristotelian account of change and corruptibility.

Following up this point, we might wonder what notion of appropriate end Averroes thinks applies to human beings. Since all substances have natures, and these natures define them and their ends, we as substances must also have natures and ends at which our actions aim. The purpose of a knife is to cut, the purpose of a tree is to reach a certain level of growth, but what is the purpose of a human being? One of our ultimate aims is to be happy, in the sense that we could bring a series of questions about why

[8] *Jāmi'*, p. 171
[9] Hourani, *Reason and Tradition*, p. 260.

we act in a particular way to an end by connecting that action to our expectation of happiness. On Aristotle's approach, it is not just a matter of coincidence that certain activities lead to happiness, but a consequence of their status as essentially human activities. They also specify what it is that we ought to be doing in a moral sense. Hence Averroes can state that 'Right practice consists in performing the acts which bring happiness and avoiding the acts which bring misery' (*FM* 19).

There is an easy congruence here between Aristotelian and Islamic principles. Moral virtue leads to happiness because, if we do what we are supposed to do by our nature and by our God, we will be able to achieve, or be rewarded by, happiness. There are a variety of ways in which this happiness may be defined, ranging from a bundle of social and religious practices, to an entirely contemplative ideal. The latter is available only to the very few, and neither Islam nor Aristotle would approve of it as the ultimate aim for human beings. Aristotle had no doubt that the appropriate life-style for human beings is a social one, and without other human beings no human life is possible (*NE* 10. 8, 1178^b5-7). A life of isolation can produce only a limited happiness. An interesting illustration of this thesis is provided by ibn Bājja and his account of the role of the *mutawaḥḥid* in an unfriendly social context. The *mutawaḥḥid* is the solitary philosopher who is living in a society which does not respect philosophy and gives the philosopher no role in the direction of the state. He and his like-minded associates are regarded as superfluous *nawābit*, or weeds, which spring up in the most inappropriate places. Since philosophers are given no satisfactory role in the government of the state, they must resign themselves to apply their intellect to their own self-government.[10] As Averroes puts it:

If it happens that a true philosopher grows up in these cities, he is in the position of a man who has come among perilous animals. He is not obliged to do harm along with them, but neither is he sure in himself that those animals will not oppose him. Hence he turns to isolation and lives the life of a solitary. The best perfection is missing in him, for that can be attained by him only in this city [i.e. the ideal city] (*APR* 64. 23–7).

It is quite clear that there is an essential social dimension to human happiness for Averroes, which makes the identification of happiness with correct moral behaviour much easier to establish.

Yet we still have to return to the basic question of how to reconcile the

---

[10] More detail on the separatist argument can be found in Leaman, 'Ibn Bājja on Society and Philosophy', *Der Islam*, 57 (1980), 109–19.

happiness of the philosophical élite with the happiness of the mass of the community. There is no doubt that Averroes held that a different kind of happiness applied in these two cases, a largely contemplative kind for the intellectuals, and a predominantly sensuous and social kind for the majority. It is important, though, to acknowledge that we are not looking at completely different kinds of activity here, but rather at a continuum along which different kinds of happiness are positioned. Thus philosophers would not base the whole of their lives on contemplation even were they to be able to do so, since as human beings they have social obligations which they should perform. Similarly, the unsophisticated majority do not spend all their time in mindless enjoyment of pleasure. They are led to consider rationally the nature of the world and its contents by their adherence to Islam, or any other religion. Many commentators on *falsafa* have implied that the references to the importance of religious observance by everyone, philosophers included, is just a nod in the direction of orthodoxy and an attempt at placating the religious authorities. What need in reality does a philosopher have for religion if he is capable of understanding the nature of the universe and the purpose of the living things within it? He can then derive from rational principles how he should behave and what ideas he should have about the creator of the world. Averroes comments:

the religions are, according to the philosophers, obligatory, since they lead towards wisdom in a way universal to all human beings, philosophy only leads a certain number of people to the knowledge of intellectual happiness, and they therefore have to learn wisdom, whereas religions seek the instruction of the masses generally . . . since the existence of the learned class is only perfected and its full happiness attained by participation with the class of the masses, the general doctrine is also obligatory for the existence and life of this special class (*TT* 582).

It may be possible for the philosopher as *mutawaḥḥid* to achieve a certain level of happiness in isolation from his society, but this should be regarded as a second-best option. Far better is the situation where he is fully integrated with his society and can allow his specifically human characteristics to flourish in company with those of other citizens. We should thus be able to appreciate how important it is for Averroes' philosopher to be more than just a solitary thinker alone with his reasoning and scientific work.

From the point of view of Islam, it is not just mortal happiness which is an appropriate aim for moral action, but also and more importantly the happiness in the next life (*al-saʿāda al-ukhrāwīya*). As Averroes suggests: 'True science is knowledge of God . . . and the other beings as they really are, and especially of noble things, and knowledge of happiness and misery in the next life. Right practice consists of performing acts which bring happiness and avoiding the acts which bring misery' (*FM* 18–19). This might well be thought to be an evasion, since it is difficult to represent Averroes as a believer in the existence of an afterlife, or at least an afterlife with individual survivors of this life in it. As one would expect, he insists in the *Tahāfut al-tahāfut* on the importance of belief in happiness in an afterlife for the appropriate functioning of moral and social life, but we should be wary of taking this as an attempt at presenting a sop to the orthodox. After all, he also claims that all religions share a belief in an afterlife and agree on the sorts of actions required to secure happiness in it (*TT* 582), and that people should choose the best religion around at the time they are in the market for a religion (*TT* 583)! These are hardly assertions carefully constructed to placate the suspicions of the *mutakalli-mūn*. What Averroes means in his references to happiness and misery in a future life cannot indeed be the idea that after our death something very much like us carries on in something very much like our life as mortals, but better or worse, depending upon whether our lives as humans have been good or evil. As he says, this idea might be important in gaining adherence to moral behaviour by many people, but it will not stand up to philosophical investigation (and he continues to belabour the simplistic conception of an afterlife right up to the end of the *Tahāfut al-tahāfut* itself). What ordinary people find difficult to grasp, and so require the religious language and imagery, is that our moral actions affect not only ourselves but the happiness of the whole community, and not just at a particular moment of time, but as a whole, as a species. When we act badly, we damage our own chances of human flourishing, and this damages our personal chances of achieving happiness. It also affects our relationships with other people, who then come to trust us, and by implication other people, less, and the whole notion of society weakens and suffers. While our misery may not follow us after our death, it may well follow the community, and the importance of belief in an afterlife could be taken as an indication of the wider terms of reference of moral action.

This sort of approach might be enlightening when it comes to wondering what sort of contribution Islam makes to informing the philosopher what he is to do. Averroes makes a sharp distinction between being wise and being religiously inspired: 'Wisdom has never come to an end among the inspired, i.e. the prophets, and therefore it is the truest of all sayings that every prophet is a sage (*ḥakim*), but not every sage is a prophet. The learned, however, are those of whom it is said that they are the heirs of the prophets' (*TT* 583–4). It is a necessary condition of being a

PRACTICAL PHILOSOPHY

prophet that one is wise, but the reverse is not the case. Being a prophet is
to have something extra, and we know that for Averroes this consists in the
ability to put over a message in a compelling sort of way. Prophets, in other
words, possess political expertise: 'Every religion exists through inspiration and is blended with reason. And he who holds that it is possible that
there should exist a natural religion based on reason alone must admit that
this religion must be less perfect than those which spring from reason and
inspiration' (*TT* 584). He strengthens this claim with respect to
inspiration (*waḥy*) when he describes the laws in the Qur'ān as 'such as
could not be acquired by learning but [only] by inspiration' (*Manāhij*,
p. 100).[11] Hourani argues that this cannot be Averroes' real view.[12]
Could he really believe that it is impossible to discover the requirements of
morality by the use of rational processes? It is tempting to agree with
Hourani that this and other assertions in the *Manāhij* are a sop to the
religious classes, but this conclusion is not inevitable. When Averroes
stresses the significance of inspiration he is emphasizing the way in which
sharī'a is capable of transmitting values and motives to the very widest
audience possible. The inspiration does, in his view, come from God, but
its effect is to present in imaginative and attractive language the tenets of
religion. The source of the inspiration is irrelevant to its utility in moving
people to act, in the sense that any religion employs language compatible
with the psychology of its intended audience. There is nothing suspicious
in Averroes' reference to inspiration here, and no need to invoke the
exoteric–esoteric distinction to make sense of his argument.

---

[11] Hourani, *Reason and Tradition*, p. 266
[12] Ibid. 266–7.

PART III
Reason, Religion, and Language

Averroism

TOWARDS the end of his life, Averroes suffered persecution from the Almohad authorities, and, although he was fairly swiftly rehabilitated, philosophy itself fell into something of a disgrace within the Muslim community. In the eastern territories of Islam there were flashes of philosophical revival within the tradition of *falsafa*, and the name of Mulla Sadra (*c.* 1571–1640) is well worth mentioning in this context, but in Andalus and the western region very little activity of philosophical note was built upon the foundations laid by Averroes. Historians who deal with this period often point out that the decline of philosophy was at least matched by the rise of theology, very much on the lines which Ghazali had recommended in his work. That is, philosophy was used not to establish religion on surer foundations than it normally possesses but rather to defend religion once the main principles of faith have been presupposed in the argument. Philosophy was limited to what Averroes would have called a dialectical role, to knock down rather than to establish arguments. It became equivalent in the *kalām* to logic, which the *falāsifa* had regarded not as a part of philosophy, but as its instrument. Logic was to be used as the instrument by which previously acknowledged religious truths were to be defended *vis-à-vis* doctrinal opposition.

This might have been a severe check to the progress of philosophy in the Muslim community, a check which is only today becoming gradually weakened, but it did not hinder the transmission of that approach to philosophy to the non-Muslim world. Just as Aristotle's thought was declining in influence in the Muslim world, it was increasing in Christian and Jewish Europe. The transmission of Aristotelian thought took a different form in different communities, and it came to have a significant influence on Christian intellectual life. Averroes was to enjoy an extensive influence for many centuries after his death through the tendency of many thinkers to regard him as *the* commentator on Aristotle. A wide variety of views have been ascribed to Averroes by the Averroist movement, and it has become the modern practice to disparage the accuracy of such views. This had come about partly through the laudable motive of reading Averroes as a medieval philosopher working within a particular context, with a consequent unfortunate refusal to acknowledge the very general philosophical interest of his views. It will be argued here that, while many

Averroist views are not Averroes' views, the broad lines of Averroism do represent fairly the main principles of Averroes' mature philosophical thought.

In the decades following Averroes' death, the beginning of the thirteenth century, there was considerable interest in Christian Europe in the thought of Aristotle. This interest was directed not only at the texts themselves but also at the commentaries which were available to help make clearer the philosophy of a very subtle thinker. The relative absence of Latin texts of the Aristotelian corpus had not encouraged the growth of a commentary tradition which, by contrast, had flourished for three centuries in the Islamic world. There was as a result a great activity of translation of Averroes' commentaries, sometimes from Arabic directly to Latin, and sometimes via Hebrew. In the same way that the original translations from Greek into Arabic were made under official encouragement in 'Abāssid Baghdad in the ninth century when Greek philosophy came to be seen as important and interesting, so the translators of the Arabic commentators were sponsored by the court of Frederick II of Sicily and by Archbishop Raymond in Toledo. The relatively wide availability of Averroes' commentaries in the universities led to a tendency to identify the commentator with the Stagirite himself. Although many of Averroes' non-Aristotelian works were also translated, they did not achieve the popularity of his commentaries, and so the ways in which he tried to reconcile Aristotelian philosophy with religion were largely unknown. The commentaries themselves, as we have seen, defend and augment theories which appear to threaten the foundations of religion itself. In the commentaries Averroes normally does not bother to discuss how Islam would cohere with the Aristotelian position, since this is a subject he takes up elsewhere. In marked contrast with the present study of Averroes, his medieval readers in the Christian world were primarily interested in his work on Aristotle, because they were interested in Aristotle and in anything and anyone who related to him.

It is hardly surprising, then, that the philosophy of Averroes came under the condemnation of a variety of theological influences. It was not difficult for readers to distinguish Averroes' views from those of Aristotle, since the commentator frequently peppers his commentaries with suggestions bearing on the religious relevance of particular Aristotelian arguments, and because together with translations of commentaries there existed translations of his shorter expository works such as his *De substantia orbis* and the *Treatise on the Prime Mover*. While his contribution to the understanding of Aristotle was widely acknowledged, the conclusions he uses Aristotle to reach were condemned by many Christian thinkers as heretical, often using language uncannily similar to that of Ghazali when he attacked the Peripatetic movement. Giles of Rome, for instance, accuses Averroes of denying the creation of the world *ex nihilo* and labelling the theologians derogatively as *loquentes*, the Latin equivalent of *mutakallimūn*.[1] St Bonaventure in his *In hexaemeron* of 1273 criticizes both Aristotle and Averroes for their adherence to the impossibility of individual immortality. In 1256 Albert the Great produced his *De unitate intellectus contra Averroem* at the direct request of Pope Alexander IV, a work which was followed in 1270 by Aquinas's *De unitate intellectus contra Averroistas* which tries to drive a wedge between Aristotle and Averroes, labelling the latter as an interpreter who inserted far too much of his own erroneous theological reasoning into the 'pure' Aristotelian text. Most philosophers in Christian Europe who argued against Averroes' views none the less thought highly of him as a commentator, and it might be said that Averroes set much of the tone of the debate concerning Aristotle and religion in the thirteenth century for both his supporters and detractors.

The introduction of a widespread Aristotelianism was not without its problems, and there existed a whole series of condemnations and bans on this philosophical approach. In 1270 and 1277 the bishop of Paris, Étienne Tempier, declared as anathema thirteen propositions stemming from the *falāsifa*, and Giles of Rome's *Errores philosophorum* of 1270 listed the mistakes of Aristotle and Averroes. The direct object of these attacks was the movement which came to be known as Latin Averroism and which seemed to defend an extreme fideism. Writers such as Siger de Brabant (*c.* 1240–*c.* 1284) and Boethius of Dacia seemed to argue that the radical views of Averroes on the creation of the world and the nature of immortality were irrefutable, and yet these propositions do not themselves contradict revealed religion. Religion is based upon revelation and its justification is to be found within that system of revelation, while philosophy employs justificatory techniques essentially different and inappropriate to faith. This should not be taken as a criticism of religion, but as a comment upon the different logics implicit in the different ways of using language. Religion puts itself forward as a route to a virtuous life-style, while philosophy claims to incorporate a system of demonstrative reasoning. The religious and the philosophical activities are entirely different in

---

[1] H. Wolfson, 'The Twice-revealed Averroes', *Speculum*, 36 (1961), 373–92; pp. 380–3, repr. in his *Studies in the History of Philosophy and Religion*, i (Harvard University Press, Cambridge, 1973), 351–87.

nature, and it is inappropriate to expect one to support or contradict the other.

Was this Averroes' view? To a certain extent the answer must be affirmative. He did argue in his work that religious reasoning and philosophical reasoning are disparate activities, each having its own rules and criteria of validity. For example, if one were to wonder in what circumstances a Muslim community is obliged to wage war on a neighbouring territory one must consult the Qur'ān, the Traditions of the Prophet, and the relevant legal discussions of this issue. One can then arrive at a justifiable view of one's duty in this matter. This is a very different reasoning process from that involved in establishing, say, a logical axiom. But it might be argued that this is not true, that similar reasoning processes are involved in both cases. After all, the way in which one works from a revealed text to a variety of commentaries and examples is itself a rational process. It involves argument and comparison of like with like, and considerable legal training to understand. What can Averroes then mean when he classifies this sort of reasoning as dialectical and contrasts it with demonstrative reasoning? What he seems to have in mind here is that, while the reasoning which goes on in both examples may be perfectly appropriate and valid, it is the nature of the premises from which they start which characterizes the nature of the reasoning as a whole. Theological and legal reasoning starts from theological and legal premises which are taken to be true, and logical consequences are drawn from them in accordance with the principles of the relevant Islamic discipline, that is, *fiqh*, *kalām*, and so on. It is the 'taken to be true' nature of the premises which leads to the description of the reasoning itself as dialectical. In demonstrative reasoning the premises themselves are established as true through logical argument before they are used. When we talk about law and theology, though, using theological and legal premises as our starting position, we are limiting the scope of our argument to the scope of the premises. This is not to say that there need be anything wrong with the premises, since there is nothing at all objectionable to the basic principles of *sharī'a* and the Qur'ān, yet, perfect and complete though those systems are taken to be, they do not give rise to justification except via a revelation and the institution of a legal system. This is not a criticism of either the systems or the ways in which they are established—on the contrary, for Averroes they are beyond criticism for a Muslim—but an acknowledgement that such systems are not generally applicable. Jews and Christians, for instance, are not bound by the principles of Islam, except in so far as they live in a Muslim state. A nonbeliever does not have to accept through the workings of his rational faculties that Islam is the only true religion. That is, if he does not accept Islam as superior to all other religions he is not making a logical error, albeit no doubt he should be regarded as going awry in his ethical decision-making. Whatever we have to say about that, he is not making a demonstrative error.

So when the Averroists argue for a 'double-truth' theory they have Averroes on their side to a degree. He would happily concede that there are different ways of establishing propositions in different universes of discourse. He would not be happy at being credited with the idea that these universes of discourse exist in splendid isolation, however. As we have seen throughout this book, Averroes did emphasize the differences between religious and philosophical language, yet also argued that both types of language describe the same reality. They describe it in different ways for different purposes for different audiences. But these different ways of talking are not autonomous activities which operate separately from each other. There would be little point to them if they had this character. For example, if it follows from Averroes' arguments that individual immortality of the soul is an unsatisfactory concept, it follows that some explanation must be given of how Islam can talk about such a form of immortality. And of course he provides such an explanation, in terms of the political relevance of the notion for the community as a whole and its role as representative of the more accurate and somewhat different philosophical notions of immortality. To argue that Averroes succeeds in disproving the coherence of the notion of individual immortality philosophically makes it puzzling to know what one is taken to believe in when one says that none the less one must believe in the truth of the individual immortality of the soul for religious reasons. If this is how the Latin Averroists argued, and from what we have of their work it is not clear that it is, then there is not much to be said for their views.

Despite the condemnations of Averroism the works of the commentator continued to be studied in Paris, and John of Jandun (1275–1328) is the major figure in fourteenth-century France to pursue the Averroist philosophical agenda. The arrival of the Renaissance had an interesting effect upon this movement which to an extent pushed it forward and to an extent made it retreat. The Renaissance promoted the study of Greek culture, which encouraged the use of Averroes as a commentator. On the other hand, it also stimulated the study of Greek and the Greek commentators, which inevitably led to a questioning of the usefulness of the sort of work on Aristotle carried out within the tradition of *falsafa*.

After all, it was well known that Averroes did not have the Greek text in front of him when preparing his commentaries, and Hellenists wondered what value his commentaries could have as a result. In the fifteenth century Averroism started to dominate some of the Italian universities, and in the sixteenth there was even a split within the camp of thinkers influenced by *falsafa* between Averroists and the Alexandrists. The former adhered to the notion that personal immortality of the soul is inconceivable, while the latter accepted this Averroist thesis together with the view that the possible intellect is a power of each individual soul, and as such mortal. The Alexandrists reject Averroes' criticisms of the theory that the possible intellect should be regarded as a thing.[2] This controversy, well within the guide-lines of the debate of many centuries earlier within the philosophical world of Islam, was thought significant enough to merit condemnation by the Fifth Lateran Council in 1513, which rejected both sides of the argument as presupposing the mortality of the soul. This did not put an end to the dispute, though, and both Agostino Nifo (1473–1538) and Pietro Pomponazzi (1464–1525) continued the discussion. The former must have managed to annoy both the Hellenists and the Church with his assertion that Averroes 'is so famous in our time that no one seems to be a peripatetic unless he is an Averroist'.[3]

What is the significance of Averroism within the Christian world? The outstanding work which deals with this question is still Ernest Renan's *Averroès et l'Averroïsme* of 1852. Although later commentators have challenged many of Renan's ideas, there exists nothing on this subject which matches the scope of his work. The main criticisms of his position attack the influence which the particular cultural context within which he wrote had on his work. He was fascinated by the competition between established religion and the opposing forces of rationalism and atheism, and he imported that competition into his interpretation of the development of Averroism as a doctrine. He argued that the Latin Averroists were a rationalist school of philosophers in the thirteenth century who were intent on producing a philosophy based on Aristotle and Averroes which is entirely contrary to Christian doctrine. Thus they propounded belief in the mortality of the human soul, the unity of the intellect, the eternity of the world and the emptiness of religious beliefs. Naturally, it was very dangerous to expound such heretical views openly,

---

[2] Alexander, *De intellectu et intellecto*, in G. Théry, *Alexandre d'Aphrodise* (Le Saulchoir: Kain, 1926), 74–82.

[3] Nifo, quoted by E. Renan, *Averroès et l'Averroisme* in *Œuvres complètes de Ernest Renan*, iii (Calmann-Lévy: Paris, 1949; first published, 1852), 281.

so they employed the device which they are taken to have discovered in Averroes, the notion of 'double-truth'. This ensured that the same set of beliefs could be true in philosophy and yet false in religion and vice versa. To anyone with any philosophical sophistication the 'double-truth' principle seems as vacuous as it is in reality, but it can be used to permit philosophical work to proceed even against the ruling ideas of religion. Indeed, Renan argues that this device was not the sole possession of the Latin Averroists in Paris but was also much used by the Averroists in Italy up to the early seventeenth century. Perhaps its most famous exponent was Pomponazzi who put forward quite extreme views on the nature of immortality, the uselessness of prayer, and the ridiculousness of belief in miracles while at the same time claiming that his arguments were only valid philosophically and not theologically.

Much recent work on the Latin Averroists suggests that the interpretation of their thought as a surreptitious attack upon Christianity is just wrong.[4] The idea that they were secretly free-thinkers behind their Christian disguise is not one which can be easily extracted from their work. Renan had placed far too much emphasis upon the sorts of comments which were made about the Averroists, and their Christian opponents were no less restrained in accusing philosophers of heresy than were the opponents of the *falāsifa* in wielding the charge of *kufr*. Gilson points out that Siger does not refer to philosophy as being true, by contrast with revealed religion.[5] Philosophy consists of necessary and rational arguments which do not themselves constitute truth. Similarly, John of Jandun accepts Averroes' thesis concerning the necessity of nature and its laws, while at the same time insisting that God can vary these regularities at any time, in such a way that the truth of such laws and the objects they describe are based upon divine action rather than the way the world is.[6] Neither Averroist argued that philosophy and religion produce contradictory conclusions which can none the less be true together. What they seem to support is a doctrine of the distinctness of religious and philosophical language, so that religion cannot influence the progress of reason while reason cannot contradict the results acquired by faith in revealed supernatural wisdom.

Far too much of the discussion on Latin Averroism in the past has

---

[4] For example, see E. Gilson, *La Philosophie au moyen âge* (Payot: Paris, 1952), F. Van Steenberghen, *Les Œuvres et la doctrine de Siger de Brabant* (Palais des Académies: Brussels, 1938), and S. MacClintock, *Perversity and Error: Studies in the 'Averroist' John of Jandun* (Indiana University Press: Bloomington, 1956).

[5] Gilson, *Philosophie*, p. 562.

[6] MacClintock, *Perversity*, pp. 89–90.

concentrated upon the personal beliefs of the principal thinkers themselves. In so far as the discussion has gone, it has established as extremely implausible the view that Siger and John of Jandun operated free-thinking 'cells' within Christian society while carefully covering their tracks. What is more important than the personal beliefs of the thinkers themselves is the actual force of their position. They may well have genuinely believed that religion and philosophy are separate areas, with truth being reserved for religion, and philosophy regarded as nothing more than an activity concerned with playing about with arguments. But is such a view tenable? If the results of philosophy tell us nothing about what is true, if religion is sufficient for this purpose, one wonders what the point of philosophizing is. Is philosophy taken to have the same status *vis-à-vis* religion as chess? It might be regarded as a game with its own rules and objectives which exist independently of more important considerations about the sorts of creatures we are and the kind of future which we are entitled to think we may expect. It is doubtful whether anyone could be an Averroist in any sense of that very confused term and have this casual attitude to philosophy. If anything at all unites the very diverse group of thinkers called Averroists (some of whom, like Pomponazzi, who would disagree with that label), it is the belief that philosophy is an important activity which is capable of revealing important information. Being a philosopher was not an uncontroversial activity, after all, and it is difficult to believe that people would take it up for frivolous reasons.

Perhaps, though, what is meant by 'double-truth' is the idea that philosophy only has a dialectical function, much in the way that Averroes saw theology and law. The Averroists might be seen to be refuting invalid philosophical arguments stemming from Aquinas or even Aristotle without feeling justified in regarding their conclusions as proving anything that is actually true. Truth might be seen as only accessible through faith, and human reason too weak to investigate in any depth the nature of things. For example, Pomponazzi argues in his work on the immortality of the soul that the mind and body are both mortal, so that no personal immortality of any part of us obtains. Yet the Church had laid down as a dogma belief in the immortality of the soul. In his interesting *De immortalitate animae* he concludes with two comments upon his book. One is that he should not really be taken to have proved anything decisively, since there are good arguments against his conclusion about the soul. Then he claims that even this is too weak a comment, since any arguments against immortality cannot be valid. Whatever precautions we take against making mistakes in our reasoning cannot compete with the perfect certainty available to us through scripture. Yet the burden of his argument throughout his works is that philosophy is the route to finding out how things really are. The religious legislator is seen as someone who is not concerned with truth, but only with virtue. Most people would not behave virtuously were they not to be threatened by punishment or rewarded in some way, and belief in an afterlife is an important constituent in any such exercise in motivation. As he puts it in his *Defensorium*, 'Aristotle proved by natural reason that the soul is mortal even though religion claims it is immortal since it tries to make the community of men good rather than wise'.[7] This is very much a theme in his work, namely, that religious language is designed to guide human beings to appropriate action rather than inform them of the truth, and the sorts of language and imagery which religion uses is much more closely related to the most effective techniques of persuasion than to the requirements of truth or accuracy.

We have come across this sort of account before, in the work of Averroes. Indeed, Pomponazzi argues that Averroes proved that religious laws are neither true nor false, but solely designed to lead people to a life of virtue. Only a small minority grasp the true state of affairs, namely, that virtue should be pursued for its own sake. Philosophy by contrast arrives at the truth and is concerned primarily with the truth. One of the obvious differences between Averroes' account and that of Pomponazzi is the lack of a theory in the latter which links the two realms of discourse. Averroes has an argument for the necessity of translating a truth from the philosophical realm to the religious realm in order that it might influence human behaviour in as general a way as possible. Had the truth been restricted to the level of philosophy, it would never have had an effect upon most of the community. With Averroes we have one truth and a number of versions of that truth designed for a number of audiences. With Pomponazzi, by contrast, the religious point of view seems something of a device to control the otherwise anti-social impulses of the community. The respectful references to religion in his books appear to be blatant sops in the direction of the authorities since they are entirely unconnected with the structure of the arguments which he constructs in the texts themselves. It is difficult to credit Pomponazzi with even a double-truth theory, since his work seems to imply that there is no truth in religion, and religious claims have to be accepted for prudential rather than intellectual reasons. A theory of double-truth would have some sort of explanation why religious and philosophical truths are distinct, and how they are connected

7 *Defensorium*, 18 fo. 93ʳ6.

(if at all). It might result in some version of fideism according to which religious language has an entirely different set of rules and criteria of sense than non-religious language, so that the religious claim that the soul is immortal is not threatened by the Aristotelian proof of the difficulties with this notion. Pomponazzi's account lacks this sort of theory, and the respectful references to religion appear to be nothing but a protective device transparent in its insincerity.

It is important to distinguish between Pomponazzi's approach and that of earlier Averroists such as Siger. The latter, like Pomponazzi, chose to adhere to faith when it contradicted conclusions proved in philosophy. But he had a reason for this strategy, a reason solidly based upon what he saw as irresoluble difficulties in discovering Aristotle's opinion on particular issues and in assessing the most valid arguments relating to the problem.[8] This could be seen as window-dressing too, yet it is a far more acceptable position for Siger to take up given the structure of his argument than is the case with his Renaissance successor. Siger does go through a whole variety of different arguments on the nature of the soul and thought, and finds a good deal of interest even in those he rejects. The Latin Averroists did not contrast the truth arising from faith with the truth arising from philosophy, they rather contrasted the truth arising from faith with the *method* of philosophy. As Siger says, 'We seek the meaning of the philosophers in this matter rather than the truth, since we proceed philosophically,'[9] and the views of Aristotle should not be concealed even where they are contrary to the truth ('licet sit contraria veritati').[10] Now, one might wonder what the point of philosophizing is if we already can know the truth by a different method. If we know that the soul is immortal (through religion), why bother to examine philosophical arguments with respect to that notion? We seem to be back in the position of regarding philosophy as a type of a game which has no bearing on anything much other than itself. Siger would be far from favourable to such a view of philosophy as a trivial pastime. Philosophy for him can reveal a great many interesting arguments which bear on issues of importance, and permit the derivation of valid conclusions from appropriate premises. Through arguing in such ways we gain a better understanding of how to establish rationally significant principles of

    [8] *De anima intellectiva*, ch. 7, p. 108; o. 83.
    [9] *De anima intellectiva*, ch. 7, p. 101, in *Quaestiones in tertium*, ed. B. Bazán (Philosophes médiévaux, 13; Publications universitaires de Louvain: Louvain, 1972).
    [10] *Quaestiones in metaphysicum*, iii, q. 15 comm., p. 140, in *Questions sur la Métaphysique*, ed. C. Graiff (Philosophes médiévaux, 1; Publications universitaires de Louvain: Louvain, 1948).

behaviour and science. But where we cannot really decide between which arguments to accept, for one reason or another, we must accept the conclusions of faith on that subject.

At this stage one might want to throw up one's hands in despair and question the description of this category of thinkers as Averroists. Since Siger and Pomponazzi display such differences in their views, is there any point in their sharing the same label? Describing anyone as an Averroist is bound to be an imprecise activity since the term was often used as a term of abuse in the Middle Ages and Renaissance, and there were no paid-up members of the Averroist Party. Besides, when one looks closely at the work of thinkers such as Siger and Pomponazzi one comes across significant departures from Averroes' thought. The former 'Averroist' refers approvingly to Themistius in his account of the possible intellect, while the latter argues against Averroes using the theories of Alexander. The only justification for calling them and many others Averroists is the way in which they allowed Averroes to set the philosophical agenda which they then set about discussing. This agenda includes the analysis of Aristotle no matter in which direction it leads, and the notion of the philosopher as a person with the right to explore theoretical issues to their ultimate degree. This led both Siger and Boethius of Dacia to describe the philosopher as one who attempts to perfect his intellectual virtues and thus achieves the highest level of perfection available to human beings. When one examines the propositions selected for condemnation in 1277 they include Proposition 40: There is no more excellent way of life than the philosophical way; Proposition 144: The highest good of which human beings are capable consists of the intellectual virtues; Proposition 154: The philosophers alone are the wisest men in the world.[11] They did, like Averroes, soften the apparently uncompromising nature of these propositions to make *eudaimonia* available to a larger section of humanity, but the principles along which the Averroists went have in common a desire to follow the argument where it will go and accept a valid conclusion whatever it may say. In this they followed the methods which Aristotle proposed for dealing with philosophical issues in terms of hunting (*thereuein: Prior Analytics*, 1. 30, 46^{a}11), discovering (*heuresis: NE* 3. 5, 1112^{b}19) and seeking (*zetesis: Met* 1. 2, 983^{a}23), that is, not through establishing doctrines but by posing arguments and problems and trying to resolve them in so far as this is possible.

Renan's thesis that Averroism was in some way the basis to both

[11] A. Hyman and J. Walsh (eds.), *Philosophy in the Middle Ages* (Harper and Row: New York, 1967), 540-9.

rationalism and fideism, and that the Averroists themselves constituted a kind of secret society, is easy to ridicule given the sources he used, and yet it may be that on reflection there is something in it. After all, the Averroists firmly upheld the right to use rational methods in coming to a clearer understanding of important concepts which already have a religious explanation, and that insistence in itself might be seen as subversive. It is worth linking here the medieval clash between religion and philosophy and the Renaissance dispute between humanism and philosophy, where the latter is equivalent to Averroism. In the interpretative literature these two strands are generally separated, but this is a mistake. The opposition to Aristotelianism on religious grounds was in many ways an opposition based upon a determination to remain faithful to a religious *text*. The philosophers acknowledged the importance of such texts, and yet at the same time argued that Aristotle was worth studying for what he could say about issues of importance for our understanding of our world and ourselves. The theologians who adhered to literalism, or at least to a theologically defined boundary outside of which interpretation is invalid, naturally felt threatened by the attempt at replacing them as experts (in a very similar way to the fears of the *mutakallimūn* at being overtaken by the *falāsifa* in Islam). With the rise of Hellenism and humanism through the Renaissance there again came into existence a group of experts on the text who were concerned very much with its composition and style, with the literal text itself. This was not now because the text was sacred, but because whatever was in it can be best extracted by philological methods and an understanding of literary techniques. The text in question, of course, is no longer scripture, but Aristotle or Plato. Yet between 1472 and 1575 there was a great deal of interest in the commentaries of Averroes if the number of editions of his work being produced is any indication,[12] so that, despite the Renaissance, there was obviously a reaction to the sort of approach which concentrated upon the Greek language and its interpretation. After all, Aristotle produced philosophy and the sorts of questions which Averroes raised with respect to Aristotle are of philosophical interest and value regardless of whether the commentator was cogniscent of the Greek original. (It is indeed ironic that the study of Averroes and *falsafa* as a whole in this century should be largely an exercise in the sort of philological and literary techniques employed by the *falāsifa* rather than in their ideas and arguments.) The notion that the Arabic commentators

[12] C. Schmitt, 'Renaissance Averriosm Studied through the Venetian Editions of Aristotle–Averroes', in *L'Averroismo in Italia* (Atti dei Convegni Lincei: Rome, 1979), 122–42.

became redundant when the original Greek text was recovered is commonly expressed today, yet it was a controversial issue in sixteenth-century Europe, and deservedly so. If our concern is with argument and a range of commentaries on points of philosophical interest, then we should side with Averroes and his attempt at making sense of Greek philosophy. If we are obsessed with the original text itself, whether a religious or a philosophical text, then we will be satisfied with employing the less demanding conceptual machinery of the theologians and the humanists.

The development of Averroes' ideas within the medieval Jewish community took a different path. The enthusiasm and interest which Averroes stimulated can be seen by the large number of translations of his work into Hebrew and Judeo-Arabic, and the favourable references which Maimonides made concerning him in his letters did not discourage philosophically minded Jews from studying the Islamic thinker along with Maimonides himself. The most convinced Jewish Averroist is undoubtedly Isaac Albalag who lived either in Provence or Catalonia and died around 1444. He sharply distinguishes between what can be known through prophecy and what can be known through reason, and asserts that religious and rational truths may contradict each other. Now, given that individuals who are observant in a religious sense will be rewarded for their behaviour in some way, what place does reason have in informing us of appropriate forms of behaviour? If we cannot use reason to distinguish between acceptable and unacceptable religious doctrines, what basis is there for preferring one faith (say, Judaism) over another (Christianity or Islam)? A difficulty with the admission that reason has no part to play in arguments between religions is that it implies that all religions are as good as each other, and nothing can be said from a rational point of view of the advantages and disadvantages of belonging to one as opposed to another. Albo (Albalag) makes a sharp distinction between necessary and natural impossibilities (*nimna'ot qayyamot be- azmam* and *nimna'ot ezel ha-ṭeva'bilvad*.[13] He uses this distinction to argue that one criterion for an acceptable faith is that it involves belief on occasions in natural but not essential impossibilities. Judaism, for instance, demands acceptance of miracles such as the opening of the Red Sea and the turning of the rod into a serpent, but does not require belief in phenomena which are logically inconceivable, such as the same number being odd and even.

This gives Jewish Averroists a criterion for distinguishing between rational and irrational religions. Christians, who believe in incarnation,

[13] See the discussion on Albalag by C. Sirat, *A History of Jewish Philosophy in the Middle Ages* (Cambridge University Press: Cambridge, 1985), 238–43.

transubstantiation, and the trinitarian nature of the deity, were held to adhere to logical impossibilities, and so reason can show the superiority of one faith over another. Now, it must be said from the outset that Christian thinkers were and are capable of presenting rational defences of these difficult doctrines. The line that Tertullian takes in *De carne Christi* that 'certum est, quia impossibile est' is not the standard reply to charges of logical impossibility! The interesting aspect of this discussion is that it seems to provide for philosophy no more than a dialectical role when it comes to assessing religions. Philosophy can rule out opposing faiths, and provide indirect justification of one's own in the sense of proving that it is at least logically conceivable, but it cannot establish a religion as the one to be followed. This is perfectly acceptable from the point of view of Averroes' thought. A prophet is the appropriate source of knowledge to be applied to when one is looking at religions, and he has an alternative and privileged route to religious truth as compared with the philosopher. What is not acceptable for Averroes is the sharp distinction between logical and natural possibility. As we have seen, Averroes argues that this distinction is highly objectionable from a philosophical point of view. In just the same way that two plus two has to equal four, so, if natural events take the course which they do, they must take that course, and if they were suddenly to alter we should be left with a similar degree of conceptual confusion as if two plus two were no longer to come to four. Whatever difficulty exists in accepting miracles exists whether the miracles affect our mathematical rules or our physical rules, and Albalag's approach here is more akin to that of Ghazali than that of Averroes.

Many reasons have been put forward to explain the swift disappearance of Averroes from the cultural scene of the Islamic world following his death. Renan catalogues the writers who follow him quite closely in time and make absolutely no mention of him even when compiling histories of philosophy and discussing Ghazali, in marked contrast to the way in which he was regarded during his lifetime.[14] He seemed to retain no influence whatsoever on following generations of thinkers from within the Muslim community. This is not just a result of anti-philosophical sentiment becoming general in the Islamic world, since Avicenna continued to have a considerable afterlife among Muslim intellectuals. Avicenna could appeal to the continual thread of interest in mysticism, while all that Averroes possesses is an insistence upon rationality and subtle thinking, a far less exciting image to attract following generations. It is also worth mentioning

[14] *Averroès*, pp. 38–9.

that Avicenna's medical work is far superior than what we know of Averroes' efforts in this area, and this lent the former a good deal of status within a community which still used medical knowledge based upon Avicenna's *Qanūn*. Besides, the theological doctrine of Ash'arism came to dominate thinking within the Islamic world, and this doctrine is in total contradiction to everything which Averroes supports. It emphasizes atomism, creation *ex nihilo*, subjectivity of ethics, and the dependence of everything on the existence and will of a God who has all the characteristics of a normal person, but to a far greater degree. The arguments which Averroes produced to try to show that religion and philosophy are compatible came to be regarded as a clear indication of the opposition between religion and philosophy, and Averroes as an exponent of the latter against the former. Besides, many thinkers felt that they had gone as far as they would go in accepting the arguments of Ghazali and ibn Ḥazm with regard to the importance of employing logical methods in theology, and in supporting the call for clarity and a degree of toleration in theological debates. Once they had taken all that on board, together with whatever else in Islamic theory they accepted, there appears to be little theoretical space left for philosophy, and in particular for a type of philosophy which makes so little allowance for the type of thinking and language which characterize most believers' backgrounds.

In an article Wolfson referred to 'The Twice-revealed Averroes', by which he means the introduction of Averroes into the Latin world in the twelfth century and his reappearance in the sixteenth. In his first revelation he appears as *the* commentator on Aristotle, and in his second as an enemy of the humanism of the Renaissance. There have also been two appearances of Averroes in the Islamic world, once during his lifetime, and more recently in the late nineteenth and throughout this century. The revival of interest in him has come about through the rationalism of the *Naḥda*, the Islamic renaissance movement which sought to combine the best liberal traditions of Islamic culture with the West. One of the leaders of this movement, Faraḥ Anṭūn, translated Renan's book on Averroes and represented him as a victim of religious persecution as a result of his adherence to reason as a distinct and areligious realm of discourse. The modernist movement saw Averroes' stress on the difference between religion and philosophy as ammunition for its notion of the desirability of the secular state. In more recent times there has been something of a revival of academic interest in Averroes, especially on the issue of the relationship between religion and philosophy in his work, but it would be wrong to say that the character of philosophy in today's Islamic world is strongly affected by his thought. The work which has been done on Averroes is firmly within the tradition of Western scholarship, emphasizing the esoteric–exoteric distinction and the question of the sincerity of Averroes as a Muslim philosopher. The revival of Islam (or more accurately of a particular type of Islam) has led yet again to a disinclination to pursue the purely philosophical approach recommended by Averroes. Islam is treated as a concept which possesses sufficient strength at a conceptual level to perform all the explanatory work which might be required of a theory, and so once again there is not much interest in the intriguing arguments which Averroes produces to lay out clearly the boundaries between religion and reason.[15]

[15] This point is more fully developed in Leaman, 'Continuity in Islamic Political Philosophy: The Role of Myth', *BRSMES Proceedings of the 1986 International Conference on Middle Eastern Studies* (BRSMES: Oxford, 1986), 219–28.

Averroes' Philosophical Methodology

ONE of the features of the nature of philosophical argument which it is always important to grasp is that philosophers not only argue with each other on a range of issues, but also frequently differ as to how to do philosophy itself. Ghazali and Averroes do not just dispute over the question of the eternity of the world, although this is frequently how their confrontation is interpreted. Much more importantly they are at odds about how to proceed philosophically. Different theories of meaning are at issue here. Ghazali and Avicenna employ an account of meaning which is heavily influenced by Neoplatonism in that it stresses the role of some external source which brings about whatever it is which exists and which is distinct from that source. As we have seen, Avicenna's distinction between existence and essence leads logically to the occasionalism of Ghazali. If the definition of things does not include the existence of these things, then something from outside that definition is required to move those things from the realm of possibility to the status of actuality. For Avicenna the mover is another thing which causally necessitates the change, while for Ghazali it is God who lays down laws of habitual behaviour for the items of our world. With his adherence to the principle of plenitude, Averroes cannot follow in the footsteps of his predecessors. For him the eventual instantiation of a possibility is not something brought about by an external force if that possibility is what he calls a real possibility. If something is a real possibility then it will at some time take place, and this is not just an incidental fact about it, but part of its definition or essence.

These differences concerning the notion of modality, the status of things as possible and necessary, have important implications for how we can carry out arguments. Ghazali's notion of possibility permits him to put together two concepts, examine their combination for any contradiction, and if none results, he can claim that the philosophers err in arguing otherwise. For example, when he is looking at the putative necessity of the causal relation, he argues that we can think about the cause, and then think about the effect not occurring. Similarly, we can think about the effect and not think about the cause as having to bring it about. It may be difficult to carry out these thought-experiments, because we are so accustomed to linking these disparate phenomena, and indeed it is important that we can do so to make sense of our world. None the less, the fact that we *can* contemplate a break in the apparent connection between cause and effect proves that, whatever it is this connection comprises, it is not a logical connection. Were it to be a logical connection there would be no possibility of breaking the connection in thought, for if we did so we would end up with some sort of contradiction, as when we claim that two plus two does not equal four. For Ghazali the only thing that links causes and effects in a necessary manner is our imagination, and the necessity involved is not logical but psychological. As a result of intellectual laziness we are disinclined to examine the radical possibilities which exist for change in our conceptual scheme, and we persist in thinking that the apparently fixed nature of that scheme is implicit in the nature of things themselves. If we examine our experience using as our sole instrument the notion of logical possibility, we shall soon discover that there are feasible alternative ways of looking at the world, alternatives which are ruled out in practice because God chooses to construct a certain framework of ideas in our minds which establish a pattern of regularity. That pattern of regularity possesses no necessity in itself, though, and is only a reflection of something which comes from outside nature and which makes our knowledge of our world and ourselves possible in the first place.

Averroes cannot accept such a quick way with the issue of determining the meaning of propositions which challenge the structure of our conceptual scheme. When we think about people without heads writing a book, or someone stepping inside a fire without apparently suffering any deleterious effects, we are indeed operating within the realms of logical possibility. But are these limits sufficient to determine the question of the necessity of our conceptual apparatus? One of the difficulties with the thought-experiments which Ghazali employs is that they fail to do justice to the nature of the concepts which they use. They identify changes to those concepts which do not affect their meaning with changes which do. Examples of the former are not difficult to come by. For example, while typing this page it might be that I look away from the paper for a moment and when my gaze returns to the paper I see that instead of having typed words I have typed music. I can certainly imagine this to happen, in the sense that I can think of possible (albeit improbable) causes for this most amazing event. These causes need not make any direct reference to the deity, but will involve natural processes of which I am aware which could have brought about the unusual effect. More is involved in working out which notions are compatible than can be discovered by using nothing more than the concept of logical possibility. Wittgenstein once tried to bring this out when he wondered what it would mean to say that it was 5 o'clock on the sun.[1] We can envisage someone on the sun turning to his watch and observing the time, in the sense that one can imagine something happening to make such a person able to exist there. Can I not imagine myself on the sun wondering what the time is, seeing it is 5 o'clock, and missing my tea? In a sense I can, but in another sense I cannot. It is the sun which gives our concept of time its reference. Nothing non-gaseous can exist anywhere near it. These are only facts, and not immutable, and yet they significantly affect the meaning of the language we use. The feat of imagination which we might realize would not necessarily show that any genuine possibility exists in a radical transformation of any of our most basic beliefs about ourselves and our world. It is this sort of argument upon which Averroes relies when he distinguishes sharply between real and logical possibility, and the implications of that distinction for how we do philosophy are crucial.

This difference over the nature of philosophy itself becomes apparent when we look at some of the language of the attack on Peripateticism by Ghazali. The title of his Third Discussion in his *Tahāfut al-falāsifa* is interesting. It goes: 'The demonstration of their confusion in saying that God is the agent and the maker of the world and that the world is his product and act, and the demonstration that these expressions are in their system only metaphors without any real sense' (*TT* 147). Ghazali argues that God is only a real agent if he can form decisions, carry them out, and have the will and intention to perform certain changes in the world. God is taken to act in much the same way that we act, except with far greater power and understanding. In the same way that I can decide that I want a cup of tea and then organize its production, so God can decide that he wants to see what a particular human being does, observes his behaviour, and rewards and punishes him in the afterlife. He has the role of an omnipotent and omniscient headteacher. What is important for Ghazali is that it is accepted that, if God is to be a real agent, he must act 'through will and through choice' (*TT* 150), since

he who says that the lamp creates the light and the man creates the shadow uses the term vaguely, giving it a sense much broader than its definition, and uses it metaphorically, relying on the fact that there is an analogy between the object originally meant by it and the object to which it is transferred, i.e. the agent is in a general sense a cause, the lamp is the cause of the light, and the sun is the cause of luminosity; but the agent is not called a creative agent from the sole fact that it is a cause, but by its being a cause in a special way (*TT* 150).

[1] L. Wittgenstein, *Philosophical Investigations*, trans. G. E. M. Anscombe (Blackwell: Oxford, 1953), I, 350.

He goes on to argue that the concept of a natural act is self-contradictory, or at the very least metaphorical, since the only proper use of the term 'action' indicates a voluntary agent (*TT* 156). Although Averroes rather mildly responds that 'The philosophers . . . only affirm that He does not will in the way that man wills' (*TT* 160) this seems a rather ineffective response to Ghazali's central claim that 'our aim in this question is to show that you philosophers use those venerable names without justification, and that God, according to you, is not a true agent, nor the world truly his act, and that you apply this word metaphorically—not in its real sense. This has now been shown' (*TT* 171).

We have already examined some of the issues which arise on this particular issue, and there is no need to raise them again as such. What is worth discussing, though, is the nature of the argument in so far as it concerns the question of meaning. Ghazali has a view of meaning, and especially the meaning of the divine attributes, which places the stress upon univocity. That is, he expects the terms we apply to God to be the same terms which we apply to non-divine creatures, and the activities with which we credit the deity to differ only in scope from many of our own activities. Indeed, he goes further in arguing that any attempt at interpreting the properties of God as equivocal or ambiguous or metaphorical is a subtle way of attacking the notion of God itself. This discussion tends to centre on the issue of the divine attributes, but it has far wider focus. Really it encompasses the entire question of the relationship between religious and ordinary language, a relationship which Averroes seeks to define and analyse again and again in his work. It is vital that we become clearer on this controversial and interesting issue.

The first place to look is Averroes' middle commentary on Aristotle's *Categories*. He comments:

Aristotle states: Things whose names are common, that is, equivocal, are things that have nothing general or common to them except for the name, while the definition of each, which states its essence in consideration of the meaning of the equivocal name, differs from the definition of the other and is peculiar to its own definiendum. An example is the name 'animal' when predicated both of a drawing of a man and of a rational man, for the definitions of these two differ, and the two have nothing general and in common except for the name, that is, our calling them both animals.[2]

The significance of the doctrine of equivocal terms is its application to the

---

[2] *Middle Commentary on Porphyry's Isagoge and on Aristotle's Categoriae*, trans. and int. H. A. Davidson (Medieval Academy of America: Cambridge, Mass., 1969), 32.

problem of divine attributes, which is itself a metaphor for the link between religious and ordinary language. Aristotle distinguishes between two types of equivocal terms, pure and *pros hen* equivocals. The former share the name and only the name, while the latter point to some similarity in the objects which forms the basis to the sharing of the name. In Aristotle's own text he clearly does not claim that the only thing which the man and the drawing of the man have in common is the name, since he qualifies his statement by the expression 'but the definition of being corresponding to the name is different' (*Cat.* 1, 1ᵃ4). By contrast, Averroes alters this passage to emphasize the denial of likeness with regard to everything except the name, and comes out clearly in favour of the doctrine that things with equivocal names have nothing in common except the name, and thus have distinct definitions. But do not the picture of a man, a man himself, and the predicate 'animal' all have something very much in common, in that the predicate picks out something shared by both the man and the picture? What a person looks like is merely an accidental aspect of him—it is his intellect which represents his essence—so it is indeed open to Averroes to argue that the relationship between the picture of a man and the man himself is entirely equivocal. On the whole, though, he is committed to the view that the language we use to describe the properties of God is in the form of *pros hen* equivocals. If they were to be univocal they would lead to an analysis in terms of a genus or species, which in turn would imply multiplicity within the unity of the deity. If they were to be entirely equivocal, then there would be nothing in common between our religious and ordinary language except the words themselves, and this would cut off the route by which we move from our understanding of the world to our understanding of God.

The notion of equivocation arises for Aristotle and Averroes again in the *Metaphysics Lambda*, where the former talks about being in the sense of the whole of reality, everything which exists, and describes it as either one genus or several genera united through their common relation to something else, such as the relation of all things which can be called healthy to health itself (*Met.* 4. 2, 1003ᵇ1) or the relation of the categories of being to being. This sort of relationship is called *pros hen* by Aristotle (*Met.* 4. 2, 1003ᵃ33) and *bi-nisba ilā shay' wāḥid* in Arabic. Averroes wavers between holding that the relation existing between the categories is like the relation existing between the species of a genus, and that it is a *pros hen* relation (*Tafsīr*, pp. 1409–10). He comes down to the thesis that the relation of the categories to being is a *pros hen* relation rather than of the species–genus type, and this enables him to distinguish between the categories in terms of priority and posteriority, a view very different from both the original Aristotle and Alexander's commentary. Although it is possible to see Averroes' interpretation of Aristotle as just being an error on his part, we shall come to understand that it is an important part of his theory of meaning, and as such consciously selected despite its deviance from Aristotle.

Averroes argues that God is the exemplar of all things, and contains them in a complete way, since 'his essence, according to the philosophers, contains all intellects and existents in a nobler and more perfect way than they all possess in reality' (*TT* 202). What is the relationship between the deity and the things which exist in the world? There are problems with calling God a thing in the way in which we call ordinary objects things, and Averroes argues that God is paradigmatically a thing, while everything else enjoys only a derivative degree of substance. Substance is 'the existent which does not exist in a substratum' (*TT* 369) and 'when, by "existent", is understood what is understood by entity and things, the term "existent" is attributed essentially to God and analogically to all other things' (*TT* 302). It is an error to think of God being in a genus as that is ordinarily understood. Referring to Ghazali, he comments:

As to his statement that no other thing can share with the First its genus and be distinguished from it through a specific difference, if he means by this the genus and the difference that are predicated univocally, it is true, for anything of this description is composed of a common form and a specific form, and such things possess a definition. But if by 'genus' is meant what is predicated analogically, I mean *per prius et posterius*, then it can have a genus, e.g. existent, or thing, or essence, and it can have a kind of definition (*TT* 369).

The concept of God has a special status which defies description as though it were an ordinary concept definable in terms of type and qualities. Were God to be thus definable, he would consist of a number of attributes which made up a plurality, in the same way that we consist of thinking, wanting, expecting, and so on. This constitutes a very grave error, though:

It cannot be denied that one essence can have many attributes related, negative or imaginary, in different ways, without this implying a plurality in the essence; for example, that a thing is an existent and one and possible or necessary; for when the one identical entity is viewed in so far as something else proceeds from it, it is called capable and acting, and in so far as it is viewed as differentiating between two opposite acts, it is called willing, and in so far as it is viewed as perceiving its object knowing, and in so far as it is viewed as perceiving and as a cause of motion, it is called living, since the living is the perceiving and the self-moving (*TT* 315).

He goes on to elaborate this argument thus:

What is perfect by itself is like what is existent by itself, and how true it is that the existent by itself is perfect by itself. If, therefore, there exists an existent by itself, it must be perfect by itself and self-sufficient by itself; otherwise, it would be composed of an imperfect essence and attributes perfecting this essence. If this is true, the attribute and its subject are one and the same, and the acts which are ascribed to this subject as proceeding necessarily from different attributes exist only in a relative way. (*TT* 330).

Our mind tends to separate things which exist as a unity into their parts, even though these parts do not enjoy an independent existence (*Tafsīr*, p. 1623). We distinguish matter from form, and form from bodies which are constituted by that form. When we think about immaterial things, such as God, we use the same sort of language as when thinking about an everyday object in the world, but these similarities in language should not obscure the fact that we are using the same terms in different ways, indeed, in analogical ways (*Tafsīr*, p. 1622).

Wolfson argues convincingly that in many of the contexts in which Averroes uses the notion of equivocation he is really referring to analogy or ambiguity.[3] The concept of ambiguity is carefully constructed by Alexander to contrast with being purely and entirely equivocal (*NE* 1. 4, 1096^{b}26–8) and being 'one in genus' (*Met.* 5. 6, 1016^{b}32) and univocal (*Cat.* 1, 1^{a}6–12). This leads Averroes to insist in places that terms like 'intellect' are predicated of God not as univocal terms, nor as equivocal, but as ambiguous (*asmā' mushakkikah*: *TT* 387). He is quite happy to interpret Aristotle's claim that such terms as 'equal', 'much', 'one', and so on are equivocal (*Phys.* 7. 4, 248^{b}15–21) as not really being a list of pure equivocals, but rather one of ambiguous expressions.[4] This technical notion of ambiguity or analogy is important for Averroes, since it establishes an *order* in our ascription of the same name to different objects:

the term 'existence' indicates essences which have analogical meanings, essences some of which are more perfect than others; and therefore there exists in the things which have such an existence a principle which is the cause of that which exists in all the other things of this genus, just as our term 'warm' is a term which is

[3] H. Wolfson, 'The Amphibolous Terms in Aristotle, Arabic Philosophy and Maimonides', *Harvard Theological Review*, 31 (1938), 151–73.

[4] *Aristotelis opera*, comm. 26, fo. 328.

predicated *per prius et posterius* of fire and all other warm things, and that of which it is asserted first, i.e. fire, is the cause of the existence of warmth in all other things, and . . . most metaphysical terms behave like this (*TT* 370–1).

He is pointing here to Aristotle's account of what has been called 'focal meaning', where an expression has a primary sense by reference to which its other senses can be explained.[5] He goes on to explain that:

there are things which have a term in common not univocally nor equivocally, but by the universality of terms analogically related to one thing, and that the characteristic of these things is that they lead upwards to a first term in this genus which is the first cause of everything to which this word refers, like warmth, which is predicated of fire and all other warm things (*TT* 387).

Calling a fire warm is rather peculiar, since a fire can be taken to be a paradigm of warmth, a perfect instance of this quality which is found in other phenomena to a lesser degree. A hot bottle is warm because of its resemblance to the warmth of a fire, and the principles which are directly present in the warmth of the fire are to a degree present in the warmth of the bottle. The fire is warm in the fullest possible sense, and the hot bottle is warm in a derivative sense.

The direct purpose of this doctrine is to enable Averroes to avoid the objection which Ghazali and the Ash'arites in general made to the notion of God existing without attributes. All the qualities which we apply to the deity are applied to just one genus because that very special genus exemplifies in the best possible way all those qualities. There exists only one God who brings about action, and all the characteristics which we may apply to him are much completer predicates than those which we can apply to ourselves and to the objects in our own world. God's properties cannot be distinguished from him in the way in which our properties can be distinguished from us because they follow from his essence rather than merely being accidental parts of it. There is no longer a problem, then, in reconciling the essential simplicity of the concept of God with the fact that he has properties, because those properties are essential parts of him and aspects of his being, and they make possible the attribution of properties to things in the world of generation and corruption in general. There seems to exist a plurality of predicates because we tend to think of God as someonè rather like us, but more so. Our intellect naturally analyses and separates aspects of things which are in reality inseparable. There is

[5] G. Owen, 'The Platonism of Aristotle', in P. Strawson (ed.), *Studies in the Philosophy of Thought and Action* (Oxford University Press: Oxford, 1968), 147–74.

nothing wrong with this provided that we grasp that what really exists are unified things, and in the case of God the qualities with which we endow him are an essential and indivisible constituent of this essence. In short, there is only one thing there, and only one type of thing.

This discussion of equivocation appears to be limited in its purpose to reconciling the simplicity of God with the multiplicity of the attributes ascribed to him, but it has a wider focus than that. It is crucial to an understanding of Averroes' thought as a whole. This is because the notions of ambiguity and analogy bring out with some force the idea of a point of view, of seeing one thing in different ways, and the importance of an appropriate interpretation. A famous passage in the Qur'ān goes:

It is He who sent down upon thee the Book, wherein are verses clear (*muḥkamāt*) that are the Essence of the Book, and others ambiguous (*mutashābihāt*). As for those in whose hearts is swerving, they follow the ambiguous part, desiring dissension, and desiring its interpretation (*ta'wīl*); and none knows its interpretation, save only God and those firmly rooted in knowledge (iii. 5; I have altered the last sentence from Arberry's translation to make it more accurate).

We have already seen that Averroes argues that the only people who are qualified to interpret the ambiguous passages in the Qur'ān are the philosophers. They possess demonstrative skills which are capable of resolving difficulties as they arise in a clear and final manner, whereas the theologians get involved in constructing theories surrounding these difficult passages which are neither faithful to the meaning of Islam nor compatible with the faith of the majority of the community of believers. He argues along these lines in the *Faṣl al-maqāl*, and in its companion volume, the *Kitāb al-kashf ʿan manāhij al-adilla fī ʿaqāʾid al-milla, wa taʿrīf ma waqaʿa fīhā bi-ḥasb at-taʾwīl min ash-shibah al-muzīgha wal-bidaʿ al-muḍilla*, which is worth quoting in full since it presents so clearly the topic of the essay, namely, 'an exposition of the methods of argument concerning the doctrine of faith and a determination of doubts and misleading innovations brought into the faith'. Averroes criticizes the *mutakallimūn* in these two works not only for their errors but for the effect that those errors might have on the religious beliefs of ordinary members of the community. Most of the arguments and interpretations which they offer contain much more 'innovation' (*bidʿa*) than the arguments of the philosophers might even appear to imply. The theologians ignore the fact that the Qur'ān speaks to the community in a variety of different ways, each appropriate to its potential audience. So, while there are demonstrative arguments for the philosophers, there are also dialectical arguments for the theologians and lawyers, and rhetorical arguments for the masses, and any attempt at blurring these divisions is not just erroneous but positively dangerous.

There is an appropriate level of assent (*taṣdīq*) for every type of person in society, and that form of assent will be sufficient for salvation to be attainable. What happens when there is a difficulty in working out what the object of the act of assent is, that is, where there is a problem of interpretation? He suggests:

> whenever demonstrative study leads to any manner of knowledge about any being, that being is inevitably either unmentioned or mentioned in Scripture. . . . if Scripture speaks about it, the apparent meaning of the words inevitably either accords or conflicts with the conclusions of demonstration about it. . . . If it conflicts there is a call for allegorical interpretation of it. The meaning of 'allegorical interpretation' is: extension of the significance of an expression from real to metaphorical significance, without forsaking therein the standard metaphorical practices of Arabic, such as calling a thing by the name of something resembling it or a cause or consequence or accompaniment of it (*FM* 7).

Let us take an example from a non-theological context. In his proemium to the long commentary on the *Physics*, Averroes suggests that the term 'man' is predicated equivocally of ordinary men, untrained as they are in the intellectual sciences. Only philosophers are men in the fullest sense of the term, and other human beings can be called men through their resemblance to the paradigm:

> In this science it is certain that application of the name 'man' to someone perfected by theoretical knowledge, to someone not perfected by it, and to someone not even able to be perfected by it is equivocal, in just the same way that the name 'man' can be applied to a living person as to a human corpse, and to a rational being as to a stone.[6]

There would be nothing inappropriate in most people regarding themselves as men and not appreciating that really they are merely pale imitations of the real thing, in Averroes' view. He is suggesting in this passage that philosophers more readily fulfil the human potentiality for abstract thought than do most people, and as such are most accurately called human beings, in much the same way that a sharp and clean knife is more accurately called a knife than a broken and filthy implement. It is alright for people to think that they are living the sorts of lives which people ought to live even where they do not involve themselves in

---

[6] *Aristotelis opera*, fo. 1ʳaH (my translation).

contemplation because of the link between their lives and those of philosophers, however remote that link might be.

One of the standard problems in interpretation of difficult Qur'ānic passages for sunnī Islam is the lack of any authority other than that of the community and its consensus (*ijmāʿ*) itself. There has always been a difficulty in assessing what the consensus comes down to, and whether a consensus among a group of Muslims with more specialized training might be sufficient. Averroes certainly seems to want to establish the philosophers as a decisive group to arrive at a consensus on particular controversial issues in section 8 of his *Faṣl al-maqāl*. The notion of consensus is important, though, and not just for its origins and role in Islamic law, but for its philosophical interest too. Basing belief upon consensus places an undeniable *social* constraint upon the sorts of interpretation which can be justified, and upon the sorts of understanding of the object of belief. That is, the majority of the population might have no problems in reconciling the spirituality of the deity with the anthropomorphic language used to describe him. This leads to no problem at all, since for such people there is a set of beliefs and practices which will enable them to attain salvation and happiness in this world. In accusing the theologians of threatening the simple faith of such people Averroes is not being disingenuous. He is indicating that the social role of religion for such people is of a certain fairly unreflective kind, and, once those believers are encouraged to reflect on their faith using the suspect and defective machinery of the *kalām*, they may well reject both their religion and the theological explanation of it. But is this not to consign them to a second-rate and problematic form of belief? After all, they rest content with their beliefs despite the difficulties which are inherent in the conjunction of all their religious beliefs, which seems rather like someone being happy about their mathematical calculations even though there are basic mistakes in their application of them to problems. This would be a misleading example. The sort of case which Averroes has in mind can be illustrated by taking an example from the realm of everyday morality. Most people believe that they ought to follow certain moral rules, and do not think deeply about the basis which such rules have in reason, nature, or whatever. They operate perfectly acceptably in society and in their dealings with their family and friends by using these rules, and might even be incapable intellectually of comprehending arguments which try to ground them in something more solid than just the feeling that they are to be obeyed. Then someone comes along (like the theologian) and presents them with a battery of bad arguments which try to show how those rules are grounded in something more solid, when they did not even think about the necessity for grounding them in anything at all. This might lead to a weakening in acceptance of the rules, and a falling off in moral behaviour. The philosopher can of course understand the need for more secure bases for the rules, and can produce good demonstrative arguments which prove decisively the validity of particular principles which are presupposed by moral rules, and the faith of the philosophers in the rules will not be weakened by intellectual analysis of them. It is not correct to say that the non-philosopher has an imperfect view of what he is to do as compared with the philosopher. Indeed, if we take the moral example seriously, a far worthier non-philosopher could be contrasted with a morally weak philosopher. Salvation might be available far more readily to the former than to the latter. Averroes would say that they both know the same thing (how to behave), but they know it in different ways, each way being sufficient to make possible happiness and salvation. Neither believer has privileged access to what lies behind the principles of happiness and salvation; they both are obliged to satisfy the basic requirements of practice and belief specified by Islam.

What are these basic requirements? In his *Manāhij* he points to belief in the existence of God as a creator and purposive ruler of the world, his unity, and his perfect attributes. Exactly how God has qualities is something about which we cannot know anything definite, but that he has them is an article of faith. The philosophers do not have to accept that God can see and hear what goes on in the world, but:

The philosophers only avoid ascribing to the First hearing and seeing because this would imply its possessing a soul. The Holy Law ascribes hearing and seeing to God to remind us that God is not deprived of any kind of knowledge and understanding, and the masses cannot be made to grasp this meaning except by the use of terms such as 'hearing' and 'seeing', and for this reason this exegesis is limited to the learned and so cannot be taken as one of the dogmas of the Holy Law common to the masses. And the same is the case with many questions the solutions of which the Holy Law leaves to science (*TT* 454).

The masses and the philosophers both know that God knows and understands everything there is to know and understand, and this is made clearer to the masses by the ascription of seeing and hearing to God. The philosophers realize that this cannot be meant literally, since God has no body. Precisely how he knows and understands is not known to either group, and is unimportant. This comes out nicely in Averroes' treatment of the longstanding controversy between the Mu'tazilites and the

Ash'arites on whether the divine attributes are identical with God's essence, or distinct from it. The Ash'arite view that the attributes are distinct from God's essence implies that God consists of essence and predicate and as a result contains multiplicity, while the Mu'tazilite argument for the identity of deity and attributes cannot be established logically, 'for when it is said that God's knowledge and attributes cannot be described by, or compared to, the attributes of the creature, so that it cannot even be asserted that they are essence or an addition to the essence, this expresses the thought of genuine philosophers and other true thinkers' (*TT* 354; also 446 and 149). It is accordingly something of a theme of the *Manāhij* that we are led by Islam to acknowledge the very profound differences which must exist between ourselves and the deity. The difference is to be explained, as we have seen, in terms of God possessing certain attributes in their most perfect and complete forms, which we can only be said to share in an equivocal manner.

One of the chief virtues of Islam as a faith is its capacity to employ highly imaginative and effective imagery. It makes plain to the widest possible group of people what it is they ought to do and believe. The necessity to behave in morally appropriate ways is clearly high on Averroes' agenda of the criteria of a successful religion, and Islam, with its blend of inspiration and reason (*TT* 584) fulfils this requirement well. He claims that:

all philosophers agree that the principles of action must be taken on authority, for there is no demonstration for the necessity of action except through the existence of virtues which are realized through moral actions and through practice. . . . the prayers in our religion hold men back from ignominy and wickedness, as God's word certifies . . . the prayer ordained in our religion fulfils this purpose more truly than the prayers ordained in others, and this by the conditions imposed on it of number, time, recitation, purity, and desistance from acts and words harmful to it. . . . the same may be said of the doctrine of the beyond in our religion, which is more conducive to virtuous actions than what is said in others. Thus to represent the beyond in material images is more appropriate than purely spiritual representation (*TT* 584–5).

Averroes argues in this passage that Islam does everything which Judaism and Christianity do, but more successfully. The ceremonial and ritual rules are more conducive to regular adherence to religious law, and the religious stories are more appropriate to the needs and capacities of the general audience. Should not that audience examine those stories and seek to discover what lies behind them? It is clear that Averroes does not take the account of the afterlife in Islam at face value; he does not believe in the likelihood of a sensuous existence following the death and decay of our bodies in this life. If the community as a whole is led to adherence to Islam through, among other things, a particular story about how they will come back to life in paradise if they behave well in this life, then this story must be incorporated in the religious teaching of Islam.

There can be little doubt that this is what he says, but is he justified in saying it? Are not people being encouraged to believe things which are just not true, and are they not being urged to base their behaviour on erroneous beliefs? The philosophers can pat themselves on the back since they do not need to be taken in by such stories, and they need only admire the way in which the majority of the population are led to virtuous action through them. It is tempting to classify this position as a version of complacent élitism, and to see it as implicitly critical of traditional religious beliefs. The *falāsifa* seem to place the less sophisticated members of the community in the role of children who need not and cannot be told the whole truth because it would weaken their acceptance of adult rules, children who need to be put in their place by stories of bogy men and fairies and so on. This unsympathetic view of Averroes should be resisted. The point about the stories which are widely broadcast in the community is that they must be true. He gives the well-worn example of the doctor treating patients (*FM* 22–3) who are not on the whole able to understand why particular treatments work. To be a successful doctor he need not train his patients to be doctors themselves. What he has to do is to get them to behave in certain ways which are conducive to their health. If he instructs them in some medical knowledge this might well lead them to misunderstand what he is trying to do and make his treatment less effective. What he tells them is true, but it is not the whole of the truth. If the patients had the right to demand the whole of the truth they would be assuming the role of doctor themselves. Similarly, someone who tries to interpret the difficult passages in the Qur'ān, who points to the variety of possible interpretations which such passages have and to the difficulties in reconciling them with other parts of the book, will be in the position of people who try to persuade the community that there is no such thing as health or illness, and that doctors have no valuable role to play in society. This will be because they throw into confusion the simple and straightforward beliefs of the majority of the community, and replace them with theoretical arguments of dubious value and little certainty.

Averroes continues this theme:

this comparison is certain . . . it presents a true analogy, in that the relation of the doctor to the health of bodies is [the same as] the relation of the legislator to the health of souls: i.e. the doctor is he who seeks to preserve the health of bodies when it exists and to restore it when it is lost, while the legislator is he who desires this [end] for the health of the souls (*FM* 23).

If the legislator is to succeed in his task he must first of all be able to dress up his message in imaginative and attractive language, in order to induce people to follow it. Secondly, what he urges them to do must be based on something which is true. He knows why people should act in a certain way, and he knows this through demonstrative reasoning. He uses his skill as a communicator to persuade the majority of the community to act accordingly. The sorts of examples which Averroes gives of action are interestingly ritualistic, with their accompanying beliefs. We need to follow certain religious practices and obey particular ceremonial regulations in order to be able to aquire a virtuous and steadfast disposition to follow the right path. In the same way that a doctor might advise us to seek health by eating more fruit and less sugar, so a legislator might advise us to seek spiritual health by fasting more often and praying more regularly. We may obey him for traditional reasons, because it has always been the practice to perform certain rituals and ceremonies, but the basis of the behaviour lies in its truth, that is, in its accordance with some demonstratively established principle in terms of what is conducive to spiritual vigour.

To understand Averroes' account of a variety of paths to the truth we have to grasp his theory of meaning. Unlike his philosophical predecessors (but curiously like his fellow-countryman, Maimonides) he places great weight on the notion of equivocation and ambiguity in our language. The relatively loose connection between the use of similar names permits him to discuss the difficulties involved in grasping what those names mean. Their meanings are different depending upon the context within which they are used, although they are not completely different and distinct. There is a thread of meaning connecting the different uses which extends from the divine exemplar to the temporal imitation. If we regard these terms as clear and univocal then we will get into the sorts of difficulties experienced by Avicenna in explaining how a simple deity could embody a multiplicity of attributes, and of how the essence of a thing is independent of its existence. There will also exist a fatal difficulty in differentiating between the levels of abstraction which obtain between the ordinary thinking subject and the active intellect and beyond. Averroes accepts with Aristotle that there can be no priority or posteriority within the same genus, and so is led to develop an account of meaning which is based upon the *pros hen* rather than the genus–species relation. This relation is extremely useful in characterizing some of the most important theses presented by Averroes.

What are these theses? One is the significance of the notion of a point of view. In Averroes' philosophy there is a continual contrast between different points of view. There is not just a distinction between God's point of view and the human point of view, but also a differentiation of the standpoints of a whole variety of different human beings based upon their forms of reasoning. In the *Faṣl al-maqāl*, for example, there is a distinction between demonstrative, dialectical, rhetorical, and sophistical people (*FM*, ch. 3 *passim*). All these people are using similar language to describe what is important to them, namely, their religion, God, happiness, the next life, moral behaviour, and so on. This language is not identical regardless of its usage, but nor is it completely equivocal. There exist links between different applications of the same name, and these links are sufficiently strong for it to make sense to say that these uses are of the same term. In that case we can talk about a variety of routes to the same destination, a variety of views based upon the same principles and beliefs, and a variety of life-styles which together add up to something morally and religiously desirable. Commentators on Averroes tend to restrict his use of the notion of consensus (*ijmāʿ*) to its theological role in sunnī Islam, and this is valid in so far as it goes. But agreement in society has a more powerful role even than that of establishing religious orthodoxy and the definition of belief and heresy. Agreement also establishes what words mean. For Averroes the criterion of ambiguity is entirely social. If a group of people within the community come to regard a scriptural passage as ambiguous, then it is ambiguous, and has to be resolved in some way if practice is not to suffer. If a passage is clear to everyone, then it is clear in itself, and there is no need to speculate what lies behind it or how it justifies what it claims. It is clear and provides a definite route along which salvation eventually lies. When one group of people is satisfied that it understands a text, and another group is worried by something in it, it is incumbent upon the latter to satisfy the theoretical problems without challenging the beliefs and practices of the majority of society, since any widespread challenge to the normal understanding of key terms would make such terms useless. It is crucial to grasp here that he does not just mean useless as a guide to action. In the example comparing spiritual and physical health he suggests that, if the theologians broadcast their confused thoughts about the meaning of the Qur'ān, ordinary believers would come to doubt that they have an adequate grasp of the meanings of the texts which they know. They may come to doubt that those texts have any meaning at all, in the same way that the patients of the dialectical doctors might come to think that there is no such thing as health and sickness.

But there is such a thing as health and sickness, and religious texts do convey important information about how people ought to behave. Averroes argues that, in addition to these significant facts of what he takes to be common-sense experience, we have to pay attention to the different ways in which different people relate to these facts. A doctor has a different view of disease than an ordinary unsophisticated patient, and an ordinary believer has a different view of the grounds of his belief than a philosopher. Rather like Aristotle, Averroes respects a whole gamut of different views on a common topic, refusing to select some as more privileged or accurate than others.[7] This variety of views is represented by the variety of language available to characterize a whole continuum of views, ranging from the entirely demonstrative to the most poetic and expressive. In his work Averroes spends a good deal of effort in trying to disentangle this variety and order it along the grid of demonstrative argument and its less stringent but still rational and related argument forms. It follows that equivocation in language is not something to be rejected as such. This feature of language must be accepted because it is a feature of our lives as different people living in a community with a whole range of ends and interests in prospect.

As we have seen, Ghazali condemns the suggestion that equivocation is a feature of the relationship between our language describing God and our language describing the ordinary world. He sees this as an attack upon the notion of God as a powerful and all-encompassing individual. In his reply to Ghazali, Averroes argues that equivocation is an inevitable aspect of our language, since that language has to describe a wide gamut of views using the same name. We must respect the different uses of the same word because they represent different points of view, different points of view of the same thing. It is an error to represent some uses as essentially more accurate than others. At one time it was popular for philosophers to argue that, when a physicist and an ordinary person talk about a table, they have in mind different objects. The physicist knows that a table is 'really' a collection of immaterial atoms, while ordinary people think of it as something solid and stable. Averroes would argue that, when we talk about and observe a table, we are looking at one thing from a variety of points of view which are equally valid. The physicist is right because the table does

[7] See on this topic the very interesting 'Good Repute' by M. Burnyeat, *London Review of Books* (6 Nov. 1986), 11–12.

have an atomic structure, and the ordinary person is right because he can eat his dinner on it. Our language is flexible enough to capture this diversity of view. In his philosophical methodology Averroes tries to show how it is possible for one thing to be described in a variety of ways. The arguments which have subsequently arisen concerning his 'real' views fail to grasp the philosophical approach he has constructed. When he tries to reconcile apparently contradictory views his strategy is to argue that all these views are acceptable as different aspects of one thing. The Averroist movement provides a useful focus for this idea, the precise nature of the apparent conflict between reason and religion. In his tentative remarks on language Averroes suggests that this conflict comes down to a stress upon different aspects of one thing, namely, the way the world really is. This is an intriguing interpretation of a longstanding philosophical dilemma, and may well be Averroes' most important contribution to philosophy itself.

Select Bibliography

The works of Averroes

Aristotelis opera . . . cum Averrois Cordubensis variis in eosdem commentariis (Juntas: Venice, 1562–74; repr. Minerva, Frankfurt a. Main, 1962).

Averroes' Commentary on Plato's 'Republic', ed., trans., and int. E. Rosenthal (University of Cambridge Oriental Publications, 1; Cambridge University Press: Cambridge, 1956; repr. 1966 and 1969).

Averroes' Epitome of Aristotle's Parva Naturalia, trans. and int. H. Blumberg (Medieval Academy of America: Cambridge, Mass., 1961).

Averroes' Middle Commentaries on Aristotle's Categories and De interpretatione, ed., trans., and int. C. Butterworth (Princeton University Press: Princeton, 1983).

Averroes on Aristotle's De generatione et corruptione Middle Commentary and Epitome, trans. and int. S. Kurland (Medieval Academy of America: Cambridge, Mass., 1958).

Averroes' Three Short Commentaries on Aristotle's 'Topics', 'Rhetoric' and 'Poetics', ed., int., and trans. C. E. Butterworth (State University of New York Press: Albany, 1977).

Averroes on Plato's 'Republic', trans. and int. R. Lerner (Cornell University Press: Ithaca, 1974).

Averroes on the Harmony of Religion and Philosophy, trans. and int. G. Hourani (Luzac: London, 1961; repr. 1967 and 1976).

Averroes' Tahafut al-tahafut (The Incoherence of the Incoherence), trans. and int. S. Van den Bergh (2 vols.; Luzac: London, 1954; repr. 1969 and 1978).

Averroes Cordubensis commentarium magnum in Aristotelis De anima libros, ed. F. S. Crawford (Medieval Academy of America: Cambridge, Mass., 1953).

Averroes Cordubensis sermo de Substantia Orbis, Destructio Destructionum Philosophiae Algazalis, De Animae Beatudine seu Epistola de Intellectu (Juntas: Venice, 1573).

Bidāyat al-mujtahid wa nihāyat al-muqtaṣid (The Beginning for him who interprets the sources independently and the End for him who wishes to limit himself) (Muṣṭafā al Bābī al Ḥalabī: Cairo, 1960).

Ḍamīma (Appendix to the *Faṣl al-maqāl*) in *Philosophie und Theologie von Averroes*, ed. M. J. Müller (Munich 1859).

Die Epitome der Metaphysik des Averroes, trans. and int. S. Van den Bergh (Brill: Leiden, 1924).

Discourse on the Manner of the World's Existence, MS Paris, Cod. hebr. 988

(89a–91a); trans. B. Kogan, 'Eternity and Origination: Averroes' *Discourse on the Manner of the World's Existence*', in M. Marmura (ed.), *Islamic Theology and Philosophy: Essays in Honor of George F. Hourani* (State University of New York Press: Albany, 1984).

Faṣl al-maqāl (Decisive Treatise), ed. G. F. Hourani (Brill: Leiden, 1959).

Jihad in Medieval and Modern Islam (The chapter on *jihād* from Averroes' *Bidāyat al-mujtahid*), trans. R. Peters (Brill: Leiden, 1977).

Kitāb al-kashf 'an manāhij al-adilla (Exposition of the Methods of Argument concerning the Doctrine of Faith), in *Philosophie und Theologie von Averroes*, ed. M. J. Müller (Munich, 1859).

Middle Commentary on Porphyry's Isagoge and on Aristotle's Categoriae, trans. and int. H. A. Davidson (Medieval Academy of America: Cambridge, Mass., 1969).

Middle Commentary on Aristotle's *Nicomachean Ethics* (Hebrew), Camb. MS Add. 496, Cambridge University Library.

Rasāʾ il ibn Rushd (Dāʾ irat al-Maʿārif al-ʿUthmānīyah: Hyderabad, 1947.

Tafsīr mā baʿd al-ṭabīʿah (Long Commentary on the Metaphysics), ed. M. Bouyges (4 vols: Bibliotheca Arabica Scholasticorum, Série Arabe; Imprimerie Catholique: Beirut, 1938–52).

Tahāfut al-tahāfut, ed. M. Bouyges (Bibliotheca Arabica Scholasticorum, Série Arabe, 3; Imprimerie Catholique: Beirut, 1930).

Talkhīṣ kitāb al-nafs, ed. F. Ahwānī (Maktabat al Nahḍah al Miṣrīyah: Cairo, 1950).

Talkhīṣ mā baʿd al-ṭabīʿah, ed. U. Amin (Muṣṭafā al Bābī al Ḥalabī: Cairo, 1958).

For an acerbic view of some recent work on Averroes, see C. Butterworth, 'The Study of Arabic Philosophy Today', *Middle East Studies Association Bulletin*, 17/2 (1983), 161–77; pp. 165–70.

General introductions to Averroes

Badawi, A, *Histoire de la philosophie en Islam*, ii. *Les Philosophes purs* (Études de philosophie médiévale, 60; Vrin: Paris, 1970).

Fakhry, M., *A History of Islamic Philosophy* (Columbia University Press: New York, 1970).

Gauthier, L., *Ibn Rochd (Averroès)* (Presses Universitaires de France: Paris, 1948).

—— *La Théorie d'Ibn Rochd (Averroès) sur les rapports de la religion et de la philosophie* (Leroux, Paris, 1909).

Hérnandez, M., *Filosofía Hispano-Musulmana*, ii (Asociación Española para el progresso de las ciencias: Madrid, 1957).

Hyman, A., and Walsh, J. (eds.), *Philosophy in the Middle Ages* (Harper and Row: New York, 1967).

Munk, S., *Mélanges de philosophie juive et arabe* (Franck: Paris, 1859).

Quadri, G., *La Philosophie arabe dans l'Europe médiévale* (Payot: Paris, 1947).

Renan, E., *Averroès et l'Averroïsme* in *Œuvres complètes de Ernest Renan*, iii (Calmann-Lévy: Paris, 1949).

Collections of articles on Averroes

Multiple Averroès (Les Belles Lettres: Paris, 1978).
L'Averroismo in Italia (Atti dei Convegni Lincei: Rome, 1979).

Averroes' metaphysics

Alexander of Aphrodisias, *De intellectu et intellecto*, in G. Théry, *Alexandre d'Aphrodise* (Le Saulchoir: Kain, 1926).

Allard, M., 'Le Rationalisme d'Averroès d'après une étude sur la création', *Bulletin d'Études Orientales*, 14 (1952–4), 7–59 (Institut Français de Damas; Damascus, 1954).

Arnaldez, R., 'Ibn Rushd', *Encyclopedia of Islam*, NE (Brill: Leiden, 1971).

—— 'La Pensée religieuse d'Averroes, i. La Doctrine de la création dans le Tahāfut', *Studia Islamica*, 7 (1957), 99–114.

—— 'La Pensée religieuse d'Averroès, ii. La Théorie de Dieu dans le Tahāfut', *Studia Islamica*, 8 (1957), 15–28.

—— 'La Pensée religieuse d'Averroès, iii. L'Immortalité de l'âme dans le Tahāfut', *Studia Islamica*, 10 (1959), 23–41.

Fakhry, M., *Islamic Occasionalism and its Critique by Averroes and Aquinas* (Allen and Unwin: London, 1958).

—— 'Philosophy and Scripture in the Theology of Averroes', *Medieval Studies*, 30 (1968), 78–89.

Finnegan, J., 'Texte arabe du *Peri Nou* d'Alexandre d'Aphrodise', *Mélanges de l'Université Saint Joseph* (Beirut), 33 (1956), 157–202.

Gätje, H., 'Averroes als Aristoteles Kommentator', *Zeitschrift der Deutschen Morgenländischen Gesellschaft*, 114 (1964), 59–65.

—— 'Die "inneren Sinne" bei Averroes', *ZDMG* 115 (1965), 255–93.

—— 'Zur Lehre von den Temperamenten bei Averroes', *ZDMG* 132 (1982), 243–68.

—— 'Die Vorworte zum Colliget des Averroes', *ZDMG* 136 (1986), 402–27.

Goodman, L., 'Ghazali's Argument from Creation', *International Journal of Middle East Studies*, 2 (1971), 67–85.

—— 'Did al-Ghazālī deny causality?', *Studia Islamica*, 47 (1978), 83–120.

Hourani, G., 'The Dialogue between al-Ghazālī and the Philosophers on the Origin of the World', *Muslim World*, 48 (1958), 183–191, 308–14.

Ivry, A., 'Averroes on Intellection and Conjunction', *Journal of the American Oriental Society*, 86 (1966), 76–85.

—— 'Towards a Unified View of Averroes' Philosophy', *Philosophical Forum*, 4 (1972), 87–113.

—— 'The Will of God and the Practical Intellect of Man in Averroes' Philosophy', *Israel Oriental Studies*, 9 (1979), 377–91.

—— 'Averroes on Causation', in S. Stein and R. Loewe (eds.), *Studies in Jewish Religious and Intellectual History* (University of Alabama Press: Alabama, 1979), 143–56.

Jolivet, J., 'Divergences entre les métaphysiques d'ibn Rushd et d'Aristote', *Arabica*, 29 (1982), 225–45.

Kogan, B., 'Averroes and the Theory of Emanation', *Medieval Studies*, 43 (1981), 384–404.

Mehren, A., 'Études sur la philosophie d'Averroès concernant son rapport avec celle d'Avicenne et Gazālī, *Muséon*, 7 (1888), 613–27 (1889) 5–20.

Tornay, S., 'Averroes' Doctrine of the mind', *Philosophical Review*, 52 (1943), 270–88.

Wolfson, H., *The Philosophy of the Kalam* (Harvard University Press: Cambridge, 1976).

—— 'The Twice-revealed Averroes', *Speculum*, 36 (1961), 373–92.

—— *Religious Philosophy* (Harvard University Press: Cambridge, 1961).
—— 'Plan for a *Corpus Commentariorum Averrois in Aristotelem*', *Speculum*, 6 (1931), 412–27.
—— 'Revised Plan for the Publication of a *Corpus Commentariorum Averrois in Aristotelem*', *Speculum*, 37 (1963), 88–104.

Averroes on the soul

Davidson, H., 'Averroes on the Material Intellect', *Viator*, 17 (1986), 91–137.
Hyman, A., 'Aristotle's Theory of the Intellect and its Interpretation by Averroes', in D. O'Meara (ed.), *Studies in Aristotle* (Catholic University Press of America, 1981), 161–91.
Gomez Nogales, S., 'Problemas alrededor del *Compendio sobre el alma* de Averroes', *Al Andalus*, 32 (1967), 1–36.
—— 'La immortalidad del alma a la luz de la noética de Averroes', *Pensamiento*, 15 (1959), 155–76.
Merlan, P., *Monopsychism, Mysticism, Metaconsciousness* (Nijhoff, 1963).
Tallon, A., 'Personal Immortality in Averroes' Tahafut al-Tahafut', *New Scholasticism*, 38 (1964), 341–57.
Teske, R., 'The End of Man in the Philosophy of Averroes', *New Scholasticism*, 37 (1963), 431–61.
Zedler, B., 'Averroes on the Possible Intellect', *Proceedings of the American Catholic Philosophical Association*, 25 (1951), 164–78.
—— 'Averroes and Immortality', *New Scholasticism*, 28 (1954), 436–53.

Works in Arabic on Averroes

'Aqqad, M. al-, *Ibn Rushd* (Dār al-Ma'ārif: Cairo, 1953).
Bisār, M., *Al wujūd wal khulūd fī falsafat ibn Rushd* (Existence and Immortality in ibn Rushd's Philosophy) (Dār al-kitāb al-lubnāni: Beirut, 1973).
Fakhrī, M., *Ibn Rushd, faylasūf qurṭaba* (Ibn Rushd, The Cordoban Philosopher) (al-Maṭba'a al-kaṭuliliya, Beirut, 1960).
Hulw, A. al-, *Ibn Rushd* (Dār al-sharq al-jadīd: Beirut, 1960).
Imārah, M., *Al māddiya wal mithāliyya fī falsafat ibn Rushd* (Materialism and Idealism in ibn Rushd's Philosophy) (Dār al-Ma'ārif: Cairo, 1971). An edited collection.
'Irāqī, A. al-, *Al naz'a al 'aqliyya fī falsafat Ibn Rushd* (Intellectualism in ibn Rushd's Philosophy) (Dār al-Ma'ārif: Cairo, 1967).
—— *Thawrat al 'aql fī falsafa al'arabiyya* (The Revolution of the Intellect in Arabic Philosophy) (Dār al-Ma'ārif: Cairo, 1976).
Musa, M., *Bayn al dīn wal falsafa fī ra'y ibn Rushd wa falsafat al 'asr al wasīṭ* (The Reconciliation of Philosophy and Religion according to ibn Rushd) (Dār al-Ma'ārif: Cairo, 1959).
—— *Ibn Rushd al faylasūf* (Dar al Ma'ārif: Cairo, 1945).
Qasim, M., *Naẓariyyat al ma'rifa 'ind ibn Rushd wa ta'wiluhā lada Tumās al Akwīnī* (Ibn Rushd's Theory of Knowledge and its Interpretation by Thomas Aquinas) (Maktabat al-Anglū al-Miṣrīyah: Cairo, 1964).
—— *Ibn Rushd wa falsafatuhu al dīniyya* (Ibn Rushd and his Religious Philosophy) (Anglo: Cairo, 1969).

—— *Ibn Rushd al faylasūf al-muftara ʿalayh* (Ibn Rushd, the Misinterpreted Philosopher) (Anglo: Cairo, 1954).

Qumayr, Y., *Ibn Rushd* (Dār al mashreq: Beirut, 1953).

—— *Ibn Rushd wa al Ghazālī* (Dār al mashreq: Beirut, 1969).

Zayk, S. al-, *Ibn Rushd* (Beirut, 1971).

Index

Due to their ubiquity in the text there are no references in the Index to Aristotle and Averroes.